MONEY MATTERS

THE FEE
IN PSYCHOTHERAPY
AND PSYCHOANALYSIS

William G. Herron
Sheila Rouslin Welt

THE GUILFORD PRESS · NEW YORK · LONDON

© 1992 The Guilford Press
A Division of Guilford Publications, Inc.
72 Spring Street, New York, NY 10012

Printed in the United States of America

This book is printed on acid-free paper.

Last digit is print number: 9   8   7   6   5   4   3   2   1

Library of Congress Cataloging-in-Publication Data

Herron, William G.
    Money matters : the fee in psychotherapy and psychoanalysis /
William G. Herron & Sheila Rouslin Welt.
        p.   cm.
    Includes bibliographical references and index.
    ISBN 0-89862-887-3.—ISBN 0-89862-152-6 (pbk.)
    1. Psychotherapists—Fees—Psychological aspects.
    2. Psychoanalysts—Fees—Psychological aspects. 3. Money—
Psychological aspects. 4. Psychotherapist and patient. I. Title.
    [DNLM: 1. Fees and Charges. 2. Psychoanalysis—economics.
    3. Psychotherapy—economics. WM 420 H568m]
    RC465.5.H47   1992
    616.89′023—dc20
    DNLM/DLC
    for Library of Congress   92-1564
                                                                   CIP

To our mothers,
Josephine W. Herron and Sarah Rouslin,
and
to our fathers,
J. Burrows Herron and Paul H. Rouslin

ABOUT
THE AUTHORS

WILLIAM G. HERRON, PH.D., received his degree in clinical psychology from Fordham University and is a graduate of the Adelphi University postdoctoral program in psychotherapy and psychoanalysis. He is a Fellow of the American Psychological Association and a Diplomate in Clinical Psychology of the American Board of Professional Psychology. He is a professor in the Department of Psychology at St. John's University, Jamaica, New York, and is in private practice in Woodcliff Lake, New Jersey. He is an editorial consultant for *Psychotherapy* and the coauthor of *Reactive and Process Schizophrenia, Contemporary School Psychology, Issues in Psychotherapy*, and *Narcissism and the Psychotherapist*.

SHEILA ROUSLIN WELT, M.S., received her degree as a clinical specialist in psychiatric nursing from Rutgers—The State University of New Jersey. She is certified for psychotherapy practice in New York and New Jersey, where she is in private practice. Her coauthored books, *Narcissism and the Psychotherapist, Issues in Psychotherapy, A Collection of Classics in Psychiatric Nursing Literature*, and *Interpersonal Theory in Nursing Practice: Selected Works of Hildegard E. Peplau*, received the *American Journal of Nursing* Book of the Year awards. A former Rutgers educator and clinical editor, she has lectured throughout the United States and abroad and is widely published in psychiatric nursing journals. She is on the editorial board of *Archives of Psychiatric Nursing*.

PREFACE

Money has always been a peculiar issue for psychoanalysts and psychotherapists. Like their patients, they also need it for physical and psychological well-being, but beyond that, they need to get it from their patients. The latter need creates a vulnerability to possible criticism that one becomes a psychotherapist of whatever persuasion in order to make money, not to help people. The presence of a fee is imagined as obliterating the positive helping image in which most therapists sincerely believe and that they want to convey to their patients. The desire for payment can so quickly create a money-unbridled greed scenario that is placed in opposition to concern, holding environment, warmth, really most of the positives that become part of an effective psychotherapeutic relationship. As a result, therapists are often particularly uncomfortable about being *noticed* as paid service providers. Although they want to get paid, and they hope to get paid, and they even try to get paid, the relative silence about this issue in the psychoanalytic and psychotherapeutic literature, as well as in actual practice, has an eerie quality.

If this matter were just an issue among therapists, then it could remain in the land of the strange without that much concern. However, money is such a disturbing topic for everybody that for patients to have therapists who have just as much, if not more, trouble discussing money matters is a serious liability for all psychotherapies. The very nature of the psychotherapeutic relationship can become severely distorted when a major defining boundary, the fee, is avoided or used improperly. In addition, the content of the sessions can unfortunately gain mutually sanctioned deletions so that "free" association has an added suppressive/repressive barrier.

It is time for the last taboo to fall, which is why we wrote this book. Early psychoanalysts were not so reluctant in this regard, as witnessed by some of the writings of Freud, Abraham, Ferenczi, Jones, and Fenichel, but for many years the topic has been relatively untouched, with exceptions noted throughout the book. We believe the topic is beginning to open up again, fueled both by an increasing awareness of the key role that money can have in the therapeutic process and by increasing competition for provider dollars as a correlate of the demands for accountability and rapid, relatively inexpensive "cures." In addition, there has been a rapid increase in the number of providers from all the disciplines contributing to the profession of psychotherapy. Although this increase has recently begun to abate as disillusionment has appeared in respect to the certainty of a psychotherapy practice leading to either relative or consistent wealth, marketing and the necessity of "making a buck" are now noticeable, spoken-of, and written-about concerns.

In this regard, we want to mention *Money and Mind* (Klebanow & Lowenkopf, 1991), *The Last Taboo: Money as Symbol and Reality in Psychotherapy and Psychoanalysis* (edited by Krueger, 1986), as well as our earlier, briefer discussions of money issues in *Issues in Psychotherapy* (1982/1984) and *Narcissism and the Psychotherapist* (1990). We went from five pages to a full chapter, then to the present book. We have divided this book into four major sections. The first has three chapters focusing on the meaning of psychotherapy fees, the second, three chapters on patients' fee attitudes, and the third, three chapters on therapists' fee attitudes; finally, we include a chapter on effective fee policies.

Acknowledgment is gratefully given to all those who taught us about the role of the fee in psychoanalysis and psychotherapy, particularly supervisors, our own analysts, other analysts and therapists, and the patients who have paid for our services as well as those who are either doing so now and/or will do so in the future. We are happy to be making our living this way, and we hope this book can be a significant addition to the continued viability of the psychotherapy profession by providing a grounding in economic realities coupled with an appreciation of the incredible significance and myriad meanings of, in one sense, a mere commodity—money—not so nutritious as soybeans or as basic as pork bellies but, oh so often, the object of the heart's desire.

CONTENTS

PART IV. INTEGRATION

MONEY MATTERS

PART I

THE MEANING
OF FEES
IN PSYCHOTHERAPY

T he possible and probable significances of fees in psychoanalysis and psychotherapy have been murky. The problem immediately becomes apparent by the limited acknowledgment given to the actual role of the fee in the psychotherapy process. Thus, we begin in Chapter 1 by making it clear that fees are indeed part of the process, that service is rendered for a fee, and that the patient pays, directly or indirectly, and in a similar manner, the therapist receives payment. We discuss the historical context that has given rise to the disguising of these realities in terms of therapist, patient, and cultural contributions and collaborations. In doing so, we highlight the fact that therapists appear to be the least willing of all concerned to face the basic role of cost in psychotherapy, and we point to the need for a change.

Chapter 2 explores the complex meanings of money that of course contribute to its problematic status. The existence of explicit and implicit meanings is noted, a variety of "money types" are described, and then considerable attention is given to psychoanalytic meanings, since these are the most detailed explanations that have been offered. This section includes Freud, Ferenczi, Jones, and Abraham among others, with a particular focus on the work of Fenichel in which the overdetermination of money is made apparent. We continue our exploration with a look at how meanings of money have evolved in our current society, noting the continuation of multiple symbolism, and conclude with the idea of money as a potential for the translation of diverse fantasies into realities, known and unknown. It is the potential, with its myriad images, that both beckons and threatens, turning money into a most complicated, unnerving topic.

Of course none of these subjects frees the therapist from coming to grips with money matters, so in Chapter 3 we discuss the philosophy of payment, which is central to the role of the therapist as a paid service provider. We consider major reasons for psychotherapists being uncomfortable with their roles, starting with the general problem of distortions in the boundaries of the therapeutic relationship. Then the dynamics of the therapist's role are explored in terms of being a helper, making room for greed, and understanding the difference between friendship and the therapeutic relationship. We conclude this section by noting the compatibility of healthy narcissism and the provision of effective psychotherapy.

Chapter 1

THE FEE
IS PART
OF THE PROCESS

D efinitions of psychotherapy do not mention fees as essential ingredients. Texts in the fundamentals of psychotherapy gave payment
limited coverage. Yet fees are a basic element of the psychotherapeutic
process and money issues deserve to be discussed as openly as any other
concerns. Money has a voice, a presence, and a power that therapists are
reluctant to notice. They restrict it, give it brief discussion, talk about it
only when they have to, and patients often follow in their footsteps. The
impression created is that while money has its place, it is a quiet place,
and therapists and patients rather silently agree to keep it that way.

Psychotherapy is in turn portrayed as an ideal, emphasizing the
provision of service and the dedication of the providers. When and if
therapists show any interest in money, it is because they need it to live.
Money is an unpleasant necessity that therapists prefer to come their way
automatically rather than through calculated effort. Therapists work diligently because they care about people, because behavior fascinates them,
and because of a host of other intellectual and emotional motivations, all
of which have an altruistic, or at least social, underpinning. Payment for
therapeutic services is involved but, in a major sense, is incidental. We
grant there are exceptions to all this, but they are in the minority.

Certainly psychotherapy stresses relationships between people, and
dissonance readily comes to mind if the emphasis is on the paid nature
of the relationship. Actually the therapeutic relationship is an unusual
one, a mixture of fact and fiction, fantasy and reality, with money falling
into both categories before, during, and after the therapy. Money as a
fact of therapeutic life is made explicit, but to the least degree possible,
whereas money as fantasy is more acceptable, though not a favorite topic
of either patients or therapists.

The reticence described is understandable and steeped in the history of psychotherapy. In tracing the development of psychotherapy from its detectable origins, Ehrenwald (1976) starts with magical healers, followed by philosopher–priests, eventuating in modern psychotherapists. The evolution from magic to science has retained elements of its early and transitional periods. Psychotherapy remains a "mystical science" with considerable artistry in its execution. The special quality of the mental healer is still there, something potentially charismatic alongside the more carefully designed technical and theoretical principles. There is little in the history of psychotherapy to suggest that it is a business arrangement or that therapists could be classified as business people. The transactional nature of the process, the fact that therapist and patient *both* want something from each other, is overshadowed by the healing motive.

Yet psychotherapy is a transaction, akin to what Fairbairn (1952) described as "mature dependence." This is an interdependence, conditional giving, an exchange that, although certainly selective in psychotherapy, nonetheless requires that both parties be rewarded for their efforts. However, Fairbairn (1952) was also pessimistic about people's ability to achieve mature dependence, and his skepticism is well reflected in the practice of psychotherapy. For example, the therapist and the patient may have a desire for an all-good, all-caring parent. The patient activates this by expecting to be helped for as little cost as possible, and the therapist gains satisfaction from identifying with the giving role and makes the fee minimal and apparently incidental.

In the above example the striking aspects of the fee are that it is given so little attention, and will probably never be discussed by that therapist and patient. A transaction did take place in that both parties got something out of the process, but this hardly ranks as an example of mature dependence. There are numerous problems with the arrangement, but our point is the readiness of therapist and patient to hide a significant aspect of treatment. Therapy as a discovery process is constricted even as it begins. This will not occur if proper recognition is given to the fee as part of the therapeutic process.

Balsam and Balsam (1984) have made the point that there really is no such thing as "free" psychotherapy. In situations where the patient pays less than what the marketplace would suggest, there is a subsidy, and in some fasion the patient pays for that. Thus, poverty can get people apparently free services, but somebody is paying the salaries of the providers. When insurance is used, the patient's labors have contributed to having the insurance, so although it is a step removed from direct payment, it is the patient's payment nonetheless. The psychotherapy profession is relatively socialistic with the presence of public and semipublic low-cost services, but society, and thus the people in it, pay for these services.

Another possibility is an arrangement in which therapists are apparently providing free service. There are a variety of motives for this happening, such as therapists' obligations to provide service to those who need it or desires to learn something about particular disorders or any interest other than monetary reward. However, therapists expect something from such service, namely, the satisfaction of their motives. It is still a transaction, only the currency has changed. A "fee" is still being charged, such as patient gratitude, recognition by peers as a good and giving person, or the obtaining of special knowledge or experience.

Certainly psychotherapists see themselves as having obligations and desires to provide service to those who need it, and certainly they do this. For example, Prochaska, Nash, and Norcross (1986) surveyed 327 full-time independent practitioners. They found that about two-thirds of the sample based their fees on the patients' ability to pay and provided some free therapy. Thus, the issue is not whether therapists are greedy but the lengths to which the profession goes to conceal the existence of any profit motive. This promotion of an unreal, inappropriately idealized image then creates a distortion in a process that otherwise specializes in illuminating motivations. The result is what Morgan (1983) has described as iatrogenics, namely, a problem caused by the provider in the process of service provision.

The problem can be better understood within the context of the historical development of psychotherapy. Ehrenwald (1976) has concluded that over time there are three major discernible components in all forms of psychotherapy, namely, therapist variables, patient variables, and their culture. These are overlapping and interactive, but we focus on their separate contributions as a way of highlighting the issue of the economics of treatment.

THE THERAPIST

Chodoff (1964) has described psychotherapists as competitive service sellers who need to give appropriate attention to the effects of payment for their services on their ideas and practices. Tulipan (1983) makes the further point that these ideas and practices of therapists affect how they view fees. The question at this point then is the degree to which the mental health providers believe that treatment essentially involves payment in one form or another. In addition, if therapists believe this, then do they carry out their belief in practice?

Psychotherapy is structured so that both parties can get satisfactions. Since the satisfaction received by the therapist is not always a direct economic one given by the patient, there is opportunity for therapists to repress/suppress the monetary component. Thus, in all instances in which the therapist gets paid by somebody other than the patient, and there are many of these, the therapist may conceptualize therapy as a process without patient–therapist economic transactions. This is an error. We have given some examples and will now elaborate with a detailed review of all these situations.

The most common case is that in which the therapist is salaried, so that an institution pays. Patient fees are often not collected by the therapist, and whether or not they are paid, the therapist's salary is not directly affected. Yet the patient's responsibility to pay is no different than if the therapist were paid directly by the patient, and if this did not happen, the therapist would not have an income. In the institutional setting, however, the opening is there for therapists to demonetarize therapy, and many therapists do just that. Mayer and Norton (1981), for example, found therapists in a mental health center to be resistive to billing and collecting fees directly from patients. The therapists' reasoning? Such procedures would contaminate the therapy.

In this attitude we have a major contributor to the problem. Therapists prefer money-free therapy. As long as they can derive a satisfactory income from their work, they will gladly keep money out of it. Fees are unpleasant, "dirty business." It is analogous to enjoying being a teacher but not wanting to grade students, or doing any job in which there are unpleasant aspects that are nonetheless part of the job description. One may understandably look for ways around them, and even find ways, but doing so changes the job. It is not what it was designed to be.

Perhaps such changes ought to be made. That is not our issue here. Instead we are making the point that therapy is essentially a transaction for which the patient pays, in one form or another. When therapists act as if this is not the case, they distort reality.

Let us consider some other examples. Payments by sources external to both patient and therapist, such as insurance companies, are relatively common. However, patients have to do something to obtain such an arrangement, the "something" usually being working at a job that provides the insurance coverage. This is money, part of the patient's salary, and if the patient loses such a benefit, he or she has lost equivalent money.

In some instances the payment may be made by a parent or a spouse. Still, the patient pays because the people putting up the money expect payment of some kind—gratitude, understanding, changed attitudes— from the patient. The transaction between patient and therapist is more remote, but the payment concept is constant. Furthermore, the people paying the money may well expect an accounting from the therapists. If therapists in this situation think they have taken monetary concerns out of the therapy, they will be unpleasantly surprised.

Another example is training, where patients usually pay a modest fee but where the therapist gets no fee. The therapist's rewards are fulfilling training requirements, learning, and other possibilities, but not money. Again the transactional nature of the process has not changed. Even if the patient pays no fee, the economic support of the service comes from somewhere, and the patient is expected to contribute to the supporting institution in some way. The state, the charity, the individual practitioner, all get their funds from somebody, and the nonpayers are expected to become payers at some point. The goal is to be productive and in turn to pay for what one gets.

Psychotherapy embodies that aim, placing a responsibility on the patient and on the therapist to carry out their respective roles within such a framework. Psychotherapy is generally considered a health service, and psychotherapists operate within a context of expected payment for such services. Also, even if one were to argue that it is some other kind of service, as people indeed have (Kovacs, 1989; Winokur, 1973), that does not change the economics of the situation. For example, Burrell (1987), in rejecting the medical model and health insurance payments as well, still states that psychotherapy is "a business." Even Hurvitz (1979) conceded "despite their awareness of the contradictions between . . . American capitalist society and their professed humanism, radical therapists are also enterpreneurs who collect a fee for services rendered" (p. 66).

Therapists know the fee is a basic ingredient of the psychotherapeutic process, but they do not like it. Why they do not like it, and what can be done about that, are topics we intend to explore throughout this book. For now we want to show that because therapists do not like the therapy model as it is, they try to decrease the aspect of it that they dislike. This aspect is not getting paid but, rather charging the fee, letting the patient know the therapist wants money.

Raskin (Jasnow, Raskin, Klein, & Stern, 1979) depicts the situation aptly. "I would prefer to forget that there is a monetary aspect to my activity as a psychotherapist. I work, actively and passively, to keep it in its place: some little corner. I want the exchange to be entirely interpersonal, characterized by a developing trust, sharing, and affection, leading to a stronger client and a stronger me" (p. 3).

Thus, the conflict exists between the purity of the therapy as the therapist wishes it and the reality of the therapy as a business. Although therapists may feel guilty, uncomfortable, and/or unworthy, reality needs to prevail. Therapists tell their patients there are no taboo topics. That means money is really part of a process that also can have all the personal, intimate qualities Raskin and most other therapists expect of it.

How can this be? Because psychotherapy is not a friendship, a love affair, or a subsitute or some other significant relationship. It is a special relationship with its own defining characteristics, particularly the rendering of a skilled service for which one gets paid. Therapists sell skills, not themselves, and they expect to get paid for these skills. Furthermore, if the skills were not effective, then psychotherapy would have vanished ages ago.

The therapist's task is to include all aspects of the process rather than to neglect or avoid any that make him uncomfortable. It is time therapists faced up to wanting the money. That is not the same as being in it *for* the money. Certainly some therapists are more avaricious than others, but we do not know any therapists for whom this is their sole, or even primary, motive. One does become and remain a therapist out of an interest in people, but part of that interest is economic. It is indeed time to bring that forward and let money be a visible part of therapy for all concerned.

THE PATIENT

A man who had been in psychoanalysis for 2 years and had just paid his analyst for the month said, "I didn't feel like paying you this month. I wonder when I'll get to the point where I don't feel like that, where I feel like paying you?"

Perhaps never, thought the therapist. Why should the patient feel like paying? Consumers may enjoy coming, but that doesn't mean they enjoy the loss of money. Thus, patients accept the idea of payment and find it worthwhile, assuming the therapy is working for them. They may even feel grateful and praise the therapist, but they would prefer not to have to pay. Thus, patients are not going to erase therapists' feelings of discomfort about the monetary aspects of therapy by feeling that the fee is a "non-issue."

There has been little written by patients on their point of view about paying fees, but, having been in that situation ourselves as well as having seen many patients over a long span of practice, we have gained some impressions. The first is that patients accept the fee-for-service concept; they expect to pay and are more open about the monetary aspect than therapists. The openness is relative, however, in that money is a taboo topic, and therapists can encourage or discourage talk about it. Patients will talk about money, including monetary transactions between themselves and therapists, given the opportunity. However, therapists have lots of content control, and patients will go along with avoidance of a particular topic, such as money, that also makes them uncomfortable in some way. Therapists can neglect the money aspect and not be challenged by patients. Therapists can easily become enablers of resistance by fostering relative silence and neglect. A tacit agreement takes place that what is a resistance will not be so considered by either therapist or patient. Patients will accept this and not complain even though they are being cheated.

Patients also tend to use the fee as a frame of reference or discussion of their financial situation. This means that they are aware that therapists can gauge from the descriptions of how much money the patients have, and how they spend money, where the fee being charged fits into their schema. Probably the most frequent scenario is for the patient to downplay her financial assets and gains. The theme is that the fee is not easily paid and there are no surplus funds if the therapy is becoming lengthy and/ or the therapist wishes to increase the fee. The source of funds is often mentioned, as "I don't know what I would do if it weren't for insurance," or, "It certainly is a good thing I got a bonus this year." The message is, I can pay the fee, and I will even pay it without really complaining, but it does restrict me financially, which I do not like.

This approach keeps pressure on the therapist, who is the one who needs the fee and who also has a tendency to hide that need from the patient. Some therapists take the view that the payment is good for the patient, a motivator, but there is no evidence to support universal ineffectiveness of free psychotherapy (Herron & Sitkowski, 1986). Certainly paying for therapy can motivate patients and creates a structure of self-responsibility, but that does not mean patients will always, or even for long periods of time, like paying the fee. They may like and value therapy, which in turn eases the dislike of payment, but it will not eradicate it. Their preference will be to pay less or nothing and get the same service. At the same time, if that were to happen, patients would be suspicious because it is not the norm. Even patients who are economically disadvantaged often expect to get relatively inferior service. Although we don't know how often these expectations are met, fairly often is a definite possibility. It is not true that a therapist who charges a lot will deliver a lot. It is more likely to be true that therapists working for relatively little will provide just that. There are exceptions, of course, but patients understand, for example, that entering into situations such as a training clinic they may get therapists who, although they are trying, are nonetheless hampered by a lack of knowledge and experience.

Patients getting "cheap therapy" then may well devalue it unless they can be convinced that the therapists involved are sufficiently knowledgeable. The patients' wish is to get the best for less, or at least to get what they need for less. Therapists would prefer this as well, but they are interactive with the current marketplace, which means a certain fee in accord with a certain life style, usually upper middle class. So, although they are sympathetic to patients' desires and have been patients themselves, therapists just see the fee as an unpleasant reality. Some patients may get some therapists to lower fees, but fees have been subject to inflation. If a therapist looks back at him fees of 10 years ago, the difference is striking, and that increase is reflective of patients' willingness to pay more for psychotherapy. It still does not mean patients enjoy paying or even that they forget about the monetary aspect of the relationship.

In terms of the fee, some patients take another direction and emphasize their wealth. For example, a patient was due to pay his therapist in a particular session. The patient had just sold his business for $2 million and had the check with him. Instead of handing the therapist the check for the fee as usual, he deliberately gave the therapist the $2 million check and laughingly pretended the mix-up was accidental.

This type of patient is rare relative to the others described. The insignificance in size of the fee is apparent relative to the patient's wealth, although that does not mean such a patient will forgo complaining about the cost. Feelings engendered in the therapist are different, however, with envy being more likely to occur in this case than guilt. If the latter occurs, it is a reaction to the envy, as is contempt. Therapists also may have to struggle with such patients' contempt based on their view of themselves as particularly important because of their wealth. Olsson (1986) has described the problems of working with very wealthy patients, particularly therapists' envy and deference in reaction to the narcissism and grandiosity connected to the accumulation of money.

The focus in this section is on how patients view the role of money in the psychotherapeutic relationship. Of course money has numerous meanings to patients, and these will be explored subsequently and have been given considerable attention in the literature. However, our present concern is how the fee aspect of psychotherapy interacts with patients' attitudes toward money. We see patients using the fee as a fulcrum for expressing their feelings about money. The manner of this expression in turn is designed to affect therapists' feelings about the fee.

Just as therapists tend to want patients to pay the fee and act responsibly without focusing excess attention on it, patients tend to want therapists to be aware that they are paying with effort and to be credited accordingly. In that sense patients are more willing to think of the payment as an essential part of the psychotherapy process.

The conceptual reality of the situation, however, is difficult to maintain because of countertransference and transference. The image of selfless helping is promoted by therapists, yet transference can spin the fee into selfishness at the turn of a thought. For example, a patient arrived at a session and told the therapist she would give her a check at the end of the session. The patient spent the session lamenting her life, definitely expressing feelings of victimization and depression. At the end of the session she started to leave without paying the therapist. Clearly she had unconsciously changed her mind. As she later told the therapist, she was in no mood to give anybody anything but grief. The therapist had stopped her before she departed and requested the promised payment, which was given. This triggered still another thought on the patient's part that the therapist indeed deserved to be paid, particularly for that session, which must have been difficult for the therapist. The shifts in feelings about the therapist as good or bad mother, deserving or undeserving, were rapid and intense, and these were reflected by the patient's actions with regard to the fee.

Such affective moves are to be expected. If therapists believe patients will get "into a groove" about fees, one that is always going to be to the therapists' liking, they will often be disappointed. The most reliable of patients at times becomes unreliable, and the less reliable have periods of fiscal responsibility. Nonetheless, the recognition of the fee as ultimate reality is present enough of the time for the majority of patients.

A problem is that some of the time patients want to think of the therapeutic relationship as some other type of relationship, one based solely on mutual positive feelings for the people involved. At those times patients want to eliminate the notion of the fee, and if it does make an appearance, it is experienced as an unpleasant jolt to a very pleasant fantasy. Just as therapists have to learn to integrate the fee with warmth, empathy, and respect, so must patients. The fee is one of the boundaries of therapy, although certainly not the only one, and it should not be considered an automatic barrier to intimacy and mutual caring.

It is not even accurate to say that the fee is an impersonal part of a personal process. There are some impersonal aspects to the process, such as the therapist's charging a fee and that amount being unrelated to how much the therapist likes (or dislikes) the patient. At the same time the financial transactions are something therapists and patients have feelings about, and they are conducted within an affective context. The size of the fee tends to be regulated by the needs of both parties as well. This is customarily a matter of financial circumstances, but even the impersonal could get personal here, as either party could get manipulated by the other in terms of attraction.

Patients need to have an appropriate perspective on the fee, or it becomes an eternal possibility for resistance. If the personal elements are overemphasized, then feelings of adequacy and worth may be distorted. Thus, a paranoid position, either persecutory or grandiose, or a depressive position, masochistic or reparative, may dominate the fee process. In the former instance, the patient feels the fee is either a punishment for badness or a reward for goodness. In the depressive position, the fee is an integral part of an already suffering personality or an atonement for previous transgressions.

If the impersonal elements are exaggerated, then the patient's position tends to be more paranoid–schizoid. The therapist is treated with distrust as someone who is interested in money rather than people, and a safe distance is maintained by witholding material and feelings. Such an approach is accompanied by an air of resignation as to what can be expected, a cynicism that holds regardless of the size of the fee.

These attitudes are a problem because they are often not directly expressed and emerge intermittently after the fee has been set or, if noticed from the start, go unresolved despite apparent agreement to the fee. In essence the patient will deny that the fee is a problem, yet she always thinks of it as an issue and acts accordingly to defend both the denial and the original feelings.

The facilitative perspective is indeed to have feelings about the fee and to express them without letting them be an obstacle to the therapeutic relationship. The payment is understood as expected, accepted as part of a contract for services being rendered, and is respected without necessarily being liked. Thus, during a vacation a patient may miss the therapist yet enjoy saving the payment. Clarity about psychotherapy of whatever type should include clarity about the place of payment in the therapeutic procedures. Therapists need to be more alert to the fact that such clarity is often not easily or well established. Because therapists tend to wish money matters settled between themselves and their patients, they are quick to close the curtain before the end of the "money show," leaving a lot of unresolved and even untouched material.

The education of patients regarding the role of the fee has to be the responsibility of therapists, like it or not, and requires that therapists have their own feelings and attitudes about it well in place. If not, they will either neglect or undermine the educative effort with their own contradictory actions. Patients come into therapy with an awareness of at least some of their problems but without much of an awareness of the details of treatment. They know payment of some sort is expected, but how much, how often, for how long, and what payment has to do with solving their problems are all matters requiring explanation. There is no reason to think the majority of patients would have useful knowledge about all these aspects of therapy. Also, even relatively sophisticated patients may have different conceptions than the particular therapist they choose, or they may consider themselves as exceptions. Actually, there are no universal guidelines. Fee policies vary with type of therapy and type of therapist. Considering the prevalence of sliding scales and other reasons for variations from the "regular fee," bargaining is certainly possible. Ultimately, then, fees are up to the therapist, and it seems patients know that more cogently than the therapists themselves.

SOCIETY

We live in a society that has become increasingly health conscious and that requires delivery systems to meet growing health needs. Lesse (1989) notes that the health-care profession has become a $500 billion industry, and psychotherapy is a part of this. Recognition of the need for psychotherapy and increased acceptance of it contribute to an awareness of a mental health "business." Although debate continues as to the degree and specifics of its effectiveness, the mental health delivery system does enough for people that they are willing to pay to receive it. Furthermore, it is a growth industry. Kiesler (1983) reports that in terms of epidemiology an appropriate estimate appears to be that about 15% of our population needs mental health services, although only about 2% are receiving them. The mismatch indicates the necessity of increased service provision. Even though this increase will not be limited to traditional services and providers, there is a large market for psychotherapy.

At the same time, the psychotherapy business is constantly subject to business concerns. The major one is cost containment, a particular interest of employers and insurance carriers. They accept the value of psychotherapy but usually have defined limits as to how many sessions, how much money allowed per session, culminating in a cost-containment trend. Other procedures used to limit costs are utilization reviews and managed health care systems.

The economic aspect of this trend is that the type of psychotherapy that will now be preferred is brief and targeted to specific problems. This is in marked contrast to the long-term psychoanalytic therapies that were once the dominant model.

This change in the marketplace is not based on evidence that one form of psychotherapy is indeed better than another. Proving the efficacy of therapy has certainly been a problem, but in recent years, we have become more adept at empirical study. Thus, it is now possible to demonstrate that therapy is effective, that the effects last, and that some therapies are more effective than others with certain problems (Lambert, Shapiro, & Bergin, 1986). The last finding is not a general effect, however, with differences in outcome for various forms of therapy being rather slight, certainly not enough to have engendered or supported a cost-containment policy.

As participants in a business, therapists are part of the economic cycle. As health costs have spiraled upward, there has been a tendency to cut wherever it seems feasible. The amorphous qualities of mental health and mental illness, as well as those of the psychotherapeutic process itself, have all offered inviting targets. Accountability has a logic and ethic to it that is undeniable, yet it is difficult for psychotherapists to demonstrate all the problems treated, the methods of treatment, and the results achieved in terms that are satisfactory to major economic supporters of the treatment system. Psychotherapists offer a variety of services designed to provide a variety of treatment from single-symptom relief to complete personality overhaul. One wishes the client to have a choice, but this option is increasingly becoming limited. Quick and cheap are now the magic words, and along with clients' choice goes therapists' choice, despite the increasing mental health needs of the population.

Another business need now becomes apparent. Competition has been created for the therapy dollar, since some types of services are better funded than others. In addition, in areas where there are large numbers of psychotherapists, there is competition for patients, even though nationwide the need for therapy is greater than the supply of therapists. Also, with numerous disciplines contributing to the supply, the exclusion of some of these by third-party payers results in further competition. The result is the need for marketing by psychotherapists.

One way to do this is to flow with the tide. Shulman (1988) stresses being "business minded," and he includes five strategies. The first is to operate as a life-cycle helper with short-term interventions applied as needed for symptom relief and solutions for specific problems. The second is to get involved in outpatient treatment of addictions that can be more cost effective than hospitalization and that responds to an acute need of the society. Programs for health promotion and educating the public to the value of mental health services in reducing the need for other medical services are also suggested, as is participation in managed mental health care.

Although Shulman was addressing one mental health discipline, the suggestions are applicable to all with respect to highlighting the increasing awareness of psychotherapy as a business. It is not necessary to follow the suggestions in order to have an active practice, and in fact, it would be impossible to do so in regard to some of them if, for example, one wishes to practice psychoanalytic therapy. However, psychoanalysts then have the task of educating the consumer to the value of their services (Welt & Herron, 1990). In essence, if any psychotherapist believes in the value of a particular approach, then he will have to market that approach. This is a result of recognizing that the fee is indeed part of the process, and society does view it in that way.

The controlling forces in mental health care are not sophisticated in regard to psychotherapy, nor have the economics of payment for services been developed with significant input from psychotherapists. Instead, emphasis is increasingly on cost containment, sometimes to make a profit for insurance carriers, other times to relieve the burden of taxpayers. The focus is more on the cost than the quality of ingredients of the service, and there is limited understanding of the diversity of conditions requiring services or the results likely to be obtained.

It is obvious that the voices of psychotherapists need to be heard in the present situation in order to develop and provide the spectrum of effective mental health services that are possible. However, it is not our point here to lament the present policies and delivery systems, though their lamentable status cannot go unnoticed. Our emphasis is the economic recognition factor. Because psychotherapeutic services have a significant cost, people other than direct users are involved.

These people are mental health power brokers who develop controls in regard to the services therapists offer. Of course, therapists can offer whatever they want, but the takers become more limited when funds are restricted, and thus control is wielded. A further restriction is the sociopolitical climate for what constitutes mental illness or conditions requiring treatment, and this climate usually has an economic linkage. A rough equation is that whatever disrupts the productivity of the work force, such as depression or addiction, deserves treatment, along with whatever makes people uncomfortable and is harmful to self and/or others. This does cover a lot of ground, so the probability of considerable cost is high and brings with it an impetus to make the treatment rapid. The concept that what takes a long time to develop may in turn take a long time to unravel is not popular with money providers because of the cost involved.

In addition, consumers do not like paying out their own money over long periods of time, so that although both the logic of learning–unlearning–relearning as a lengthy process may be apparent, and their own experience may support such logic, cost will contribute to termination. There is considerable recidivism, but so far that is more acceptable than lengthy continuous treatment. Which course might be better is very difficult to establish and, at the moment, is largely a matter of opinion.

Freud (1937/1964) anticipated this issue many years ago. "Experience has taught us that psychoanalytic therapy . . . is a time-consuming business. . . . Attempts have been made to shorten the duration of analyses. . . . Whatever one's theoretical attitude . . . the termination of an analysis is . . . a practical matter" (pp. 216, 249).

"Practical" includes time and effort but primarily money. Thus, therapy is a matter of need up to a point, and after that people will get along without it because they think it is not sufficiently cost effective. It can be endlessly effective from an adaptive, learning point of view, but from an economic perspective, therapy ends whenever the consumer decides it costs too much.

As a result the stamp of money is put on every session by all concerned. Society at large is the least knowing and the most bottom-line oriented, although individuals within the society have more sophisticated and flexible realities. Unfortunately, psychotherapists have been the last in the mix to act as though they recognize the integral role of the cost of psychotherapy. This situation must change.

Chapter 2

THE MEANING
OF MONEY

Money is customarily defined by its functions, namely, a medium of exchange, a standard of value, and a storehouse of wealth (Mayer, Dusenberry, & Aliber, 1984). As an exchange medium, money replaces direct barter and instead becomes the intermediary. As a value standard, it is a way to measure what goods and services are worth, and finally it is a way to hold wealth.

Most of the money in use today is credit money, without commodity value equal to its monetary value and not redeemable for commodity value. This situation exists for efficiency reasons and is of relatively recent origin. The evolution of money was from precious metals to precious metal coins, then to paper money that could be redeemed in these coins, and now to paper money. Thus, our current money has minor inherent value but has a stated value because people in the society agree it has that value and treat it that way.

The concept of money having an implicit meaning is present in its credit attributes and is congruent with the fact that people attribute meanings to money. The designed functions of money—namely, exchange, value measurement, and storage—lend themselves to a variety of personal and emotional needs of people. For example, people can be exchanged, bought, and sold for money as slaves or as in the expression, "buying someone off," or in the statement, "she married him for his money."

People also measure themselves in terms of money, as their yearly income, and are thought of as rich and powerful or poor and weak. The accumulation of wealth is seen as an indicator of security and comfort as well as freedom. The accumulation of money is a common goal, with the manner of acquisition and the use of money often involving intense affects, as greed, competitiveness, fierce work ethic, as well as philanthropy, charity, parsimony, and irresponsibility. Disdain and disregard are also possibilities, although most people appear to have a strong but anxious interest in money. The anxious part is reflected in the need to disguise the motives for wanting the money, which is invariably justified, sometimes with the most peculiar twists of logic. It is these motives, and their disguises, that concern us next.

ATTITUDES TOWARD MONEY

Wiseman (1974) described a number of personality constellations organized around a person's attitudes and behavior toward money. Although these overlap, they do illustrate the possible variety of focus, including the romantic, company man, collector, hustler, double-dealer, criminal, gambler, and loser, as well as the nonplayer.

Wiseman's emphasis is more descriptive than explanatory, although he sees money as overdetermined in meaning and origin. He cites a number of psychoanalytic explanations for particular types, such as Freud's anal character and Melanie Klein's concept of the inexhaustible breast, as well as a social psychological theory of personal valuation. His major point, however, appears to be that money is essentially an unsatisfying dream, and his typology stresses this ultimate discontent.

Thus, the romantic idealizes money but justifies this in terms of a mission to be successful. The company person emphasizes making money for others while downplaying, yet not eschewing, personal acquisition. A timely example is the corporate raider who claims to be just enhancing stockholders' value. The other types have similar approaches, namely, a great desire for money and a justification. Even the criminal sees life as having dealt him a bad hand so that crime is necessary to live. The nonplayers, few in number, subscribe to the "can't buy happiness" creed that is in accord with evidence that the dream and reality of wealth can be painfully discrepant. Altruism is another possibility for these people, with the belief that although money can be useful and even make people happy, there are other viable ways to live. Thus, there is another money type, the poor, who vary in how much money they do not have and how voluntary and personally desired is their level of substinence.

The nonplayer category refers to a minority subtype of the poor, whereas the majority of the poor are players who consistently lose and who tend not to make the type of list just described. Yet they are a major money type, with subtypes as well, and with their own developmental origins, attitudes, and behaviors about money. The neglect of the poor as a money class with psychological characteristics has been common and may well reflect a tendency among psychotherapists to consider the middle class as the representative class (Ehrenreich, 1989).

Kaufman (1976) provides another example of monetary nosology based on how people use money emotionally. The first is the well-balanced person who accrues and spends in a realistic fashion. This translates into maintaining a high standard of living that is at the same time in accord with income and includes saving. There is a flexible, modulated approach that can use credit, take some risks, yet adjust to income variations. This person competes fairly, is not envious, and is willing to help others.

Then there are a number of not as well-balanced types, beginning with the nonspender, who can fall into a number of subtypes such as the conservative, the economic, and the miser. The conservative insists on value for the dollar and limits purchases to necessities, whereas the economic spender insists on bargains, and the miser loves her monetary hoard. Nonspenders are hypothesized as having been deprived of love and in turn having money symbolize security and love.

In contrast to these people are the compulsive spenders, who are depicted as having a variety of backgrounds, including being given money as a love substitute as well as having been deprived of both love and money. Again a number of subtypes are depicted, such as narcissistic, exhibitionistic, and affection-buying, as well as gamblers.

Other types of money users include the guilty, indecisive, and anxious, the pretenders who depict false poverty or wealth, the controllers who reward or punish, and the defensive, who use money in ritualistic ways. Charitable utilization of money and the giving up of money are also noted, and the point is made that the particular use of money—as a gift, for example—may be healthy or disturbed depending on the motives involved.

Kaufmann (1976) favors a balanced use of money, distinguishing between money-health and money-sickness based on the social acceptability of how a person behaves in regard to money. He sees the origin of what he terms "psycho-economic" behavior in childhood patterns fostered by parents. His approach is adaptive, accepting the existing economic structure and paying limited attention to instinctual components of behavior. It is also a broad-based view that could have a variety of specifics. The origins of the meaning of money and its uses for an individual include culture, religion, parents and teachers, life experiences, and goals.

The development of the child's use of money under parents' direction is traced from learning that money can buy things that are pleasurable and can be used as a reward or punishment to realizing that there are limitations on the money supply and that money has to be earned. Ambivalence, connections between love and money, the awareness of socioeconomic differences, envy, anger, and the desire for economic power are all recognized along the way.

Both Wiseman (1974) and Kaufmann (1976) view money as multideterminined in origin and meaning, although Wiseman gives more weight to such psychoanalytic constructs as anality and envy than does Kaufmann.

Although the latter makes no direct links to experience prior to the age of 3, pregenital motivations are nonetheless discernible. It appears that most materials exploring the subject of motivation for and about money rely on the idea of a "drive," sometimes mentioning the drive to acquire wealth or the capitalistic instinct, if not making direct attribution to an aspect of libidinal or aggressive instincts.

Bergler (1959), for example, distinguished between normal and neurotic attitudes and uses of money, delineating a "money neurosis" in which money is the focal point of existence. The money illness has its roots in the infantile fantasy of omnipotence, which the money neurotic cannot relinquish. Rather than make adjustments to the demands of reality, there is an unconscious stabilization at the level of rejection of demands. Pleasure is now derived from displeasure in what is termed the masochistic triad. The components are provoking deprivation of some sort, avoiding notice of the provocation and instead focusing on the apparent injustice, which is then met with retribution, self-pity, and self-justification. Money becomes an instrument in the process, characterized by its accumulation and its possessor's unwillingness to spend it. The acquisition is an expression of getting as opposed to refusal, and the miserliness represents defensiveness against passivity.

Bergler spins off a number of personality types from the concept of psychic masochism that bear resemblances to money types already noted, as the success hunter, gambler, golddigger, and dependee. However, the reasons for the persistence of infantile omnipotence are not clear. In addition, the explanation of the development of psychic masochism and its involvement with money are not very convincing. After making a case for what appears to be quite a distinction between normal and abnormal approaches to money, Bergler (1959) uses the "dissatisfied infant" concept as an explanation, for "at times, even our most correct people act, let us say, 'peculiarly' in matters concerning money" (p. 18).

Peculiar behavior can be agreed on when it comes to money, but Bergler's megalomania genesis leaves too many exceptions. However, it does set the stage for the consideration of psychoanalytic explanations of money that are specific and comprehensive, highlighting probably the most famous money type, the anal character.

However, before doing that it is useful to note an added feature of money typing, namely, a sociopolitical attitude about money that limits both range and objectivity of observation. Bergler (1959) was aware of this possibility and tried to dismiss it with a disclaimer that money neurosis is not engendered by any external system. Perhaps he wished that were so, but his assertion is as unconvincing as stating that money issues are solely the result of societal structures. Bergler (1959) tips his hand by stating, "The not too-neurotic person will try to make money as best he can and as extensively as he can" (p. xiv).

Wiseman (1974) appears as a reluctant capitalist who is pessimistic about people ever using money constructively and happily, particularly if they have a lot of it. A similar view appears on the work of Lapham (1988) as he links money and class as the "civil religion" of America. Kaufmann (1976) comes across as an unabashed proponent of the good life. Thus, none of his money types are the poor despite their large presence in the world, and he clearly sees a high correlation between monetary and emotional security. In contrast to all of these writers is Bornemann (1976), who has stated: "The analysis of money must develop into a therapy that will cure us of the interest in it" (p. 357).

Undoubtedly we, the authors, also have social, political, ethical, and moral attitudes about money that will become apparent in varying degrees throughout this book. The existence of these attitudes emphasizes the point that money is an emotionally charged issue, probably more so than many other more widely debated issues. After all, money affects so many areas of life and for such a long time during the life span.

Certainly one's approach to money has a developmental genesis and reflects a variety of personality characteristics. As noted, these may appear in other significant areas as well, as sexual expression or in political activity or sports. However, our concern is with money as the medium for expression, namely, the meanings of money for people and the origins of these meanings.

Lapham (1988) has commented that in regard to money and class: "Few words come armed with as many contradictions or as much ambivalence" (p. 3). The term "contradictions" is a common one, but "ambivalence" requires some clarification. In a recent review, Sincoff (1990) defined ambivalence broadly as overlapping approach–avoidance tendencies, which is akin to Lapham's use of it to refer to essentially mixed but contradictory feelings. However, in terms of the meanings of money, it is more profitable to consider the term from its clinical origins with Bleuler (1911). He identified both conscious and unconscious types of ambivalence. Conscious thoughts and actions indicating conflict were viewed as normal processes. In some contrast was emotional ambivalence: love and hate feelings directed toward the same object, in our case, money. This was of greater interest and stressed by Freud (1913c) as unconscious feelings.

Whereas ambivalence as originally conceptualized was linked to the pathologies of indecision and disintegration, more current psychoanalytic views have stressed the fusion aspect of ambivalence. In contrast to splitting, where money is viewed as all good or bad, ambivalence allows a totality of feelings, good and bad, about the same thing. It is essentially a precursor of the development of a relatively consistent attitude that includes the recognition of mixed qualities in the object of consideration. Although a certain degree of ambivalence is expected, useful, and tolerable, to be locked into ambivalence is painful and conflictual. With all this in mind, we are ready to look into the psychoanalytic meanings of money.

PSYCHOANALYTIC MEANINGS

It is apparent that people are frequently ambivalent about money and that the ambivalence, often unresolved, is traceable to the multidetermined meanings of money. Freud stressed the connection between money and anal eroticism beginning with *Three Essays on the Theory of Sexuality* in 1905. This idea had been taking shape in earlier comments, for example, in a letter to Fliess in 1897, and this statement: "Uncleanliness in childhood is often replaced in dreams by avariciousness for money: the link between the two is the word 'filthy' " (1900a, p. 200). Also, in terms of symbolism, Freud noted, "Dreams with an intestinal stimulus . . . confirm the connection between gold and faeces which is also supported by copious evidence from social anthropology" (1900b, p. 403).

In 1908 he described the anal character as a person who constitutionally had particularly intense anal erotogenicity that is diminished in subsequent development only to be replaced by a triad of personality characteristics. These are orderliness, parsimony, and obstinacy. Orderliness includes cleanliness, conscientiousness, and trustworthiness; parsimony is displayed in avarice; and obstinacy has an aggressive cast, including defiance, rage, and revenge. Of the three he considered parsimony and obstinacy the most closely related and most constant. Money lends itself to the expression of any or all of the three, which are construed as results of sublimating anal pleasure.

Thus, money and dirt are related, with an interest in money replacing the original interest in defecation and its product. In the case of the Rat Man (Freud, 1909), the connection between what is dirty and money is again indicated with the patient's equation of money and rats. Other associations of the patient with rats link money to sex and power as well, although Freud's emphasis was on the anal connection. This is elaborated in 1918 when Freud discusses the distinctions between normal and abnormal interests in money, considering the latter connected to libidinal interests, beginning with anality.

The equation of money and feces is described in more detail, indicating that feces are the child's initial gift to parents, bodily content sacrificed for the sake of loved ones, but are also used to defy others, introducing a sadistic component as well. The genesis of a power motive appears here, with the idea of money also taking over the meaning of baby (both being gifts). Freud stressed the sexual concept of the baby symbol, but a phallic or power conception could be construed as well.

While Freud's emphasis was on anality in understanding the meaning of money, he did give brief mention to oral motives as well, namely, the "primitive greed of the suckling" (1901, p. 158). Furthermore, he was clear about the presence of ambivalence, stating "Among the majority even of what are called 'respectable' people traces of divided behaviour can easily be observed where money and property are concerned" (Freud, 1901, p. 158).

That he was not immune from such ambivalence was also clear. In his technical recommendations he is "strict" about the necessity for a fee and for explicit arrangements about its payment as well as the general foolishness of "giving away" therapy. However, when a female patient described a situation in which she was without money she needed because she was embarrassed to ask her husband for it, Freud said, "After she had told me this once, I made her promise that if it happened again she would borrow the small sum necessary from me" (1913b, p. 306).

Also, although he generally believed that fees were necessary to motivate patients, he did admit that free treatment could be successful in some cases. He accepted the idea of money as being necessary for self-preservation and as a way to gain power, but it was the hidden libidinal components that he focused on. In turn he noted the hypocrisy and ambivalence surrounding money and urged analysts to cast off such attitudes and educate their patients to do so as well (Freud, 1913a). As events have turned out, Freud was a more successful sexuality teacher than monetary teacher.

Ferenczi (1952) described an ontogenetic and phylogenetic development in the child beginning with pleasure derived from both defecating and retaining feces. There is a movement of interest from feces and mud as an equivalent to sand, then stones, marbles, coins, stamps, and ultimately, money. This is part of a civilizing, repressing process with both an instinctual and rational component, since money does provide realistic comforts as well as satisfying anal erotic needs. Jones (1918) and Abraham (1923) both continued the anal connection, with amplifications of anal character traits that used money as the medium. Thus, money can be used to express impulses and affects that no longer can be expressed in their raw form. Anal impulses are the most notable, but oral and genital ones are also included.

Fenchel (1981) links money and excretory impulses by stressing the secrecy about money matters that is so common in our society. In noting the powerful symbolism of money, Bornemann (1976) traces its metaphorical meanings throughout history. Money has always seemed to exist as more than its designated function with a very potent affective charge.

Starting in the oral phase, Fenchel (1981) sees money as having both an exploratory and a proprietary meaning. An exaggeration of proprietary feelings results in a fusion or inability to part with money as well as an entitlement to it. Thus, we have the fantasy of money as the idealized, ever-flowing breast depicted by Melanie Klein (1957/1975).

The ambivalence that we have noted in regard to money is present in the oral stage with its sucking and spitting out as well as the treatment of the breast, which can be sadistic as well as tender and nurturing. This ambivalence is heightened in the anal stage, where there is a definite power struggle. There is pleasure in getting, taking, possessing, and giving. Money can be used to fulfill any or all of these in a variety of ways, including the reflection of inconsistency and the perpetuation of ambivalence.

Fuqua (1986) summarizes the classical psychoanalytic view of the meaning of money as representative of anal pleasure in either retention or defecation. It is interesting that not a great deal has been written in contemporary psychoanalytic literature that goes beyond the concept of the anal character, which is primarily conceptualized in drive theory. Krueger (1986b, 1991) adds a self-psychological note with interest in money being part of the development of narcissism, but his focus is on pathological narcissism engendering monetary addiction. Nelson (1979) has described the psychoanalytic equation, money = feces, and a capitalistic equation, money = power as both being part of the process of civilization.

In reviewing psychoanalytic conceptions about money, Bornemann (1976) disputes the derivation of money attitudes from the anal character or a combination of orality and anality or, in fact, from any somatic economy. He does see value in understanding such an economy, and he proposes one of his own with four metabolic stages. Orality is the first, with ingestion the model for acquisition. There is a lack of adequate nursing here, so that the repetitive act of acquisition is more pleasurable than the acquisitions themselves. Then there is a digesting stage that is the prototype for investing and can be viewed as a mixture of oral and anal activities. This is followed by anal phases of withholding and expelling, corresponding to saving and spending.

Character types are in turn linked to three stages, but this is not the main point of the work by Bornemann (1976). Instead, he sees the role of the parents as a tool of a society that uses the oral and anal stages to educate children in a particular way. For example, he points out that both Reich (1949) and Fromm (1941) portrayed capitalism as an obsessional neurosis, and he concurs. Fromm contrasted the relatively late training during the age of feudalism with early training in the era of capitalism. Toilet training was seen as shaping the culture and as being affected by it as well. In feudalism, competition was limited, surplus was not invested, and incentives were few. However, capitalism required new values in accord with early training in cleanliness, such as orderliness, persistence, and thrift, which in turn affected the education of the children. Thus, the thrust of the model suggested by Bornemann (1976) is that economics determines education, which itself is used to civilize instincts in service of the economy.

An interesting feature here is the interaction of instinctual and in-terpersonal elements as displayed in the society. The manner of that interaction as suggested by Borneman raises problems, however, because he is determined to demonstrate the desirability of socialism and fits his clinical evidence into that framework. Thus, he states, "All psychoanalytic experience suggests that the desire for possessions which exceed require-ments . . . and can only be satisfied by the private ownership of the means of production is neurotic in origin" (Bornemann, 1976, p. 46).

Lathrop (1979) sees money as a fundamental way to express psychic energy and as a manifestation of power. Other comments about the psy-choanalytic meaning of money can be found, as in Chodoff (1964), Bar-Levav (1979), and Forrest (1990), but there has been a lack of comprehensive synthesis of the psychoanalytic meanings of money.

A neglected exception to this is the work of Fenichel (1938/1954) which, although written over half a century ago, nonetheless has considerable present and future applicability. He saw the accumulation of money as multidetermined, with four primary motives. These were the rational satisfaction of needs, the desire for power, the possessive instinct, and the ideology of society. The accumulation of money was considered a drive, with pathological and normal forms, but an interactive drive between instinctual structures and social influences. In the reductionistic sense the drive for money can be construed as an example of anal eroticism, but social forces modify this, and the modified drive acts on social structures so that a reciprocal loop is created. Thus, Fenichel adhered to the money = feces equation, yet he did not consider money as merely a convenient intervention for instinctual satisfaction.

As a great synthesizer, then, Fenichel had vision that allowed for an expansion of drive theory without having to lay it waste or subsume libido and aggression to relational needs in order to consider the motivational role of society with its interpersonal emphasis. This aspect of Fenichel's thinking has seen light in other theories, particularly those of Adler, Horney, Fromm, and Sullivan, but with a more singular emphasis on detaching from instinctual drive theory and without a particular concern for the many meanings of money.

The rational motive is based on the logical assumption that money is useful or necessary in satisfying people's needs. The logic is correct when society requires money for that purpose, which most societies do. Thus, people are expected on a realistic basis to have an interest in money as a way to be able to satisfy their human needs, many of which can be classified as basic and instinctual, such as hunger and shelter as well as supporting a family structure and developing a society. There are limits on the degree of interest and the amount of money to be accumulated to meet these needs. The limits are determined by the prevalent quality of life in a particular society, which varies over time. The limits in some societies are closer to a basic survival level then they are in others, and certainly there is a powerful subjective element in deciding what is or is not needed for satisfaction once the minimum is in place. Consensus is frequently available, however, in regard to the rational acquisition and use of money. Guidelines exist in the society as to how much money per year is needed to feed, clothe, and maintain families of various sizes. These guidelines are formed on the basis of providing a generally recognized life style, varying by class and in terms of the purchasing power of the currency. Thus, judgments can be formed with relative accuracy as to the rationality of the monetary motive.

Although conforming to the rational motive is reasonable, it is not necessarily satisfying on an emotional level. The uneven distribution of wealth that appears to prevail in virtually every society can be understood, and even accepted, without being liked. Depending on how uneven it becomes, the acceptance of the situation will also vary. Add in the rather common presence of emotions such as jealousy and envy and the probability of a dominant rational motive for money acquisition is limited.

Linked to the rational motive are the possibilities provided by money, or the idea that money can provide power. The desire for power, inherent in an aggressive drive or represented in narcissism and/or self-esteem, is well recognized. For example, Lapham (1988) states: "Ask an American what money means, and nine times in ten he will say it is synonymous with freedom, that it opens the doors of feeling and experience, that citizens with enough money can play at being gods and do anything they wish" (pp. 26–27).

The quote does not have to be limited to Americans. Fenichel saw the acquisition of money as one way to improve or maintain self-esteem, derived from an earlier form of maintaining the self with narcissistic environmental supplies. Money now became the current ideal food for fantasy. Although it is true that people are not always satisfied with what they attain once they have it and often find that it is not enough, they are still motivated by the possibility of power. Regardless of whether everybody fulfills the fantasy or gets the power and misuses it, the power is there for the getting. As Fenichel points out, if a society equates power with money, then of course money can be power.

Fenichel goes a step beyond societal creation of the need for possessing wealth, however, and deals with a need for possessing. This need represents the protection of the integrity of the self, with possessions as ego parts based on the concept of the ego as originally a body-ego. The psychic structures are often felt to be under siege, and possessions are the barrier preventing disintegration. The social acceptability of money, its necessity as a means of living, makes it easily transformable into a type of narcissism.

All the psychosexual stages appear as contributors to the desire to possess, including withdrawal of the breast as well as castration anxiety. However anal eroticism continues to maintain center stage.

It may be that the anal retentive pleasure is always secondary and is always mixed with a fear of experiencing the pleasure in excreting; at any rate the retentive pleasure does come to exist, at least secondarily, and analytic experience concerning anal retentive pleasure leaves no doubt but that it is the erogenous source of the desire for possession for possession's sake and the source of all irrational behavior concerning money. (Fenichel, 1938/1954, p. 98)

As Fenichel admits, arguments could be made for accumulation pleasure (as well as spending pleasure) in all the psychosexual stages, although anality has the traditional emphasis. Similar conceptions could be advanced in regard to the give and take of object relationships. In fact, Fenichel mentions that money can represent object relations and self-regard, actually everything about the self and others that can be transacted.

A key contribution of psychoanalysis has been to elucidate the unconscious symbolism of money, yet this represents a danger that the reality of money becomes lost. No doubt that often happens, and that is a misuse of the function of money. Understanding of distortions in the operation of money is facilitated by psychoanalytic investigation, but the true function of money is not accurately deduced from its misuse, as Fenichel noted very clearly. Although it ought to be possible to view money as "only money," it is simply not easy to do that, as demonstrated earlier in our discussion of the "rational motive."

In reviewing the development of attitudes toward money, Fenichel makes note of a "pre-pecuniary phase" in which there is a desire to keep everything, and money is merely part of the everything. This phase is also shaped culturally in terms of attitudes toward giving and taking, but it has little to do with the reality of money as distinct from any other possession. This is followed by a "pecuniary phase" in which the child learns the designated or real function of money, though this phase in turn is colored by previous, and continuing, unconscious tendencies. In particular, Fenichel links power and possession in attitudes toward money, basing his model on components of anal pleasure that are both erogenous and self-regarding. Although Fenichel is speaking primarily in terms of libidinal drive theory, the updating of his conceptions in ego psychology, object relations, and self-theory is certainly possible. The overdetermination of money is clearly established, and a number of motives are brought into play in addition to the ideology of societies and their corresponding economic structures.

Recently Lapham (1988) chastised people for their "obsession with money" as our national religion and for giving so much value to "something as abstract and as inherently meaningless as money" (p. 218). Albeit not in the same querulous vein, Fenichel is making the point that of course, we attribute meanings to the "meaningless." And whereas he does not avoid taking a few swipes at capitalism and the ruling class, his point, and in the same sense Lapham's, is that money is the innocent, our motives are the guilty, society constitutes the collaborator.

Society, then, is the validator of money, creating it for structural reasons, out of a rational need. But of course society is the creation of individuals who are interested in satisfying their needs. One of these is definitely an economic system that needs money. Thus, there is a reciprocal relationship between money and instinct. As Fenichel noted, production and distribution systems are significant aspects of the history and future of mankind. Economic reality, then, will always be a powerful motivational force as well as a force shaped by instinctual needs.

It is striking that analyzers of the monetary scene are struck by the negative uses that people in society make of money. Fenichel (1938/1954), concludes, ". . . reflection on the significant influence of economic evaluation upon all the conditions of mankind show us that such a drive (to become wealthy) at one time did not exist and at some future time will exist no longer" (p. 108).

Berle, in predicting an evolution toward democracy in an increasing number of nations resulting from demonstrated productivity and stability, stated: ". . . a degree of wealth is likely to be accepted because it results from productive institutions. But it is highly unlikely that wealth will run wild . . ." (1969, p. 217).

These were hopeful men, each wanting in different ways an equitable, humane economic system with money as just an ordinary hammer that can drive a nail. As Lapham comments, they and many others have been disappointed. "We squander our fortune in order to become a nation of somnambulists deprived of the cultural and spiritual means to escape our confinement in a gilded cage. . . . As has been said more than once (but probably needs to be said yet again) it isn't the money itself that causes the trouble, but rather the use of the money . . ." (Lapham, 1988, p. 243).

This is where psychoanalysis can have its impact, providing the understanding of what money means to people and how in turn they will attempt to use it. General motivations, such as drives and relations, press money into their service so that money can mean anything and everything, much of it far from the simple tool it was supposed to be.

MONEY NOW

In a recent newspaper article, Tom Wolfe (1990) predicted the spirit of the 1990s as that of "money fever." Ehrenreich (1989) emphasizes a growing gap between rich and poor. Perloff (1990) states: "Given all the pathology, dehumanization and deprivation that flow from poverty, my own subjective impression is that poverty is the most important social issue of our time" (p. 7). At the same time, Glazer (1988) has pointed out the failure to develop a national system of social policy, with one of the causes being an individualistic trend that blames the poor for their poverty. The "American Dream" Award for 1990 went to a New Jersey congresswoman for her efforts to protect the mortgage interest tax deduction. Not surprisingly the National Association of Homebuilders sponsored the award, their version of the dream. Added to the above mixture are the numerous books, pamphlets, and offers to make one rich as well as all the exhortations about the evils of money.

Although these various attitudes toward money are certainly confusing, a few clear ideas emerge from all this. Most people want money. Money has a dream-like quality beguiling its reality. People disagree as to the "proper way" to regard, handle, acquire, even think about money, but money is important. The importance is personal and disproportionate to the intended meaning of money as created by society.

As psychotherapists, we face the task of dealing with the overdetermination of money as it occurs for us and for our patients. The personalized meaning of money is in turn reflected in the use of money and illustrated in the fee transaction between patient and therapist. A particularly useful conception for understanding this is adaptation, defined by Phillips: "The term 'human adaptation' refers to a person's response to the complexities of living in society" (1986, p. 1).

Adaptation has its origins in the work of Hartmann (1964) who developed ego psychology and aptly attempted to construe psychoanalysis as a general psychology, which had certainly been one of Freud's original goals. Hartmann emphasized the individual operating within an environmental context, especially understanding and working with reality. The motivational aspect of reality, of the socioeconomic system, was expanded, and adaptation to social reality was something for which people were innately prepared. A key part of this reality is economic.

From the advent of psychoanalysis, productivity has always been lauded as a human goal. Within the development of the variety of schools of psychoanalysis there has essentially been an expansion of the reasons for people being interested in money as well as the reasons for their discomfort with this interest. Although not directed at money, this expansionist, essentially integrative view is very well illustrated in two recent papers by Pine (1988, 1989).

Beginning with sexual gratification, money serves a clear purpose. It can "buy" sex literally as well as more subtly. The latter is apparent in the creation of a "rich image" based on wealth, which is also a sexually attractive image. The intertwining of power and sexual gratification is also apparent, with the idea that wealth and sexual prowess can be equated, at least in fantasy. On an instinctual, pregenital level, the anal, as well as the oral and phallic, erogenous appeal of money has been well documented. On a broad libidinal level money serves as a provider, a way to demonstrate that one cares about and loves others. The repetitive sensual pleasure fits in quite well with acquiring money and going after more of it. Of course, to say that money is an equivalent of sex is inaccurate, but to be aware that money and sex are well connected is very accurate.

The satisfaction of aggression via money is even more apparent. Money is an avenue to power without being a guarantee. With money, it is possible to acquire and to control, and it is certainly possible to feel powerful, to "throw one's weight [measured in dollars] around." The pregenital origins of possession have been noted, as has the genital pride that money can readily symbolize. Money serves reactive aggression particularly well because it provides means to redress wrongs or exact revenge.

Considered from an interpersonal view, money is a way to demonstrate object attachment as well as to demonstrate levels of relationships. Money can be used to care for others or to distance from them. Money is an engaging force between people because it is used in transactions. Money provides for envy, jealousy, dependency, gratitude, and charity. It is an integral component of the functioning of society, and it is a key determiner of "class." Money is the mainstay of social engineering and social policies.

Of course, money serves the self. People frequently value themselves in dollar terms and, in turn, in terms of competency and mastery. In many ways, money is narcissism. The role of money cannot be thoroughly understood, however, without our keeping in mind its multiple functions.

In 1930 Waelder (1976) stressed the multiple function of all behaviors. Drive gratification, repetition, adaptation, and conscience were his major categories. We have already made it clear that money is an expression of drive gratification. The repetitive aspect is in regard to mastery and maintenance. Using money in a way that is gratifying is the goal, and that requires repetition. Money is not acquired once but repetitively. At the survival level nothing of what is earned is left, whereas at higher levels there is discretionary use of the money, including hoarding, wasting, and giving it away, as well as investing it to gain still more income.

Survival needs dictate a certain maintenance level, and class needs or value systems combine with survival, so a standard of living is established that has a homeostatic character. One strives to keep it or achieve a better one and maintain that. Thus, although some people always seem to want more and resist the idea of any level of acquisition being yet enough, even they appear to have a minimum that provides them some sense of mastery.

However, coming to terms with money is a complex task, and money tends to be an enduring concern. Forces larger than the individual have their effects, such as inflation and recession, so there is a reality in the need for most people to plan their economic lives. Making money is a necessary task in the society, and it requires repetition to master, that in turn requires maintenance of the mastery in order to sustain security and the sense of well-being connected to having "enough money."

Of course it is well documented that people often are not at peace or in congruence in regard to what constitutes "enough." Nonetheless, there is a comfort zone and a psychic equilibrium that is maintained as long as a person stays within the zone. Therein lies the motivation for the repetition. Often people will strive to recreate that comfort zone by repeating efforts at production, investment, or saving. Thus, in the clinical situation, money issues will be repeated between therapist and patient as well as by the patient (and therapist) outside of therapy. Gedo (1981) provides a review of psychoanalytic theorists who have stressed the centrality of repetition in motivation, so the consideration of the role of repetition in money matters has a definite theoretical foundation.

Gedo (1981) sees repetition as essential in the development and organization of the self, which in turn is part of the process of adaptation that we have already indicated is a key concept in understanding the use of money. The tendency is to fit with as well as shape the psychic environment, including conflict resolution, self-development, and relationships to others. Money is involved in all of these as a possible means of adaptation as well as a possible source of disturbance. Thus, money can be used to cause a conflict as well as to defuse one. Essentially the use of money is the issue, and it is employed by each person as an adaptation.

The success and reality of the adaptation are determined in reference to how much ego control is involved, as compared with money in service of id or superego forces that are relatively untamed. Thus, if one were to list the seven capital sins of pride, envy, greed, sloth, gluttony, anger, and lust, money could certainly be used to service any one of them. In contrast, the idea that money is inherently evil symbolizes the rampant superego, and it appears that the touch of the instinctual that always follows money around is accompanied by a conscience as well. Money is unrealistically but routinely split into a force for good or bad, meaning there are good and bad ways to do anything with it, and there is disregard for the basic neutrality of money.

The self-image is depicted through having a "proper attitude" toward money, which usually involves not talking about it, not admitting exactly how much of it one either has or wants other than in vague generalities, and demonstrating its use in key situations, such as charitable contributions.

In addition, the self-image is represented by monetary worth, which is proudly shown through certain possessions such as one's home, car, clothes—the public persona that a person considers compatible with the self-image. In other situations, the self-image is carefully downplayed, as in dealing with the Internal Revenue Service or friends and relatives who might want to borrow money or at least who might display envy and unpleasantness. Of course there are people who ignore these "rules," but they are usually denigrated as being ostentatious or indiscreet. Money is something people think about much more than they talk about, and they conceal some of the nature and content of their thoughts even when they are verbal about money. Also, it is much easier to talk about other people's money than one's own, so there is a lot of public displaying of money matters, as in the media. On the personal level, money usually remains a taboo topic, and thus the difficulty in handling the subject in psychotherapy.

We have stressed the overdetermination and multiplicity of the meaning of money for each individual. This indicates that the therapist should expect money always to mean something to a patient other than "mere money." Psychoanalytic theory offers many of the possible meanings that could have developed historically in patients' lives. Thus, it is possible to see the instinctual connections to money, to view money as the tool of psychic structures, the component of self and interpersonal relations, the content of conflict, defense, and adaptation, and to trace its genesis and subsequent place in individuals' lives. It is also possible to notice the interaction of motivations and meanings and to arrive at a picture of each person's personal motivational organization, what Pine (1989) has described as "personal hierarchies."

Despite this complexity, we are struck by a central theme in reference to money, namely, that money is *potential*. As a psychic component money represents what can be done, and therefore, it has a wishful quality. It is certainly true that money does not satisfy every need and that people are not automatically better off once they have more money. Having money can foster anxiety just as easily as not having it, and as we have indicated, there is a large amount of history documenting the problems of having money.

Yet, it is not money per se that is the problem, but how it is used, including how it is obtained. Money has power because of its possibilities for creating good or evil. The uses of money essentially have to do with wish gratification that may or may not be costly to the self or others. It is those wishes, and the affects attached to them, that give money its neurotic taboo quality and open the way to individual variations in using money.

For example, although money is gender-neutral, there are sex differences apparent in the handling of money. Rowland, in a *New York*

Times column of May 6, 1990, reports that financial planners find women generally have more problems in managing money than men. This was attributed to a developmental pattern in which women are raised to spend money and men to invest it. These planners saw this as a pattern that is still perpetuated in younger women, although no suggestions were made that women were less able to understand money. Women's perceptions were unfortunately slanted in the direction of seeing great mystery in the process of investing and in personalizing investments as indicators of intelligence. Once again, money has been transformed into something else, a symbol of the self and in this case certain gender-typed characteristics. In accord with this, it has also been noted that female therapists have more trouble than males with fee issues (Burnside, 1986; Lasky, 1984; Liss-Levenson, 1990).

Since therapists have no special knowledge about money and have been subject to many of the same developmental influences about money as their patients, the probability of avoiding or failing to work adequately with money issues in therapy is high and, of course, needs to be reduced. We cannot expect therapists to be financial experts, but we can expect them to understand both their patients and themselves in regard to the personal meanings of money. This includes an awareness of intrapsychic issues as well as societal distinctions that may be related to gender, culture, race, and class. They need to be open to exploring what money is all about for their patients and to help patients do this when avoidance is displayed.

Exploration and understanding are certainly facilitated by adequate personal psychotherapy, but as far as money goes, this often has not been the case. In addition, there are numerous therapists who have had no, or very little, personal therapy, so there's work to be done in educating therapists about the meaning of money. A significant part of that education is learning to come to realistic terms with money. It is a neutral tool with incredible potential whose power rests with the user. Money is indeed what you make of it, and particularly in therapy, that should not be a secret.

Chapter 3

THE PHILOSOPHY
OF SERVICE

P sychotherapists are recognized in our society as paid service providers. All of the disciplines involved in the umbrella profession of psychotherapy have worked long and hard for such recognition and will continue to do so in order to maintain this role. The paradox is that too many psychotherapists are uncomfortable with the inherent philosophy of service, namely, that they provide a specialized skill for which they deserve to be appropriately paid. This discomfort unfortunately can result in diffusion of the legitimate methods of psychotherapy, ineffective work, and personal dissatisfaction. As a result we want to focus on the reasons for this problem and its remediation.

BOUNDARY VIOLATIONS

The problem begins with a disrespect for the boundaries of psychotherapy. When this happens the patient is exploited, the quality of treatment suspect, and the therapist a dubious recipient of payment.

Epstein and Simon (1990) state, "it violates a treatment contract based on both overt and implicit agreement that the therapist's sole purpose is to treat the patient's disorder in return for monetary compensation. . . . The therapist may also obtain satisfaction from being involved in an interesting and helpful profession" (p. 456).

Their role description is the customary model for private practice, although certainly there are other settings for psychotherapy in which the direct payment from patient to therapist is not as obvious or does not exist. However, even when the therapist is treating the patient for no fee, this represents a donation of the therapist's service within the framework of a fee-for-service model. The concept is always one of an exchange in which the patient, or some agent of the patient, is responsible for paying for the services, and the therapist is the recipient of the payment, directly or indirectly. The transactional nature of psychotherapy, then, is a major boundary of all psychotherapeutic relationships, with the fee symbolizing a major limit of the relationship.

However, the fee is not the only satisfaction for the therapist, and in fact it may not be the primary reward, which is more often the work itself. In addition, there are satisfactions that are incidental to the process, such as enjoying one patient more than another for any number of possible reasons. At the same time, these satisfactions are not the focus of the relationship. If they move from incidental to primary, then the therapy will be limited.

For example, a male therapist may derive pleasure from the appearance of a female patient, but if his focus in the therapy session is in looking at her as contrasted with listening to her, he hardly deserves to be paid for his vision.

The therapeutic situation is one that calls forth a variety of feelings and motivations in therapists. If these can be used in service of the therapy, such as providing empathy, or are recognized but not focused on in the interaction, then there is no problem and therefore no reason for therapists to feel uncomfortable about getting paid.

In contrast, these feelings and motivations may be acted on without recognition that their exploitative aspects are caused by pathological narcissism resulting in self-deception as to the noxious probabilities. Accompanying such actions there may well be guilt about the fee, the stirrings of the preconscious, but the therapists involved do not recognize these as connected to their boundary violations.

Since what is and is not appropriate therapeutic technique is open to some question, there is room for self-deception. Nonetheless, there are enough established standards and agreed-on procedures so that most therapists could become aware of possible exploitations, institute remedies, and return to earning their money.

A much larger problem is that the boundaries feel excessively fluid because feelings and motives are experienced that therapists consider antithetical to the proper therapeutic stance. In accord with such experiences, therapists depreciate or exaggerate the transactional nature of the therapist–patient relationship. It is the thought of exploitation, the wish for sadism, eroticism, idealization, or whatever unacceptable desires, that triggers guilt about payment. The fee then becomes the focal point of acting defensively. Either therapists will feel guilty and undeserving and therefore become lax and tentative regarding fee structures, or their policies will reflect a rigidity and lack of understanding designed as reactive defenses.

Essentially, then, it is the personality of the therapist that embodies a lack of healthy self-regard that in turn will be reflected in discomfort with the philosophy of payment for therapeutic services rendered. Although the therapist will try to act like a reasonable and responsible paid service provider, she will feel like someone else—and too frequently get treated that way by patients.

The role of the therapist as perceived and displayed is discussed in more detail from patients' and therapists' viewpoints in Chapters 6 and 7. Our concern here, in the interests of understanding and prevention, is to investigate the dynamics of the therapist's role in respect to payment philosophy in three key areas: helping, greed, and friendship.

HELPING

How being the helper is a role that gets in the way of receiving one's monetary due has been investigated by Lasky (1984), Burnside (1986), and Liss-Levenson (1990) as a gender issue, although all psychotherapists have a problem here. It is a question of striking a proper balance between giving and getting as well as being clear about what is given and what is gotten in return. As Liss-Levenson (1990) notes, this does appear to be more of an issue for women, which of course will become of increasing concern because of the larger number of women who are now entering the psychotherapy field.

Cultural factors appear to be involved in the fit between the role of psychotherapist and the socially learned role of women to be caretakers without expecting much, if any, monetary reward. Their return would be an emotional one, whereas men tend to be more focused on financial success. However, in the psychotherapy field the situation is particularly complex because the role itself fosters maternal transference for both men and women. Men as providers are accustomed to getting paid for what they do, but what they do is not usually psychotherapy. Also, in the traditional role men use money to nurture and care for others, usually women and children, rather than derive money from nurturing. Although their giving to others may be symbolized via money, their return also has affective components; they receive affection from the people they are nurturing via money.

It is true that women are generally paid less than men, and this "tradition" can get carried over into lower fees. Also, it is true that people who see themselves as less needful of, or connected to, money will often make less of a demand for it, and women are more often in this situation than men. At the same time, the role of good parent, mother and father, that is frequently placed on psychotherapists is not one that usually carries with it expectations of monetary rewards. Parents give a lot, emotionally and monetarily, with primarily an emotional return. The high degree of parenting that gets integrated into practicing psychotherapy creates a conflict about getting paid for the creation of a holding environment. Guilt is created because one is engaged in doing what comes naturally, and getting paid for it.

Of course this is a simplification of the therapist's role, yet there is no question that the relational, transferential, caretaking aspects of psychotherapy can exert a pull in this direction. In addition, although these aspects are theoretically construed to be undifferentiated as to the gender of the therapist, differential parenting of therapists makes this difficult. Chodorow (1989) points to the differing learned relational capacities of women that suggest that women as therapists will be more focused on the needs of their patients and men on their own needs. Thus, both men and women have to work to keep the psychotherapist role intact. Women may have trouble getting proper payment because they consider relating to be enough of a reward, whereas men feel guilty at being paid for a role in which they do not feel they are giving enough.

Benjamin (1988) has suggested that women are more drawn to self-effacement in the acceptance of needs of others, whereas men reverse the process. In psychotherapy, neither position is tenable, and either can result in distorted fee policies. There is a balance to be struck and maintained for therapists to understand and derive satisfaction from being paid for their work. They are not going to be able to do what comes naturally, or even what was learned as role-appropriate behavior, or ultimately be true to themselves unless they accept the unusual role dimensions of psychotherapy. The fee, indeed, is a key one of these.

In attempting to clarify the question of what the relationship is in psychotherapy, Steiner-Adair (1991) asks the following: "How do we as therapists conceptualize ourselves in the therapy relationship as different from our patients, yet simultaneously connected to them and involved in a real relationship?" (p. 241). Based on our discussion, one part of the answer is clearly, expect to be paid appropriately for your services.

Thus far we have made the point that getting overly invested in being the helper is likely to create discomfort about fee policies. Since the helping concept is clearly something valued by both therapist and patient, any other motives or feelings on the therapist's part that she would at any point consider contrary to helpfulness will also cause guilt, confusion, and conflict about payment.

Epstein and Simon (1990) developed an Exploitation Index (EI) that presents a number of possibilities that suggest the helping component of the relationship is at risk. The EI has the seven categories of general boundary violations, eroticism, exhibitionism, dependency, power seeking, greediness, and enabling. Although some of their specifics are open to question depending on one's therapeutic style, many are clear indications of probable exploitation that could certainly result in guilt and/or defensiveness about fee practices. At the same time, it would be unreal to expect a "purification" of feelings and motivations before any therapist can be comfortable with getting paid for providing his or her services.

A balanced position suggests that deliberate exploitation is unacceptable, that undetected exploitation is possible, and requires discovery and remediation, and that thoughts of exploitation are normal in response to patient provocations. Thus, any therapist may *think* positively about imagining social or erotic contacts with patients, have some desire to show off her prowess or power, want to be a magic healer, be tempted by a stock tip, or feel like sharing the experience of having a bad day. Some of these temptations, if acted on, can have a major negative impact, some minor, and none of these is what therapists should get paid for. However, since many of the topics are *felt* by therapists, the area that is particularly pertinent to fees, namely, greed, will be given detailed attention.

GREED

"I have to ensure having an income over the summer, after all," a colleague said with righteous indignation. "So of course I charge the patient when either of us goes on vacation!" What was there to say in response, except that this narcissistic therapist, with her sense of entitlement, embodied a therapist's secret desire: to be cared for according to seemingly rational, self-designed rules, monetarily and at a distance.

Even though we do not think that on one level therapists are essentially greedy, on another, because of certain emotional/interpersonal privation in growing up, some are indeed predisposed or at risk for greed and have the potential to act in this direction. Although the greed starts out as an emotional/interpersonal yearning in infancy, by the time it reaches adult status, it is transformed into, among other things, material or monetary demand that symbolizes the earlier desire. However, under ordinary circumstances the desire is vigorously ignored to the point that even "normal" greed, healthy greed that is part of life from the outset, cannot be allowed in a state of awareness. We therefore must explore the dynamics of the therapist's greed. In the process we compare and contrast the roles of friend and therapist and, in so doing, consider the service actually rendered by the therapist.

Greed as Motivator

If a person were truly greedy, why go into the therapy business, where the money made is limited by hours of service rendered? In other words, although one can make a decent living, the field is not replete with Wall Street possibilities. Obviously, money per se is but one motivator. On a rational level, there is indeed fascination with the work and a desire to be helpful. On an irrational level, there may be a core of helpfulness that turns altruism into a self-serving endeavor.

In previous writings Welt and Herron (1990) have stressed that

> our point has been that the quality of the therapist's narcissism facilitates, if not compels, him or her into a field where the task is to help others. In [giving] treatment, however, it becomes clear that there is a hidden agenda, namely, that it is the patient who is to help the therapist, simply by being a patient in need of the therapist's help. The therapy situation, then, becomes an arena for the expression of the therapist's narcissism, a dilemma where the therapist's developmental lacks in mothering result in his or her becoming mother to his or her own needy mother, now the patient. The therapist, in a single operation, becomes the competent, all-giving mother and through identification, the mother whom the child (patient) must attend. (p. 26)

In other words, enter helper and helpee, and the therapy context then is fertile territory for the therapist's greed to manifest itself. If, according to Klein (1957/1975), deprivation increases greed, that "impetuous and insatiable craving, exceeding what the subject needs and what the object is able and willing to give" (p. 181), then the therapist's premature development into a helper predisposes her to greed. We speak here of course of greed in an emotional/interpersonal sense.

When the mothering one has had inordinate power over the child, the result is a child who not only envies that power but a child who is greedy for power over others and power over the self. As an adult, one way a person tries to acquire such power is to transform the emotional/ interpersonal need into a material one, to desire, if not require, to need and to demand lots of money. However, to therapists, this presents a problem. First, the therapist's identity is infused with parental power at the level of desire and defense at the same time that it is racked with helplessness and subservience at the hand of parental power. So, while therapists unconsciously may yearn for and feel greedy for confirmation and regard, at the same time, they feel unworthy and unprepared for that respect and consideration. Money then becomes something they want but feel uncomfortable about receiving. True power over the self eludes the therapist and in its stead is a "false" power, thinly identified with parental power. Greed, then comes to represent what one did not get emotionally and interpersonally, standing for an anxious attachment (Bowlby, 1969, 1973) to the mothering one. Greed also embodies the power of that parent to have or not have the coveted things and for the decision to give or withhold these items and emotions. Greed is what the therapist feels but cannot be aware of because of a sense of unworthiness. It is difficult to be aware of feeling greed, as well, when one has been trained from infancy to be a selfless helper. Greed would seem to run counter to the idealized image of altruistic caregiver, greedy only in the zeal to help.

Expressions of Greed

Greed, then, is a problem for therapists. It is a problem for those who experience *unbridled,* but *unidentified greed,* for those in other words who feel entitled and have no reservations about the fee or its limits but who are unconscious about their greed. For such therapists, the patient is there in the service of the therapist, just as the therapist's mother was not, and just as the therapist was for that mother. In this emotional scenario, payment becomes a "right" now due. By doing a good job, the therapist justifies the fee, which unconsciously disguises yet replicates the scenario where pathological hope remains that the mother will come through if the therapist (child) is good enough. Further, if the therapist makes the patient (mother) whole, the patient (mother) can do the caretaking (Searles, 1975/1979), but the patient (mother) will pay big dollars for that transplant! "The child helper [now therapist] becomes mother to the mother [now patient], not out of healthy desire or concern but because there is no choice" (Welt & Herron, 1990, p. 25).

Moses and Moses-Hrushovski (1990) discuss persons who have an excessive sense of entitlement, those indeed "brimming with a sense of entitlement" (p. 67). Such a therapist may even appear grandiose, portraying the self as the omnipotent, omniscient, untouchable "Doctor Knows Best." Fees, representative of the adulation a mother has for a child, a feeling a child narcissistically absorbs, now are used as a vehicle for reparation and as a defense against unconscious anger for what the therapist did not get as a child. The therapist has rights after all, is special, and therefore the patient should pay lots. Often, these therapists actually work very hard and long, which disguises the self-righteous sense of entitlement. On another level, they may overwork because the money "extracted" under such conditions never quite brings security, because unconsciously the price the therapist pays is high in the sense of feeling at the mercy of the flawed patient (mother).

Greed defended against by reaction formation is a problem for those therapists who run from the recognition that unconsciously they perceive that money obligates the therapist to the patient, putting the patient (mother) in power over the therapist. It is not that such therapists are not greedy; it is not that they do not want or care about money. Their heritage of privation has taught them that the object's actual greed and their own projection of greed onto the object are dangerous. As Klein (1952/1975) says, "The bad breast will devour him in the same greedy way as he desires to devour it" (p. 64). Consequently, to avoid the anxiety of the aggression, such a therapist backs away from those symbols signifying needs, thus backing away from her own privation and the cognitive and affective memory of it.

Not only might such a therapist tend to charge too little and be negligent about collections, she pays a relational and psychological price of detachment. Not much money is there, and a part of the therapist is missing too. In the process, the original privation is replicated; the therapist (child) is not getting what she needs while meeting the needs of the patient (mother). All the while, in true passive–aggressive manner, the therapist unconsciously collects data on the mother who cannot or will not deliver and fulfill and on the parent (now patient) who should magically know what the therapist (child) needs. Of course, in the best of all worlds, the parent can and does deliver, but a patient cannot be expected to.

The passive–aggressive stance binds the therapist to the patient and thereby to his or her own parent. Healthy aggression is therefore not freely available to the therapist for taking care of herself by setting and collecting adequate fees. Such aggression is laced with extreme anxiety, as if taking care of oneself implied excessive greed. From the parental and later the child's limited standpoint, it probably was an extraordinary demand, but the likelihood is it did not start out that way. As one therapist has said, "If I were to see patients every 45 minutes and hear that cash register ring, I would feel like a shrew [that] must replace its body weight by eating other animal parts every few hours or die!" She was questioning how she could be that aggressive, almost promiscuous, in her need for gratification.

If receiving adequate money is seen as a gesture of greed, monetary compensation will be perceived as a destructive process, increasingly achieved at the expense of others, without consideration or generosity, at the expense of cooperation. Given such interpretation, adequate compensation is truly feared. So, the person who defends against greed through reaction formation leaves the fray, turning away from unresolved pathological greed while ignoring the possibility of arriving at a desire for healthy greed. And in the process, such a therapist repeats the privation, this time at her own hand.

There are those therapists who use *compartmentalization to sidestep greed*. Such persons compartmentalize the money from the task and the symbol from the privation. They avoid making the connection between emotional/interpersonal greed and money as a symbol of that state as a result of early patterns of privation. They are relatively comfortable, therefore, about setting and collecting fees, but they tend to do so either by emotional detachment or by having a third party be responsible. Obviously they want the money but do not want to "know" the source. Consequently, they ignore that the money they rely on to live comes from the patient. This protects them from feeling they are there in the service of the patient or that the patient is there to serve them, the familiar patterns in their own parent–child histories.

Superficially, it appears that money is not an issue. The fact is, the issue is being ignored, split off from awareness by detachment and dissociation of affect connected with the original privation. In conscious awareness is an apparently rational approach to the fee situation. A third party is the "heavy," the institution, or the receptionist or the administrator. What, then is the problem if the compartmentalization works and the therapist gets paid?

We think that at some level, if unresolved greed is a problem for the therapist, the patient is ultimately affected. In one way or another, at one time or another, the patient is not immune from the problem and is not protected from the greed. For example, if indeed the issue is emotional/interpersonal privation, now translated as money, what will be the therapist's response to a patient's similar problem? Will the patient's privation be noticed and adequately processed by the therapist? Will the adult patient's response or defenses against it be identified, particularly if the patient's reaction involves money? And what about the patient's acting out with the therapist regarding the fee? One such patient wanted to pay a month ahead, actually to assure she would "get something" from the therapist (parent) and, not so incidentally, to control her. Another wanted the therapist to falsify the insurance forms so that the therapist would say he had charged a higher fee than the patient would actually pay in order that the patient "get his due" from the carrier (parent). The therapist was instructed to indicate the amount the patient thought she (the patient) deserved, while the patient, not so incidentally, collected data on how fraudulent the therapist could be.

Our contention is that if the therapist compartmentalizes the fee, then therapy opportunities are lost. Valuable data, potentially helpful to the patient, are not attended to. The patient never has the opportunity to show envy about the therapist's receiving money or the resultant desire to do harm, and she cannot, therefore, note or explore the anxiety generated by these phenomena (Klein, 1957/1975). Furthermore, the patient cannot notice, associate to, or explore "uncertainty about the goodness of the object" (p. 187) because the therapist remains so pure, so untainted by the money her mama (third party) is collecting. Such "therapy privations" increase the potential for emotional/interpersonal greed and acting out. Also if the therapist looks so pristine, untouched by greed or money, as Klein might say, transferentially she would be seen as so good that she is "all the more greedily desired and taken in " (p. 187). The patient may prolong the session, the more to "take in," or carefully leave on time, an apparently rational, normal thing to do, similar to the therapist's apparently rational, normal fee arrangement. All the while, the demand for care, for reparation, and the defenses against those needs remain unrecognized by patient and therapist alike and unexplored by both. A third party becomes, in a sense, caretaker and savior for both patient and therapist, but in the process, it reinforces the problem of both, that is, the yearning greedily for a mother to take care of business that meanwhile assures that a vital element of the therapeutic process remains under wraps.

HIRED FRIEND VERSUS PROFESSIONAL PROVIDER

Sometimes, a therapist sees a way out of the greed dilemma by perceiving and presenting herself as a hired friend. Supposedly, the friend dimension softens the fee dimension. First, however, we note that "hired friend" is a contradiction in terms. Although there are many ways one becomes a friend, by definition a friend is not and cannot be hired and paid for the job. So the concept "hired friend" is artificial and flawed from the outset. We are indebted to Peplau for her writings on professional versus social behavior (1964) and professional closeness (1969). Although these works do not focus specifically on the psychotherapist–patient relationship or process, rather on the more general nurse–patient relationship, the concepts and formulations fit all therapeutic work perfectly. Although we have added our own format and elaborations, we rely heavily on Peplau's early distinctions to show the differences between therapy and friendship, between being a therapist and being a friend. We discuss four variables to make the comparison.

Selection

As Peplau (1964) says, "Patients, unlike friends, are not chosen" (p. 26). Usually, patients are selected by therapists as presented. Even though there may be chance similarities or attributes of the therapist's friends and vice versa, the relationship is not initiated for that reason. Although of course there has been a good deal researched on therapist–patient "fit" as a predictor of therapy outcome, the match has nothing to do with the therapist trying to be a friend. When a therapist does try to be a friend, it becomes clear that such a friendship can lead to trouble because the patient is burdened by the therapist's need of the patient. Furthermore, the patient is deprived of an experience with an honestly motivated authority. Thus, what starts out as a way to ease the therapist's pain about getting paid ends up as a way of causing pain and deprivation to the patient, even though initially the patient might feel flattered to be so selected and might have even invited the response.

Boundaries

In the therapy situation, there is a certain formality, indicating that boundaries exist and are limited. There is some sort of rational contract (Welt & Herron, 1990) between patient and therapist about the time, the duration, the place, the money, and the focus. Confidentiality is the rule, with material presented by the patient exclusively, very rarely by the therapist. The data are "held" for eventual piecemeal therapeutic use. The therapist does not react "freely" according to automatic responses.

On the other hand, in friendship, the boundaries are fluid and limitless. The meeting place varies, with the decision being made by either party. The character of the contact is informal, allowing for free expression, free reaction, limited only by individual capability and how well the other party tolerates the response, rather than by some inherent admonition against the freedom. Were the therapist to loosen the boundaries, to make the experience more like friendship, the question is, where would that end? Would the therapist emotionally, verbally, or otherwise exploit the patient, now made anxious or overwhelmed or intimidated or narcissistically gratified by the therapist? Would gifts be exchanged, money lent? Could a session end up at a bar or in the bedroom? A therapist obviously reacts to various dimensions of the patient and the process, but she has an obligation to explore the reaction privately, while holding to the formality of the process. As a therapist, this is seen as regard for the patient. Therapist-as-friend undermines that regard.

Focus

The focus of therapy, one way or another, is directed to solving the patient's problems in living. Therefore, the therapist focuses on the patient and the patient's experience, concerns, conflicts, needs, and the like. The method is investigative. The therapist uses knowledge and skill to assist the patient; she uses and refines theoretical concepts and clinical capacities to better do the work. The therapist withstands the disequilibrium of the patient's internal state and external circumstances so that the patient can learn to live with disequilibrium without having to pathologically defend against it.

Conversely, therapist-as-friend would not feel compelled to do much of the above. The focus would not be on the patient alone but on either party, perhaps on shared experiences. Even though a friend may investigate another's experience, it is to share somehow in it rather than solely to understand it, unravel it, and put it in theoretical/experiential perspective. Such a friendship would surely be one-sided and stilted. A friend does not necessarily make a point of withstanding the chum's anxiety. In fact, the friend may not be able to tolerate it and is not there as an example of mental health competence. In this area, should the therapist be acting as a friend, there is a tendency to want to fix the problem, shoo away the anxiety, or dump the patient. One hopes of course that neither friend, therapist-as-friend, nor therapist would do this. The point is, however, as a friend, the potential is there to more easily and readily discard the relationship without much consideration of the other or of unconscious motivation if things get really uncomfortable. With a friend, one does not necessarily feel obligated to analyze the discomfort or the deed; in the therapeutic relationship, both therapist and patient have a responsibility to do so. For example, borderline patients often plea and pine for friendship, not out of sincere desire for a reciprocal relationship or deeper intimacy but because friendship with the therapist actually has the potential of decreasing intimacy, thereby making it easier to dump the therapist precipitously, and also, through projective identification, to cause the therapist to rid herself of the encumbrance. In contrast, discomfort notwithstanding, the therapist-as-therapist sticks with the patient, ultimately to explore the patient's discomfort and privately analyze the therapist's related discomfort, all of which have the potential of increasing intimacy.

Content

A therapist is always alert for significant content. Verbal and nonverbal content and its process context are of primary concern, as are themes and patterns. Such systematic observation helps the therapist infer patient need and is directed toward corrective action having growth-producing intent. There is the appropriate comment, the crucial question, the reasoned observation, the expressed, educated hunch, the direct interpretation. In none of these tactics is it productive for the therapist to be unnecessarily indirect out of concern for the patient's approval or disapproval. "Courtesy tactics" (Peplau, 1964), such as pleading, begging, or constantly apologizing, have no place in the therapist's repertoire. In contrast, being too careful or too nice, which in the short run protects the therapist from ire and abuse, is actually a hostile gesture ultimately causing the patient to feel demeaned, controlled, or less good than the therapist by comparison, as well as less able to stand up and face the music.

Regarding content, a friend is concerned with what the other person says in order to have fun, to share views, to reminisce, to gossip, to keep up to date with one another. A friend supports and receives support and sympathy. A friend does not look at content for special meaning or for themes or patterns. Yes, one would hope, a friend is sensitive and can question without being hypercritical or intrusive, but though friendship may be meaningful and the outcome somehow "therapeutic," the intent is not growth of the other. A friendship is self-serving to some degree; it feels good, and personal growth is an incidental outcome. The therapist-as-therapist on the other hand has as the major concern the growth of the other. Feeling good and feeling bad are outcomes inherent in that process.

In essence, characteristics of the relationship with the therapist as a professional health service provider differ sharply from those in a relationship where the therapist is a so-called friend. In the provider relationship, the therapist is not free to be herself in the full sense of the concept, to react without "consideration." The therapist–patient relationship is not reciprocal, and it is not equal. In the ideal, the therapist is an expert in human behavior whose knowledge and skill and tenacity facilitate the patient's movement through her life experiences toward a new and enlarged perception of that experience for the purposes of change and improvement in living. Theory-based practice by an expert who is largely indifferent to approval or disapproval, who does not need the patient or need to be liked, admired, seen as special or particularly caring, who does not need the patient for confirmation, and who has a life beyond therapy is the best one could ask for. That somewhat neutral expert is who the patient needs, not a friend. In this regard, Levenson (1983) has stated, "The truth is we are not the patient's friend but his analyst. It is not a lesser category or a less concerned one: it is simply different" (p. 60).

GREED REEXAMINED

Paradoxically, being a friend instead of a therapist does not loosen the shackles of the therapist's greed dilemma. Yes, it disguises the desire for money in a cloak of ostensibly caring behaviors. However, the underlying emotional/interpersonal caring remains, intensifying the greed and paving the way for realistic patient deprivation and greed. The demand put on the patient to respond, perhaps even to subjugate her own needs to those of the therapist, to be circumspect with this therapist who is grandiose or overly caring, is all too reminiscent of the position the therapist was in as a child, a child in the service of the mother instead of the other way around. So, through the patient, the therapist-as-friend replicates the original therapist relationship and privation, this time as the parent in power. Should the patient be responsive in feeding the therapist's narcissism, the therapist's greed will increase because hope has been nourished, "the more breast to scoop out." Should the patient object, the patient becomes the parent in power, and the therapist relives the frustration, the envy, the rage, the shame for having needs to begin with and for greedily demanding that these be met. Meanwhile, the question is raised, "Whose therapy is this anyway?"

Greed of course has a bad name. It has an obviously pejorative connotation. It imparts a sense of being previous, special, of demanding excessive entitlement or perhaps reparation. In any event, these are the forms we see greed take in therapists we have observed over the years. Of course, there are defenses against the greed and less than obvious ways that the greed manifests itself.

For some helping professionals who by their nature and nurture reached premature maturity, there is a confounding issue: conscious greed runs contrary to their dynamics. They are supposed to be helpful, chronically helpful in fact. This is their history, their destiny, their reason for being from infancy onward. Greed would appear to go against an ostensibly helpful attitude even though it is actually an unconscious motivator of that helpful behavior. Greed simultaneously represents and goes against the dynamics. Consequently, conscious recognition and consciously living it out are anxiety provoking: the good mother selflessly giving to the patient while secretly demanding that the patient be responsive and confirming and paying. Aggressive strivings for developmental lacks, for parental emotional excesses at the child's expense, are shunted aside for fear of retaliation. Note how often therapists feel anxious when they initially discuss the fee or even think about bringing up the subject.

Raising the issue of fee for some therapists never seems justified and is always deemed an indulgence. Dynamically, they have no right to charge for service; it is part of life, a crucial, central portion in fact! Yet, because dynamically "service" was demanded, they are narcissistically enraged. What starts out as a natural, healthy desire to be cared for, to be special, becomes distorted through its frustration. Greed now becomes an unbridled if unrecognized demand or a nondemand through reaction formation, or a compartmentalized demand. Were the greed recognized, the therapist would feel envy of the parent/patient for holding the goods, shame for needing them, and guilt for craving, then demanding them.

On the other hand, were the therapist truly to recognize greed as one possible variable in the work of helping another, it would then become possible to attend to the phenomenon of healthy greed, greed untainted with frustration, omnipotence, or grandiosity. Here, as in "normal" entitlement (Moses & Moses-Hrushovski, 1990), there is a sense of having appropriate privileges, a legitimate right related to position and role and task performed. Recognition of such normative greed would not be contaminated by fears of projected aggression, or with envy, shame, and guilt. Instead, healthy greed could be carried into adult life as part of healthy narcissism.

In infancy, greed is inherent in the earliest desires directed toward the mother (Klein, 1952/1975). "It is part of the emotional life of the infant that he is greedy and desires more than even the best external situation can fulfill" (Klein, 1960/1975, p. 271). If Klein were colloquial, she might say, "After all, the breast is there, so why not take it all and see if there's more where that came from?" Greed appears as the natural inclination to want and take what is there, part of the drive to meet one's needs and respond to instinctual cravings and demands. The issue, then, is not that greed exists; rather, it is how that greed is responded to: how it is aroused, frustrated, or met. The earliest emotional/interpersonal patterns of response influence future cravings and the relationships that invite them.

As a therapist, then, it is fine in one's rationalized estimation to want money, to know this, and to want more money. As a therapist, one might not get all that is fantasized, but one can legitimately ask for payment for knowledge, skills, and services. Such a therapist is a better helper when awareness of inner desires and dynamics calls a halt to noxious seepage of the therapist's pathological unconscious motivation into the therapist–patient relationship and the therapeutic process. The dedicated helper is not selfless, and a life of service does not have to be a life without desire for money. Healthy narcissism and providing psychotherapy are necessarily compatible concepts (Welt & Herron, 1990), and healthy greed is part of healthy narcissism.

PART II

PATIENTS' ATTITUDES ABOUT FEES

W   hat do patients feel and do about fees for psychotherapy? In Chapter
     4 we consider the ways in which fees can operate as barriers to
     either starting or remaining in psychotherapy. The causes of the
barrier effect are both economic and emotional. In regard to economic
factors, we consider possible differences in public and private treatment
opportunities, the general underutilization of psychotherapy, and the
possible effectiveness of free psychotherapy. Following this, we discuss
the economics of mental health care, including managed care, short- and
long-term treatment approaches, research, cost containment, and accountability.

Taking note of society's current regrettable focus on a minimalist
model for mental health, we counter this shortsightedness with an appeal
for greater provision of services, including extended insurance coverage
and provisions for the poor and disadvantaged. We offer practical suggestions
for doing this, pointing out that mental health costs are a very small
portion of national health expenses, that outpatient services in particular
are cost effective and not overutilized, and that sliding-scale methods
could be included in insurance coverage in ways that would increase the
number of people covered as well as available services without increasing
carriers' costs. We invite therapists' concern and participation in reducing,
if not eliminating, the barrier element of fees from an economic perspective.
Then we turn to the emotional obstacles posed by fees and what therapists
can do about them. Finally, we summarize by stressing the need for
psychotherapists to be involved in developing social and psychological
policies that will increase the accessibility of quality service at a fair return
for providers.

Chapter 5 is concerned with changes in patients' economic situations
during the course of therapy. Most of our attention is devoted to patients
undergoing financial problems, which as part of the therapy process will

involve awareness, acknowledgment, understanding, and possible solutions. We also look at the happier prospect of patients becoming richer, and we conclude with a look at the interaction between therapists' and patients' financial situations during therapy.

This section concludes with a detailed consideration in Chapter 6 of how patients deal with their images as the payers in the therapeutic relationship. The focus is on the patients' feelings about what they are purchasing, how these feelings are expressed, and the therapists' reactions.

Chapter 4

THE BARRIER
EFFECT

O ne effect of patients having to pay for psychotherapy is that the fee restricts both entrance into therapy and continuance of therapy. A reluctance and/or inability to pay on the part of patients has a companion in therapists' discomfort when requesting or receiving fees or over the size of fees or in recommending continued therapy in the context of total cost over time. It has been difficult for therapists to develop an appropriate perspective on the issue. Psychotherapists' guilt and unresolved ambivalence result in distorted sensitivities that interfere with successful therapeutic practices. This chapter illuminates the fee primarily from the payers' point of view so that this can be correctly assessed and understood by psychotherapists. Then they can take effective steps to insure a functioning, efficient system of therapeutic service.

A recent review of the effects of fees on psychotherapy (Herron & Sitkowski, 1986) noted that for some people the fee operates as a barrier to either beginning or continuing psychotherapy. Despite an apparent need for the type of assistance provided by the psychotherapies, certain people experience the fee as an insurmountable obstacle. These people then fail to use a potentially helpful resource. This is disturbing to the entire society and is a particular concern and frustration to service providers. They are deprived of the opportunity to be helpful by the fact that their services cost money, and they are also deprived of potential income. As a result, the providers need to find ways to remove this barrier.

The solution begins with recognition of the problem and its causes, which are economic and emotional. These can and do overlap, but we will consider each separately, starting with economic motives.

ECONOMIC OBSTACLES

Public—Private

It is to be expected that the real money supply of potential and ongoing patients is going to affect their use of available services. In response to the needs of the poor and the relatively less affluent, public and private agencies have been developed to offer low-cost psychotherapies. In addition, sliding-fee scales based on patients' abilities to pay are the most common approach in the private sector. Also, insurance coverage through employers has been made available in limited amounts for mental health services, with 27 states mandating some form of this coverage (*Psychotherapy Finances*, 1990a).

Thus, there has been a historical awareness of economic variations in populations to be served by psychotherapists as well as past and continuing efforts to provide affordable service. These efforts, however, are not a guarantee of the quality of the service, particularly since there are corresponding efforts by payers to limit costs by curtailing both the amounts of service and the payments for the services. As financial rewards are limited, there is a danger that providers in economically restricted settings will be less experienced or less interested or will restrict their time in contrast to settings where the monetary return is greater. At present, even with increasing emergence of managed mental health care, the private practice setting remains the most profitable and allows providers the greatest discretion in determining and carrying out treatment plans.

The incentives to provide the same type of service that is probable in the private sector do not seem to be there is settings serving the economically disadvantaged. A reflection of the disparity can be seen in a survey by Taube, Burns, and Kessler (1984), in which the average number of visits to clinics was around 4 in contrast to about 11 in private practice settings. Some of the difference may be attributed to the interests, motivations, and problems of patients in each type of setting, but some may result from variations in providers' interest in retaining patients long enough for them to benefit appreciably. Therapists in low-cost settings are not usually in a direct patient-to-provider fee arrangement, so that their income is not clearly dependent on the presence or progress of specific patients. And although lower-socioeconomic-level patients tend to make less use of total mental health services than middle- and upper-class patients, this phenomenon may be connected to the attitudes of the providers. In addition, the settings themselves may impose explicit or implicit restrictions on providers.

Within diagnostic groups, the more disturbed patients, such as borderlines and psychotics, require more sessions for psychotherapy to be effective (Newman & Howard, 1986). Since these patients are difficult to work with and are more frequently seen in settings other than private practice because they are represented in greater numbers in the underclasses, therapists may be motivated to "assist" their departure, contributing to therapeutic ineffectiveness. Therapists do not get more money in these settings to work with difficult patients or greater numbers of patients or to do intensive long-term work, so there is actually motivation to have easier patients, fewer patients, and accelerated turnover.

When the clinic–private practice usage is placed in the context of the analysis by Howard, Kopta, Krause, and Orlinsky (1986), which suggests 26 sessions as a time limit for effectiveness in settings with limited resources that serve large numbers of people, the realities of services for the economically disadvantaged are not appealing. Even psychotherapy that is designed to be time-limited tends to have a limit of 16 to 20 sessions, and Howard et al. (1986) indicate that 52 once-weekly sessions appear to be the optimum for maximum percentage improvement. Actually, the median attendance for unlimited therapy in their study tended to be 12 sessions, so it appears that too many people disappear before they should if they want therapy to be effective. However, of the 15 studies analyzed by Howard et al. (1986), the majority of settings were clinics or counseling centers rather than private practice, so the sample is restricted. At the same time, the number of sessions is very similar to the average reported by Taube et al. (1984) for private practice. It appears then that it is not only the poor who get less than they need, although they still get the least.

Free Psychotherapy

Of course, there are many reasons for some patients to be unwilling to remain in therapy long enough for it to be effective. At the moment our interest is in just one of these, cost, and in what to do about it so at least that barrier can be mitigated or removed. Let us start with the group of patients who, based on reality issues, appear to need "free" psychotherapy. Is it effective to provide such therapy to the economically disadvantaged when they need it?

The question is posed because there is a tradition of the necessity of a fee for positive therapeutic results to occur that has been discussed in a number of recent sources (Herron & Rouslin, 1984; Herron & Sitkowski, 1986; Welt & Herron, 1990). The fee was seen as an essential motivator for the patient that at the same time relieved the therapist of having to indicate it was he who needed the fee. Because the fee was meant to be a sacrifice, it varied according to the patient's financial situation, thus limiting therapists' income according to the socioeconomic level of the majority of their patients, but it made the fee something that existed more for the patient's benefit than for the therapist's. It still favored the rich over the poor as clients in terms of therapists' incomes, but not much was made of that. The emphasis was on the idea that *some* fee was essential for any psychotherapy to be successful, which in turn made it rather obligatory for therapists to get all patients to pay something.

However, exceptions were always made to this rule beginning with Freud (1913a), and recent studies indicate that a therapist can treat a patient effectively without directly charging a fee (Manos, 1982; Yoken & Berman, 1984, 1987). In addition, it can be concluded that psychotherapy can be effective when someone other than the patient, such as an insurance company, directly pays the fee (Yoken & Berman, 1987). Thus, it is possible to remove part of the barrier when that barrier is based on a real economic problem for the patient. Therapists can take no fee or a low fee or the insurance payment allowance, and therapy can still be effective as far as some patients are concerned (Friedman, 1991).

At the same time, this does not mean there are no problems with patient subsidies or that such treatment will invariably be as effective as direct payment or payment of the therapist's desired fee. For example, the existing research does not provide information as to whether nonpaying patients might have become even better if they had paid, nor does one know how the paying patients would have fared had they not paid. Also, the research has focused on relatively brief treatment durations in settings other than private practice so that the therapists' investment in fee payment was minimized.

The study by Manos (1982) illustrates the mixture of assets and liabilities in free psychotherapy. A special situation was created in which therapists were not paid but received specialized training, and no fee was charged to patients, but they were accepted for treatment only if they could not afford it privately. There were 8 therapists, all second-year psychiatric residents, and 28 patients, most of whom were neurotics or had character disorders, with an average of 6.5 months of therapy when evaluations were made of the treatment. Therapists reported no negative influence from nonpayment in 18 cases, with some negative influence in 10 cases. The latter were lack of appreciation, difficulties expressing negative transference, and interfering feelings of gratitude. Thirteen patients felt there was a positive effect, ten felt no effect, and only four saw a negative effect, which was a feeling of obligation and suspicion of therapists' motives. The positive effects were that patients sensed a friendly rather than a business atmosphere and felt the possibility existed of getting treatment they otherwise would have been unable to afford.

A distinction was made in the study between what therapists and patients felt about the treatment and what effect free treatment had on the therapists. In 16 cases, the therapists felt a negative effect; in ten cases they felt no influence, and in two cases, they felt positive effect. The negative effect was no pay, whereas the positive effect was that it alleviated their guilt and anxiety about their inexperience in treating patients. Twenty-four patients felt the lack of payment had no effect, and when patients were asked if they would prefer to pay, 17 said no, 11 yes. The patients liked free therapy better than the therapists did, substantiating the "barrier effect" for patients.

Clinical and research evidence makes the point that not all patients have to be charged a fee directly in order to gain from psychotherapy. This takes away any universal application of the traditional justification for fees, namely, that the patient needed to pay so that he would be properly motivated and in turn derive therapeutic benefits. At least some patients seem to get along well without a fee. The question then becomes, can the therapists?

Some can, as the Manos (1982) study illustrates where therapists were able to separate their negative feelings about not getting paid from their behavior in the treatment. Gleninon and Karlovac (1988), using a hypothetical situation, did not find therapists relating low fees ($15) to greater warmth and high fees ($120) to less warmth. Thus, it was possible to separate the business and the warmth issues. The research reported by Yoken and Berman (1987) also indicates that the therapist factor can be mitigated. However, these were all special situations, not the everyday private practice of psychotherapy.

What these suggest is that it is possible to develop contexts in which the barrier effect can be reduced. Most of these situations require that the impact on the therapist of not getting paid be reduced, so the therapist's direct need for a fee from the patient is eliminated. Unfortunately, that means many low-cost services are staffed by the less-experienced trainees, and the quality of service becomes open to question. Furthermore, salaries at clinics and hospitals do not provide the level of compensation available to therapists in the private sector, thus reducing the incentive for staff to enter and, more particularly, to stay in settings that serve a majority of low-socioeconomic patients. Since public mental health institutions, particularly inpatient hospitals, currently focus on relatively rapid discharge, the major need is to provide quality outpatient mental health services to people who cannot pay for them.

Economical Services

An increase in individual altruism is not going to accomplish this job. Paris (1982–83) points out that although individualism, free enterprise, and the workings of the marketplace are highly prized in much of western society, particularly the United States, this approach can miss significant aspects of external reality. Therapists can retain the helper image without feeling significantly motivated to treat the poor.

Yet there is an ethic here that cannot be cast aside. Psychotherapists are in existence to help people. To keep their standard of living in place and still do all of the job, therapists have to involve themselves in setting social policies that provide quality mental health care. There is a growing societal concern with the provision of national health care, but it has been narrowly defined when it comes to mental health for a variety of reasons including the fuzziness of the concepts and the assumed probability of unending, escalating costs. Nonetheless, el-Guelbay, Prosen, and Bebchuk (1985a, 1985b) illustrate how universal health care in Canada is being implemented in regard to the provision of psychotherapy. Although such an approach has its share of problems (el-Guebaly et al., 1985b; Paris, 1982–83; Rainey, 1982–83), their point is that it can be an operational way to provide psychotherapy for people with limited financial resources.

Mollica and Redlich (1980) have found that although there has been an increase in mental health services since 1950, the group that was inadequately served then is still in the same situation. Treatment is in public facilities, with limited treatment available and staff that is primarily semiprofessional. Not only does this country lack national health coverage that would make psychotherapy available regardless of the ability to pay, but insurance that is available to some of the population is being decreased.

Both situations are related and are based on some misconceptions, as illustrated by el-Guebaly et al. (1985b). Studies on both the utilization and cost of mental health services when insurance is involved indicate both predictability and considerable stability of costs. When insurability comes into effect, there is an initial increase in use of services, but predictable levels then stabilize. Also, there is more usage when people pay less and the insurance company pays more, but this is no different for psychiatric–psychological services than for other health services. Psychotherapy has been demonstrated to be cost effective in increasing the general health of individuals and their productivity. The total cost of mental health services is a mere 15% of total health costs. Considering the potential benefits and prophylactic aspects, restriction of coverage promotes neglect and the potential for increasing severity and/or the use of other health services, including hospitalization, so the probability of insurance companies and employers saving money ultimately seems small.

In considering the provision of mental health services for the poor, therapists face numerous obstacles that are not going to be removed easily. A willingness to give a certain amount of service to those who need it but cannot afford it is in the tradition of most professional service providers, but even this is insufficient to meet the need. In the market economy of our society, every service has to be paid for in some fashion, so that even the more motivated psychotherapists have a limit as to what they can provide without getting paid.

Such a limitation means that social policies need to be put into place that do make provisions for needed services for those without means. This issue is not one that psychotherapists should ignore because it may not directly affect them at the moment. Social activism has to become an ongoing important concern for the psychotherapy profession. Tomes (1990) highlights the ongoing problems of state mental health practices and emphasizes the need to create adaptable mental health systems. He stresses that this means hospitals providing acute and chronic care, with community services providing outpatient therapy, social support, and rehabilitation. This type of effort is not restricted to one state because there is strong lobbying from family and consumer groups, the National Alliance for the Mentally Ill (NAMI) being one example. The expansion of services, or even the redistribution would cost money, and insuring quality care would be even more expensive, so increased taxation would be needed. Given the current economic conditions, implementation will be very difficult.

Thus, social activism is not merely the identification of needs and the existence of services; it increasingly becomes a concern with efficiency, with the amounts of money required and how it is to be spent, and particularly where it is going to come from. Advocacy itself has become a vast thicket of wants; NAMI presents just one example. Willis (1990) describes the Task Force on American Indian Mental Health, and analogous organizations for other ethnic minorities as well as for the homeless, AIDS patients, and others who are looking for increased resources and services. Consequently, it is prudent to acquire sophistication about the economic factors involved so that reality-based plans can be proposed.

Essentially, social policy has to be reformulated to give priority to what is important within the limitation of what any nation can afford. Importance is defined by a society in terms of its beliefs, and therapists' input can shape those beliefs. Psychotherapy and other mental health services are aimed at developing a vibrant, economically productive society, a loving, working nation. Although undoubtedly this perspective is relative, better mental health means a better society, and that improves the living standards of more people. It is, therefore, in the public interest as well as the interest of the profession for psychotherapists to work for funding priority for their services. The recent extension of Medicare mental health coverage to more providers has made services available where they had been missing. This entitlement could have been enacted more easily, however, if all the disciplines involved had supported the extension of services and lobbying not been hindered by too much "guild" emphasis. The divisiveness between the disciplines involved in providing therapy services is a continuing problem and an example of economic stupidity as well.

An ideal goal would be unlimited coverage for mental health services on an as-needed basis regardless of ability to pay. This would require inpatient coverage as well as outpatient because of the large portion of seriously disturbed people who are also poor. The realistic possibility is that a minimum type of coverage may get extended to all, based to some degree on ability to pay, although providing funding is going to be difficult.

Assuming psychotherapists seriously address the issue of treatment for the poor on philosophical, ethical, and economic grounds, and with sophistication and perseverance, the next barrier issue is the reaction of employers who want to cut their costs for mental health benefits for their employees (Winslow, 1990). As Bacon (1990) noted in the *Wall Street Journal*, the cost of treating substance abuse in private centers rose so sharply in 1989 that many companies cut back on benefits. Insurers typically paid for up to a 28-day stay, with prices ranging from $250 to $550 a day, which for a 4-week stay would fall in the range of $7000 to $15,000. Although longer stays reduced recidivism, they did not eliminate it, so further costs were probable. This type of expense illuminates the fact that outpatient psychotherapy at $100 per session (the higher end of the current outpatient fee range for all licensed providers) is relatively cheap and not the major culprit in rising health costs.

Nonetheless, employers seeing a rising cost want that expense decreased, and mental health coverage traditionally has had limits just in case it got out of hand. There has always been a belief that it could, as well as a belief that many people could get along without therapy and would if insurance were unavailable. Of course, the possible effects on worker productivity of those who need mental health services but do not receive them are unknown. Also unknown are the numbers of people who have received service although they have no insurance coverage. Because mental disorders carry a social stigma, many people are discreet about treatment, and some will not use insurance coverage or anyone but a solo practitioner because of possible loss of confidentiality.

As learning and insurance have made psychotherapy more socially and economically acceptable, more people use it, and more are relatively visible about the usage. As far as cost to employers is concerned, it too has increased. In reaction, employers want to decrease therapy coverage and seek out insurance carriers that have a number of managed health care strategies, all of which limit the freedom of consumers and providers. These plans may simply provide less coverage, possibly a designated number of sessions, which assumes time-limited improvement, or less money, requiring larger copayments, or develop a network of providers who cap their fees, or provide more extensive coverage for services such as inpatient services that are more expensive but get less usage (but also discourage such usage by incentives for providers not to hospitalize), and give less coverage to the less expensive but more frequently used outpatient services, thereby discouraging their use as well. The aim is to contain the total costs to an amount that will both provide a profit for the insurer and reduce the previous cost to the employer. The saving comes from the consumer picking up more of the cost or using the service less and from the provider charging less, either per session or through briefer treatment.

Short-Term versus Long-Term Psychotherapy

A major related concern is the disagreement between the short-termers and the long-termers. The psychoanalytic tradition of lengthy treatment and "more is better" was a dominant training and practice model for many years and is obviously more costly than short-term approaches. However, if a longer term actually results in people making less use of total health services over their life spans, it may be an ultimate bargain. Considered on the basis of immediate results, time-limited and unlimited therapy show no striking empirical differences (Koss & Butcher, 1986). As Lane-Palés (1989) has pointed out, the current situation is one in which short-term therapies of any orientation, including psychodynamic, are where the money lies. Therapists thinking primarily of economic security will think short-term. Shueman (1989) has suggested that therapists eliminate the myth that everybody needs long-term care. However, a new myth may start to take its place—that nobody really needs long-term care. As Stricker (1989) comments, "A treatment should be long enough to satisfy the needs of the patient, and depending on those needs, some treatment will last longer than others. . ." (p. 30).

If therapists want options, then it is essential to educate consumers, including third-party payers, that psychotherapists are capable of making appropriate assessments of who will benefit from what and that psychotherapy indeed will do what providers assert is possible. The current tendency in the field has not been to do that but to follow the dictates of the less knowledgable holders of the purse strings who erect the barriers, determine the costs, and leave the therapists struggling to accommodate. Increased competition from the increase in service providers to give less-funded services has led to the proliferation of health maintenance organizations (HMO), etc., which tend to be choice limiters and income reducers as far as many psychotherapists are concerned. This is another economic issue that may backfire on the organizers because if the services available are not as good as they ought to be, the ultimate benefit of these approaches originated to reduce costs will instead be a loss.

Freud (1937/1964) may have been accurate when he recognized the potential for interminable therapy; few patients would or could subscribe to that idea, however. People may indeed wish that insurance coverage made unlimited therapy available to them at little or no cost, but that is a fanciful idea in a capitalistic economy. Insurance coverage will be limited and require monetary contributions of one sort or another by patients and therapists. However, proponents of longer-term therapy, patients and therapists alike, should not find this so hard to live with. Indeed, we practiced psychotherapy when our patients did not get coverage because we were not medical doctors, and so did many other therapists. The concept of insurance has facilitated matters, but it is not crucial to the practice of long- or short-term therapies for people who have at least middle-class incomes.

At the same time, the purpose of health insurance is to provide adequate benefits to the recipients. Thus, it is unethical as well as foolish for people to accept coverage that is less than adequate without raising an issue about it. All providers have an obligation to educate and promulgate what they believe is effective mental health care. Although cost has to be justified, so do limitations in coverage, and by now most therapists have had their share of unpleasant and arbitrary dealings with insurance carriers.

It appears that the popularizing of short-term therapy is primarily based on the belief that consumers will not pay for long-term work. Influences moving the consumer in short-term directions are, of course, the limitations in insurance as well as the media propagandizing it as better, the appeal of rapidity in both time and cost, and the fact that some professionals believe in it and are vocal.

Bolter, Levenson, and Alvarez (1990) developed a Beliefs and Attitudes Toward Therapy Questionnaire (BAT) to differentiate short- from long-term therapists. Although eight areas have been suggested as differences (Budman & Gurman, 1983), only two of these were significant. The first was time, with longer-term therapists favoring an open-ended approach and short-term therapists preferring a time limit. The second was a view of psychological change, with long-term therapists believing that personality is structured in a way that psychotherapy is needed to change it. Otherwise resistance to change will prevail. This view requires an individualized approach to patients and no time limits because the strengths of resistances vary and one can speak only in relative terms as to the time and degree of improvement. In contrast, short-term therapists view people as essentially growth-oriented but as encountering obstacles that focused therapeutic interventions can remove to permit growth to continue. This does leave the possibility that obstacles may be encountered more than once in a lifetime, so that frequent short therapies could become the norm, which could become costly depending on the frequency. At the moment there is a relative insistence that high-quality effects will be achieved through relatively infrequent short therapies for most patients, which would cost less than long therapies. Whether this is true, nobody knows, but until proven otherwise, it is the way therapists are increasingly being asked to think and work.

The short-term view affects therapists significantly because it is related to one's theoretical orientation and how and where one practices. For example, in the Bolter et al. (1990) study, a behavioral orientation was more in accord with a short-term approach, whereas the other orientations, existential, humanistic, and psychodynamic, matched better with long-term values, as did being primarily in private practice. Differences in theoretical orientation are expected, but there is a growing tendency for behavior therapies to become longer than they had been (Kovacs, 1982), so future studies may show less of an orientation effect.

The sample in the Bolter et al. (1990) study was not primarily behavioral, with 54% indicating a preference for long-term therapy, 32% for short-term, and the rest not having a definite preference. It appears that most orientations prefer long-term work, but their preference will avail them little unless consumers are convinced such work is worth the cost and effort. Part of the problem lies in a comparative concern when different experiences are really being discussed and advocated under a general rubric.

Stricker states:

> Just as is true in medicine, there are some therapies which [sic] correct life-threatening conditions, and these surely are needed, others which [sic] improve the quality of life, and these may or may not be needed, and still others which [sic] respond to cosmetic considerations and probably are not needed, but still can be useful and valuable. We adopt an indefensible position when we assert that any treatment which [sic] produces patient satisfaction is needed, and invite third party payers to counterassert an equally indefensible position, that only those treatments which [sic] are essential to life will be supported. (1989, p. 32)

It is necessary to be realistic about what society considers important and will support, although at the same time we must recognize that psychotherapists' views are part of society's views. One could replace "indefensible" in Stricker's remarks with "wishful" (or perhaps, "wistful") and make better use of opportunities to educate society to the quality of life that can be brought about through the various psychotherapies or to what constitutes ongoing good mental health and what are all the possibilities for fostering and maintaining that. For example, relief from debilitating anxiety could be classified as necessary for functioning, but would not require psychoanalysis to be achieved. However, if for some people long-term intensive analysis produces other positives beside symptom relief, such as enhanced creativity that improves functioning, then this is another aspect of mental health. One goal may look more basic than another, but it is not necessarily better or more deserving of society's support.

Shueman (1989) has suggested that provider accountability is a major issue in the who-pays-for-what controversy. Because providers sincerely believe in what they do, they have taken the view that payers have the same attitude; as long as the therapist–patient dyads consider themselves productive, health benefits are forthcoming and should be supported without question. The current atmosphere limits such a view, but it once was relatively prevalent that in essence the professional's opinion was trusted. Shueman (1989) argues that therapists have failed to establish credibility with insurance companies and their employers, who now tend to see professionals as self-serving in their arguments against payment restrictions.

Really both groups are self-serving, but the degree is questionable. Both groups have ethical concerns and real interests in serving people as well as making money. For example, there is no question that therapists have to be able to have flexibility in determining treatment plans and to take seriously the necessity of being cost effective. If this were not the case in the past, and if the current external "policing" improves flexibility, treatment planning, and accountability, the new methodology is a positive. At the same time, it is reasonable and important for psychotherapists to expect payers to pay attention to professional opinions and to use them in determining guidelines for payment. It is also prudent for therapists to keep all viable treatment avenues open to patients. The economic and status temptations for exclusive territory are high here, but it is a fair and unified voice that ought to prevail.

Collaboration is not going to happen automatically for any of the parties involved but will require consistent effort by providers to establish and maintain credibility. Working together also means understanding that the involved parties, including the insurance carriers, are entitled to reasonable profits.

If many therapists were once addicted to practicing long-term therapy, it would be regrettable to see them now switch to a short-term model because that is where the payment is guaranteed. The same concern has to be voiced for creating and/or joining provider networks whose emphasis is cost cutting for the services and profits for the designers. Security cannot become a substitute for quality—always a possibility when care is being managed by someone other than the therapist. Ultimately the consumer is going to be the decision maker in regard to the value of the service. For the moment, the burden of demonstrating effectiveness is on providers who do not conform to the guidelines or stay out of the networks, but if they are correct, the burden will fall back on managed health care systems to prove they can provide quality service. This is an open issue not only for psychotherapy but for all health care. It is especially poignant in psychotherapy because the relationship between patient and therapist is such an important variable. Any health plan that limits this choice for either of the parties could have inherent problems, regardless of the type of psychotherapy.

Whatever the problems are with today's insurance coverage and its plans for the future, to the extent that insurance exists, it unquestionably provides more people with access to psychotherapists. This is a positive mental health development for patients that benefits therapists as well, ideologically and financially. It has created more parity among providers, the standard being set by the providers who were first covered by the insurance. These were usually medical doctors, so with the norm already established, other providers were aided in increasing their fees. Thus, the extension of coverage to more disciplines would tend to result in an initial rise in costs as people who were not using medical doctors now could use insurance for any other covered providers. However, insurance companies increasingly cap the total fee covered or pay a set amount per session that is well below the usual fees, so the discipline of the provider is now not much of a cost issue for third-party payers. However, if certain disciplines are excluded and they charge less than what patients would have to copay an insured provider, patients may choose the uninsured and so not use their insurance.

The fee is based on what the society deems the service is worth, and that varies with how many people need it as well as how many people there are who use it and the differential in status of the providers. Costs did increase with an increased numbers of providers, but that can be controlled and levels off. In fact, if insurance coverage contracts and the number of providers remains relatively the same or even increases again, overall costs to the consumer will decrease as a function of the competition. Managed health care is one example of taking advantage of that competition, for more providers have indeed been appearing on the scene. Any educated consumer can utilize this facet of the system by "shopping" therapists, although it does require considerable sophistication to insure positive results. Of course, if the profession becomes less profitable and fewer people in turn stay in it or enter it, then assuming the need remains, costs will again increase. However, it is clear that there is a supply–demand regulated range for costs that can have some predictability.

Research

Turning to research to demonstrate what dosage is needed for what condition has surface appeal, but it is particularly complex when it comes to psychotherapy. Lane-Palés (1989) uses the Howard et al. (1986) study to indicate that 52 sessions of psychotherapy are sufficient for improvement for most patients, yet we use the same study as an indicator of the underutilization of psychotherapy because most patients do not attend that long. At the same time, long-term therapists could feel some relief that if the Howard et al. (1986) study were to be the standard, at least it provided a year, whereas short-term therapists probably saw it as more coverage than was needed. The opinion about dosage is a major issue because psychotherapists tend to believe that what they do is what works best for their patients, regardless of what may appear in the literature. However, they are being nudged, if not pushed at the moment, by the lesser cost of short-term work. Shueman (1989) adds to this the notion that most of the evidence for the effectiveness of psychotherapy also comes from short-term work.

Yet, considering the complexities, should the Howard et al. (1986) study, or any existing study for that matter, be used as an index for how much therapy is necessary to be effective? The traditional idea that therapists and patients together work out what is needed and how to implement this still has considerable appeal to many consumers and therapists. Yet it is unconvincing to a significant number of others because, as Shueman (1989) indicates, it could well be contaminated by therapist and patient needs that are basically irrelevant to the need for continued treatment. For example, these could be that the patient is overly dependent and the therapist needs the money. These are indeed possibilities, and they could well be masked by patient or therapist without conscious intent. Thus, leaving the matter up to the integrity of the therapist when therapists vary in their convictions as to what works does not appear satisfactory from a cost basis.

Shueman (1989) has three suggestions to facilitate the credibility of psychotherapists. The first two are recognizing that it is a myth that most patients need long-term therapy and that it is the only treatment of "real" value. The third is that therapists collect data themselves about what they do, how they do it, and how effective it is. Assuming this is carried out with sufficient objectivity and openness to change as is possible for an individual practitioner, it can be endorsed by all psychotherapists. However, what if it keeps contradicting the first two suggestions? This is a distinct possibility. For example, there are short-term psychodynamic therapies and psychoanalytic therapists who adapt their techniques to patient exigencies, but these therapists are often doing what they can given the circumstances rather than what they think is most effective. Their evaluation of their own work, their personal accountability, may tell them that most patients do not get enough of what is needed and that more would indeed be better.

Perhaps psychoanalysts are well-intentioned but myopic and rigid. However, similar allegations could be made about short-term therapists if they think only short-term work is valid and anything else is fluff. Flexibility is the apparent solution, but it tends to be based on practicality and is not necessarily a belief in what is best. Therapists are motivated to try to help but prefer to do this in ways they consider most effective. This is understandable yet variable, because there is no solid support for the differential effectiveness of therapies. At the same time, psychotherapists have indeed made changes over time in styles, approaches, methods, etc., so reasoned flexibility is certainly possible. However, it is hoped that changes come from relatively conclusive evidence rather than expediency.

Strupp (1986) has provided a sophisticated evaluation of the limits of the research approach. Granting the need and potential for research in gaining knowledge for and about psychotherapy, he points out that outcome is very difficult to evaluate and at present only a rough indicator of what happens as a result of psychotherapy. There is not a great deal of valid information to use to make decisions about eligibility, type, frequency, and duration of service. Although psychotherapy is a health service, it does not fit well into the medical model. As Strupp (1986) notes, it is more of an educational health service aimed at personality growth, but society gives it a different emphasis. The concern at the moment is with relatively rapid symptom modification. This is a restricted view that severely limits the potential of psychotherapy. A broader view is not designed to avoid the evaluative aspect of the psychotherapies but both to take advantage of their possibilities and to evaluate them fairly. Strupp (1986) states, "Because society, at present, is prepared to subsidize health care but not personality growth (that is, greater maturity), there may be no viable alternative to the prevailing approach" (p. 128).

That observation is in the context of misunderstandings that prevail in the society in regard to psychotherapies. Their availability is really a matter of social policy, namely, the degree of "health" aspired to by a nation, which in this nation is of course intertwined with economics. Researchers are looked to for answers they really cannot provide in this area.

As Strupp notes:

What can policy makers expect from research? . . . Research is not likely to adduce precise data on the safety and efficacy of psychotherapeutic

modalities or their "cost effectiveness." Nor should researchers . . . fuel
trends of know-nothingism in contemporary society. They certainly can
carry out evaluation research and, within limits, provide data on the
cost effectiveness of psychotherapy. . . . I hedge this statement, because
at least some of the gains of psychotherapy cannot be readily translated
into dollars and cents; the gains also encompass the client's sense of
well-being, their role performances as marital partners, and the like. . . .
Public policy must necessarily take account of existent research results,
but . . . the issue revolves around the value society is willing to place
on positive mental health and its maintenance. This issue has not yet
been squarely confronted. (1986, pp. 127–129)

Cost Containment

Regardless of Strupp's informed comments, the trend is toward attempting
to standardize mental health care and "manage" it. As *Psychotherapy
Finances* recently (1990d) pointed out, although there is a lot of talk in
the managed care industry about quality, the essential idea is to reduce
costs. The approach moves in the direction of discovering therapists who
are "good buys." This is being translated more and more into relatively
rapid, symptom-focused therapy. Problems are to be resolved as quickly
as possible, and bill payers will be concerned with therapists' records in
an attempt to predict costs as well as reduce them. Emphasis will not be
on training, experience, or orientation, professional quality indices, but
on predictable, rapid "cures." The possibility that the least expensive,
least lengthy treatments will, over patients' life spans, *not produce less
total cost* will have to be demonstrated. Recidivism will have to be proven
rather than assumed before the payers will reconsider, which means an
untold amount of time could pass before the current trend changes.

Where is all this coming from? As Welling reports in the June 11,
1990 issue of *Barron's*, health care costs too much now and continues to
cost more every year with no predicted reduction or even stabilization.
The national health care tab for 1990 is estimated at $700 billion, with a
prediction that by 2000 it will use one out of every five dollars produced
by the economy. Essentially, nobody wants to pay for this, which is
demonstrated by all the possible payers trying to cut their share of the
payment. Some of the increasing costs are tied to inevitables, as the aging
of the population, but much of the blame is laid to inefficiency in the
payment and delivery systems. Payers give therapists a health service
accountability model to follow, and it is a forced fit that usually makes
patients and therapists uncomfortable. Furthermore, there is a tendency
to live with this discomfort to keep operations afloat, as well as another
tendency to appear to embrace the model and act as if psychotherapy

indeed could be so prescriptive. Both of these tendencies are bad omens for maximizing the potential consumer value of psychotherapy.

Accountability

Practitioners are sophisticated about what psychotherapy can do and with whom, but the value of psychotherapy may have to be sold and resold. In terms of fees as barriers, the current situation appears to be that psychotherapists can expect patients to have a limited amount of support from insurance. Therapists can try to reduce the barrier by lobbying the third-party payers, their regulators, and their employers to provide more support. This has been carried out effectively in the past, but it is clear that it continues to be necessary. It is useful to demonstrate some of the effects of psychotherapy in cost benefits, but others require educating the payers to a value system that embraces a broad definition of health. At the same time, psychotherapists need to get their own house in order, meaning in particular a real concern with cost effectiveness for the payers. That does not automatically mean following the accountability models that at times are now visited on therapists, but it does mean having a demonstrable model for effectiveness.

Psychoanalytic psychotherapy can serve as an example. The goal is the development of insight leading to behavioral change that includes symptom relief, although that is not the focus. This type of therapy operates within an expressive–supportive range that includes techniques such as clarification, confrontation, interpretation, and working through as well as encouragement, suggestion, affirmation, and empathy (Gabbard, 1990; Welt & Herron, 1990). Although the goal puts an emphasis on interpretation, there is a varying mixture of interpretive (expressive) and structuring (supportive) techniques. For insight to occur, any patient has to be ready, and the structuring is in the service of this readiness; the same is true in regard to change taking place.

How long this takes is difficult to predict because it is basically an open-ended process, but it is possible to describe this progression and to include time estimates. The interplay of what goes on—transference, resistance, countertransference—can all be described with examples, as can work around central features of psychoanalytic therapy. The insight triangle (Menninger, 1958) is one possibility, where connections are established among current relationships, transference, and past relationships; other possibilities for tracking the progress of psychoanalytic therapy have been suggested (Gabbard, 1990; Luborsky, 1984; Welt & Herron, 1990), including whatever connections are possible to diagnostic entities (Frosch, 1990a, 1990b; Gabbard, 1990).

Thus, it is possible to explain what psychotherapists of any and all orientations do to all concerned—patients, providers, peers. However, the explanations are not generic but, rather, specific and variable. It is important that providers cease using this variability as a way to savage each other and lay claim to patients and funds. The aim ought to be to give people more opportunities for better mental health, not fewer.

Along with the professionally liberating aspects of a capitalistic or market economy is the infamous "bottom line." Because the cost of social policies, such as public assistance, can outstrip the revenue base, government is customarily the ultimate funder. The potential to operate at an apparently endless deficit makes it difficult to cut anything and to establish priorities. Yet as days of reckoning beckon, as these indeed have been recently, cuts are being proposed. Health costs are increasing in disturbing spirals, so that mental health providers are increasingly faced with limitations of both personal and third-party payment bearing directly on how much the consumer has or is willing to pay. This is an issue of priorities that, while it is being lobbied and explored, is going to make demands on practitioners that will probably be experienced as unusual and unreasonable yet will have to be confronted.

Social Attitudes and Fee Policies

The limitations begin within the societal structures, particularly business and government, who in turn employ the insurers who offer less covered service to the consumers, and thus the fee barrier is raised. Patients have to be both knowledgeable and motivated in order to be willing to directly pay greater percentages of fees. The inducement is to accept what is offered and try to be content with that unless the level of distress is so high that the need is convincing. No room is left for prevention of mild to moderate problems or the importance of emotional maturity. There is also economic pressure on providers to conform to a minimalist model for mental health.

A lack of sophistication in many health plans is also apparent in a trend to limit the number of sessions per year per individual regardless of the presenting problems. Mental illness is depicted as a homogeneous entity treatable by another supposed entity termed psychotherapy, of which the insured get a defined number of sessions. There has to be a recognition of the heterogeneity and overlap in diagnostic categories. For example, one does not treat only anxiety but the constellation of behaviors and affects that are connected to anxiety, and these are not the same in each person, nor can they be "timed" in a definitive way. Thus, assigning benefits by specific mental disorder would not work other than as a very rough standard, namely, that adjustment disorders and neurotic symptoms tend to be alleviated more rapidly than character pathology and psychosis, but of course, sometimes the former tend to be embedded in the latter, and treatment needs to be responsive to that possibility.

The ideal is that insurance coverage is made available to all who require it, which could mean extension of current benefits by including smaller businesses and providing national health insurance for those who are not employed as well as removing the limits from existing coverages. One immediate reaction to this will probably be: Out of the question, too costly! This reaction is erroneous when it comes to outpatient psychotherapy, which makes up a very small portion of national health costs. Even if inpatient services are added, the percentage remains low. Furthermore, inpatient services can be reduced if families and significant others are willing to involve themselves appropriately in the treatment, and outpatient services could be given the emphasis because they can serve more people.

Several factors help to contain costs. One is that after an initial increase in service utilization when services become available for the first time, the use levels off. Furthermore, regardless of cost, there are cultural barriers to the use of psychotherapy, such as exposing intimate details and displaying vulnerability and dependency, so many people will not use it. Their barrier is a personal philosophy and is not related to the availability of the service. Also, psychotherapy under the best of circumstances always has unpleasant aspects and the potential for narcissistic injuries. As Pine (1990) points out: "I am referring here to the indignity of being an adult in therapy, while simultaneously allowing the emergence, in the transference, of infantile aspects of ourselves that the adult part of ourselves experiences as so humiliating and demeaning, *and further*, having to share it with another adult" (p. 74).

In addition to the committed nonusers, there are many people who would use it either infrequently or briefly. Long-term intensive therapy with many sessions per week will be used by a minority. The larger group want rapid results with limited effort on their part, and even the length and frequency are inconveniences, so short-term therapy has greater appeal. Also, conditions that are particularly disturbing to society, such as drug and alcohol abuse, generally occur in people with limited anxiety and/or stress tolerance, so they are not that interested in long-term therapy either. The people so described could benefit from open-ended work, but they are not likely to avail themselves of it just because it is affordable.

Providing limitless access to the psychotherapies is unlikely to produce too great a rise in overall health costs. Certainly it would produce some, but that would tend to stabilize so that the number of potential users in the population, and the amount and frequency of usage, all could be relatively predictable. The start-up costs are there, particularly if health coverage is extended to the 15% of the population now without it. Of course not all of those people will use mental health services. In addition, people who now have affordability nonetheless use less therapy on the average than what is needed for improvement and certainly less than what is provided for by existing coverage. This is particularly true in outpatient services, which is where we are suggesting the coverage be unlimited. Unfortunately, employers and insurers have reacted prematurely to the increases that have occurred in any mental health costs.

Furthermore, sliding-scale components could be put within insurance systems for both patients and psychotherapists. On the patient's side, the amount of coverage from the insurance payment could be based on the patients' abilities to pay, with taxable income as an indicator, information that is available to employers and insurers. This would have the effect of increasing the availability of psychotherapy for poorer people without increasing the cost to insurers. Traditionally, lower socioeconomic groups have made less use of psychotherapy, particularly the long-term type, so even if more people from these groups used it, the cost increase would not be drastic because the increase in usage would be relatively small. It also could be offset by greater copayments by wealthier individuals, even if with unlimited coverage more of these people went into psychotherapy. Just as there is graduated taxation based on wealth, there could be graduated benefit distributions that could hold costs at more predictable levels.

In regard to providers, fee schedules could be matched to training and experience levels, so that those less experienced and more limited in training would receive less pay regardless of what they thought they were worth. This would also provide some quality control for consumers as well as incentive for therapists to be better trained. Continuing education requirements could also be included to accompany experience, so that time in practice without demonstrable learning would not guarantee greater income.

None of these suggestions is without loopholes and problems, but each represents improvement over the current system and serves as an indication of methods to approach the fee barrier and bring it down for more people. Most of the professions' efforts have been first to insure some coverage and then, with ambivalence and discord, to expand the provider network as well as to indicate that mental health services can reduce the use of other, more costly medical services. The social value of mental health services is underemphasized, and ideal plans are either not proposed or compromised because there is such concern with cutting overall medical costs.

The idea of a mentally healthy society needs to be resurrected in a serious and constructive way that is cost conscious and quality conscious, by no means an incompatible mix. In addition to the many limitations already visited on the use of psychotherapy, many people will go to extraordinary lengths to avoid admitting they have a problem. Even if there were an intensive effort to get people to enter psychotherapy, the increase in users would not be that large. As mental health educators, professionals will always be struggling to convince people of the value of therapeutic services, regardless of cost. However, economic limitations add to the problem without making a significant decrease in overall health care costs.

Mention should be made of those therapists who do not view psychotherapy as a health service but as an educational one, and therefore eliminate the insurance issue. Most providers disagree with their opinion, but even if one were to agree with it, the service still has a cost, so the issue of removing the economic barrier still remains. Also, there are therapists who will not have anything to do with third-party payments because it diminishes the patients' responsibility in a way they view as detrimental to therapeutic effort. Certainly it can be understood that this type of payment has implications in the therapy, but these do not have to be seen as sufficiently different from other resistance–transference issues that can be resolved rather than avoided. It can be admitted that the ideal patient currently is one who pays directly, whatever the fee, and makes no mention, no less use, of insurance, because numerous hassles are reduced for therapists. However, this is a minority of patients. If therapists were to restrict their practices to this group, many people would be excluded who need insurance payments to afford appropriate psychotherapy, and many therapists would have less income.

Psychotherapists' Attitudes and Policies

One part of the effort then needs to be devoted to altering current provisions for third-party payments. A second part should involve a review of therapists' personal fee policies. How congruent are they with the current economic situation for each therapist and his or her patients? Are psychotherapists appropriate and realistic in regard to what they charge? This review ought to be periodic, and although it needs to be in tune with a market economy, one must keep in mind that providers are both contributors to and determiners of the market. Furthermore, psychotherapists have a commitment to be of service, which has to be factored into the process of determining what to charge.

This is a personal issue for which there can really be only individual guidelines. It is important to note that which ones a therapist chooses will influence the "flexibility" of the barrier. A variety of scenes are possible, but two examples will show the variability that can exist. Zager (1990), with a relatively recent start in practice, sees whoever is referred and feels she can treat, regardless of the fee they can pay. She removes the barrier, though with the understanding that the fee will be raised when patients can afford it. She also uses a model, when it fits, of short-term work for all members of a family. She appears to do what is most obviously needed at the time for whatever the patient can afford, and she reports personal satisfaction as well as a busy practice. This is not the model for many therapists and/or patients, but it is an attempt to face the realities of the marketplace and accommodate to them.

A different example is given by Cantor (1990), who describes herself as psychoanalytically oriented with a well-established full-time practice, seeing most patients twice a week. She averages 125 referrals a year. She states nothing specific about fees, although she is clearly optimistic about the survival and even growth of independent practice. It is possible that she would agree that fees can be barriers, but it appears to be an issue that is not pressing for her. She is a definite advocate of freedom of choice and mandated mental health coverage, so one can discern her interest in making psychotherapy affordable, but it is a different type of interest than Zager's (1990).

Right now psychotherapists can review with patients the available insurance coverage and formulate a treatment plan that takes the economic factors into consideration. For short-term therapists this will not be a large problem, though some health plans limit the cost per session in ways the therapists may find unpalatable. Long-term advocates have a harder sell because the length of treatment is under scrutiny and often restricted. Many patients have a set amount available per year that is not sufficient to defray the extent of the expense that they had in mind. Therapists then have to explain why the patient should continue regardless of insurance reimbursement. The barrier has to be recognized, and the patient motivated to go through it, and that is better carried out from the start, as we describe in detail in Chapter 8.

EMOTIONAL BARRIERS

Patients' Self-Esteem

The second type of barrier involves a feeling on the part of patients that there is something inherently wrong about having to pay for what they believe is the content of psychotherapy. This belief takes two forms. The first centers on the fact that a person in psychotherapy is a designated patient, meaning the patient admits to having a problem he cannot solve alone. This admission is difficult to impossible for large numbers of people who live by denial and would rather suffer than ask anyone else for help.

They usually avoid anything as formalized as psychotherapy and will appear there only if forced in some way, such as a spouse threatening to leave them or some other apparently overwhelming life circumstance.

Their barrier is their self-image, one of relative perfection that allows little room for the feelings attached to difficulties in living that are part of being human. Thus, a reevaluation has to take place in which people understand that they are not diminished by the ingredients of their humanity. When therapists are confronted by this type of barrier, which appears early in the possible course of therapy, they have to recognize it, treat it with respect as an integral part of the patient's self-representation, and still try to alter the belief that self-esteem must be automatically less because there are personal problems in one's life. This is often difficult to do and sometimes not possible, but unless it is addressed, therapy will either terminate quickly or continue without the necessary involvement on the patient's part until the therapist calls a halt. The fee is a barrier here because the person resents paying for something he does not feel is needed.

Psychotherapy as the Remedy

The therapist's task is twofold: to convince the patient there is indeed a problem and therefore a need to solve it, and that the existence of such a problem does not mean the person is of less value. Of course the tasks are intertwined, and if the therapist is successful, then another task immediately appears, namely, convincing the person that psychotherapy is the appropriate remedy. This addresses a second form of the belief that psychotherapy is not acceptable: that although a problem is recognized, it ought to be solved by anything but psychotherapy, such as advice from friends, religion, magic, change of environment, etc. This reaction involves a misconception of psychotherapy. Now the psychotherapist has to explain the specialized service provided by psychotherapy, a professional health service for which the providers are appropriately paid.

Therapists have some troubles with actually providing such an explanation and confronting the fee barrier when it is directly posed by the patient. This is often true in settings where therapists' incomes are not directly derived from patients' fees. Avoidances can also occur in private practice. Even where sliding fee scales are used, they are based on stated ability to pay rather than how much trouble a patient will be for the therapist. It is true that economic problems in a practice may foster a need in therapists to see patients who are unpleasant to work within varying degrees, but there is a limit to this. There are some patients whom no fee can make palatable, no less enjoyable. If these people in any fashion say the fee is a barrier, their therapists are likely to agree that it is insurmountable and quickly help them go elsewhere.

Therapists' Motivations

Budman and Gurman (1988) suggest economic value differences between long- and short-term therapists in the direction of financial gain from patients becoming long-term. However, the Bolter et al. (1990) study previously cited refuted this, although they indicate the denial may have been a reluctance to admit to a socially undesirable motivation. This is not necessarily the case, however, because as long as one has a sufficient supply of patients to fill available hours at desired fees, income remains stable. The concern about therapists holding on to patients for monetary gain seems less of an issue than the findings that patients more often do not stay in therapy long enough to get effective treatment.

This seems to be happening less in private practice, but it does happen there as well, so there is a need for therapists to help people stay in psychotherapy for longer periods of time on the average than they do now. It is possible that therapists in private practice do not make that much of an effort to keep certain patients in therapy despite the possibility of these therapists gaining financially if the patients remain. This may occur because they have other probable patients as replacements, so there will be no economic loss. It also may happen because therapists sense their efforts would be fruitless at that particular time, or because the patient owes them money and is incapable or unlikely to meet the totality of the financial obligation. Sometimes some patients become unbearable or threatening, and therapists want no further contact with them. Also, therapists can feel guilty about their fees and so become reluctant to work at keeping patients lest they be accused of "just wanting the money." Therapists may even keep some patients too long to balance those they have assisted in departing too quickly.

Probably therapists often will hesitate to deal with the fee as a barrier because monetary gain is not their primary motivation. If the situation is such that a patient will get the impression that the therapist is inordinately motivated by money, the therapist will simply agree to termination. Therapists are motivated by the good fit of a therapy situation, and that includes a relative degree of comfort with the fee for both parties. If patients want to persist in using the fee as a barrier, they will indeed get their way, even to their own unrealized detriment at that moment.

The issue for therapists is a loss of identification with the role of helper, and this loss can be stimulated by being identified as a business person. These roles are compatible and certainly can be integrated, but therapists think of themselves, and want to be thought of, primarily as givers, not takers. When a patient becomes insistent about an inability to continue because of economic reasons, the therapist is faced with the possibility of appearing as though he is focused more on getting than giving. Assuming there is detailed exploration of the resistance aspects of the patient's use of money as a barrier, and that does not result in a change, what is the therapist likely to do?

Alternatives to the usual fee arrangements are possible, and therapists are often willing to provide them to set the barrier aside as quickly as possible, but if these are declined as well, what is left? For example, prospective patients may decide after one or two evaluative sessions that they cannot afford the fee, and that the fee they are willing to pay is well below what the therapist feels he needs. Or the patient indicates he can only afford to come at a pace that is definitely less than what the therapist considers effective. Cost is used in these instances to make therapy impossible, but it is really the feelings the patient has about money and/or therapy that are the obstacles. It takes discretion and courage for therapists to discern and challenge this, so it often is not done, and doing it is also no guarantee that the patient will respond appropriately. Still, patients deserve an expert opinion rather than avoidance. If therapists also have interfering feelings about money and/or working with particular patients, then avoidance will predominate.

On the patient's side, the fee may seem to be a barrier to intimacy, considering the possible warmth and understanding involved in a therapeutic relationship. Another possibility is that some patients doubt their right to spend money on themselves, and as therapy is primarily for the patient and secondarily for others, masochism/altruism may conflict with narcissism to create a superego limitation. The patient expresses the problem as "the cost," but it is the meaning of the cost that is hidden and the most crucial issue. These types of patient concerns are discussed in detail later in this book, particularly in the next two chapters.

Therapists can also experience fees as emotional barriers for themselves. Their job is to clarify the transactional nature of therapy and the structuralizing aspect of the fee that establishes and supports the professional character of the relationship. Yet they too struggle with the degree of emphasis that is to be placed on the "business" of therapy, as well as having questions about their worth to the patient and the patient's economic and personal value to them. Therapists' concerns are considered in detail in Section III of this volume. Of course the barrier has to be taken down for the therapist as well as for the patient, and the therapist's barrier is customarily an emotional one. That is, although there are some patients who are too poor to afford therapy without a subsidy of one sort or another, most therapists can find affordable ways not to have the fee interfere. Instead, their problems lie in uncomfortable and unresolved feelings about fees, feelings that in turn distort their handling of monetary transactions and issues with patients.

CONCLUSIONS

For certain patients (and therapists), fees pose a barrier to beginning or continuing in psychotherapy. Our focus has been on patients' experience and what the therapists need to do to reduce or eliminate the patients' barriers, which we categorized as financial and emotional.

In regard to the financial barrier, we advocated strong involvement in developing social policy that would enable people to have relatively unlimited access to all the psychotherapies. We recognized that accountability is vital, that the process of psychotherapy needs to be explained and documented, and that cost is indeed a major consideration. However, rather than accepting the narrow vision of mental health that is currently popular with payers, we argued for a broader view and the ideal provision of services.

Continuing in that vein, we made the point that outpatient mental health services are an incorrect target for cuts in funding. As noted, treatment of mental disorders is a minor part of national health costs, with most of that coming from inpatient services, such as substance abuse centers. These services need reorganization in terms of efficiency and community and family involvement. Extremes have been tried in the past, including excessive institutionalization and, more recently, deinstitutionalization, without success. Cuts in funding or an influx in funds without working out what can effectively be accomplished will be useless. Although they provide empathy for inpatient services since they serve the most seriously ill patients, they have considerable entrenched bureaucracies and significant wastes that need addressing and revamping.

Our society needs a better system of quality mental health care in all sectors, public and private. Since psychotherapists are part of the health care industry, they certainly cannot ignore the cost factor and any excesses they may be in the process of initiating or perpetuating. Thus, our proposals for providing quality care while containing costs and our urging psychotherapists to have ideas, to offer them, to get involved, and thereby to address the economic barrier as a policy issue.

Of course it is also an emotional issue, and we have given a broad sketch of the problems involved with details to follow from therapists' and patients' viewpoints. The message here is that patients can and will treat the fee as an obstacle to getting needed treatment. Therapists need to recognize and address this whenever they have an opportunity. When it is a real economic issue, therapists need to be advocates of efforts to bring about means of payment. When it is an emotional issue, therapists should attempt to correct misconceptions about patients' self-images and impressions of psychotherapy that are engendering the barrier. Therapists will be able to do this effectively when they recognize and work out their own barriers to charging and receiving fees.

In the solutions we have offered for overcoming the fee barrier, we have supported, but not stressed, the more traditional use of a sliding scale and service for free with therapists donating time. We believe a certain amount of this is appropriate and necessary but unrealistic as an overall solution given the potential magnitude of the problem, including the feelings and exigencies of all involved. People became therapists to make a living, among other motivations, and our solutions to the fee barrier therefore incorporate economic goals. Their reasonableness bears scrutiny in all sectors, but the fact of getting paid cannot be bypassed in this market economy society.

Thus, direct payment, mandated mental health coverage, sliding-scale payments by insurance carriers based on patients' income and providers' competencies, reorganized inpatient financing and unlimited outpatient insurance coverage, redistribution of national priorities in regard to social policy, all with an eye on the bottom line, also are all designed to make sure psychotherapists get paid. In addition, they are not managed care approaches that restrict service to contain cost. The service possibilities are actually expanded, although in a selective manner because the demand itself has many self-curtailments.

Wright (1990) has a concise, perceptive summary of the development of national health insurance coverage in which he concludes, regrettably, that any national plan is not currently of that much interest to legislators. He indicates that costs have consistently been underestimated, that national health insurance plans in other countries have proven to be more costly than expected and of poor quality, and so the idea is being considered an already too expensive mistake. He predicts further efforts to control costs, less quantity and quality of care, and a poor future for mental health providers, unless of course the current approaches are so disturbing to consumers and providers alike that they alter the trend.

It is quite possible that mental health services were originally underestimated in terms of cost and utilization, and further services could bring increased use and cost, but we have suggested a number of ways to cope with possible rises and have raised questions about the relative extent of ultimate increases. Furthermore, it is encouraging that so many countries outside of the United States believe in the concept of their societies' responsibilities for health care. The fact that their methodology has had problems does not negate the concept. This point remains—that psychotherapists have to commit themselves to doing whatever is needed to bring down real economic barriers to their services, and they have to do this in a way that is sophisticated and capable of providing quality care with an appropriate economic return for the providers.

Chapter 5

FOR RICHER OR POORER

When a fee is agreed on by the therapist and patient, it is generally part of a contract including the idea that this fee will be in place for a relatively predetermined amount of time. The amount of the fee, the timing of the payments, and the money flow between the two people is something both can expect. There is both demand and security in these expectations, but they cannot always be met, and that can be disturbing to both parties and the therapy process as well. This chapter is concerned with what happens when patients' financial circumstances change in a way that affects payment; it also offers some reflections on changes in therapists' financial situations. Although this section of the book is devoted primarily to what patients do with fees and how therapists react, the payment process is always interactive to varying degrees in that it depends on the attitudes and feelings of patient and therapist toward money.

FOR POORER

The most disturbing possibility is that a patient suffers financial problems that limit her ability to pay. An immediate question for exploration is how this has occurred, particularly what part the patient played in it. Since patients are aware that they become "at risk" if they cannot pay, their motivation in regard to any inability to pay has to be considered. Is this the patient's way of saying, "I want out of therapy," or, if it happens rather quickly, "I don't wish to start." Another possibility is that it is a test of the therapist's concern and attitudes about money. The patient's question then becomes, "If I *can't* pay, will you see me?"

Awareness

The exploration begins when it is made apparent to the therapist that the patient is having trouble paying the fee. Some patients anticipate it and ask the therapist what is acceptable in order to continue. This is the easiest to deal with because the patient brings up the issue. Other patients let it show in a variety of ways, such as forgetting the check, making it out for the wrong amount, getting confused about the payment arrangements, etc., any of which affect the contract. The therapist then has to raise the issue of what the patient might be feeling and doing with this. It is an error to consider the "little alterations" as relatively meaningless. However, it is also tactless and annoying to patients to behave in a hypervigilant manner. Usually it is appropriate to take notice and see what evolves from the patient's side. The hope, which often gets actualized, is that the patient detects something and ascribes motivation and thus becomes like the first group of patients who raise the issue themselves.

There is some temptation by therapists either to dismiss the issue when patients raise it or to avoid noticing it as an issue when patients do not directly present it as such. In the first case, there may be such a desire for this not to happen that the therapist dismisses it, basically telling the patient somehow everything will be all right. This is of course confusing to the patient, who already knows there is a problem, and it is pointless for the therapist because days of reckoning will obviously follow. This kind of denial also can lead to subsequent resentment by the therapist who was so reassuring, only to be left with the unpleasant reality. Not too many therapists will do this, but there are degrees of it, and it is not helpful. If the patient states there is now, or is about to be, a financial problem, therapists should pay attention. (They can still explore the possibility that the situation reflects patient pessimism.)

The avoidance of noticing the issue when it is not directly presented as such is more common and, of course, part of the same wish for continued good times. The payment issue does not have to be immediately raised, but it should be taken into account. The therapist should be aware that the patient is expressing something through the medium of money and start to hypothesize. It is best if the patient arrives at the issue first, but if time passes and the problem persists, then the therapist has to raise the subject.

Causality

Assuming the stages of awareness and acknowledgment by both therapist and patient, the next question is, how did the problem really arise? Both parties may have a desire to attribute it to circumstances beyond the patient's control, thereby avoiding the possibility that the patient was self-destructive. However, it is necessary to examine the patient's role and the therapist's as well. What led up to it? Did the patient withhold information from the therapist? Did the therapist avoid discussing anticipated consequences? Thus, an unfortunate event such as the loss of a job has unconscious and conscious meanings, both in the preceding activity and the event itself as well as in the ultimate consequences.

There are patients whose workplace attitudes and behaviors make them likely candidates for unemployment. There are patients whose handling of money makes them likely candidates for perpetual debt. These are matters for exploration and change during therapy, but while that is taking place, these patients may have problems paying their fees. Some of this can be discerned in the initial or consultation stages before the therapist has made a commitment to work with the patient. If it is apparent, then the therapist has to decide whether she can be comfortable with such financial dry spells. Some therapists are not and/or do not see such behavior as sufficient for therapy to be effective. These therapists and patients clearly do not belong together. However, this type of "responsibility issue" needs attention, and there are therapists who are flexible enough to work with these patients and gain successful outcomes.

However, there are times when the issue is not recognized early or by either patient or therapist, and then the problem is more acute because a relationship has been formed and the process is on its way.

This returns us to the issue of patient accountability for what happened. Therapists are rarely financial experts. Thus, if a patient states that he is going to invest in a particular stock, the therapist has no way of knowing whether that will improve or deteriorate the patient's financial position. Therapists ought to have an awareness of their patients' general financial situations, but whether particular financial moves are good or bad is an unknown to them in most instances. In any case, the roads not taken need to be looked at because patients' motivations are of interest. In doing this, however, it is crucial to make it clear that this is not intended to lower the patient's self-esteem. The emphasis is not on the "mistake" but on its place in one's life. Factories close, workers get laid off, the stock market crashes, and patients may react with anger to exploring their part in any of this, yet they probably had a part or at least a reaction. It is not a question of blame but of understanding.

It is also true that for some patients their responsibility will be illuminated, particularly if the focus needs to be on issues of responsibility. Still, the emphasis is on learning, not accusing. The therapist has to phrase the inquiry in such a way that the patient is not unduly threatened or depressed by the interest in her role. If this is not carried out properly, the patient will feel misunderstood and may experience the therapist as blaming the patient for being unable to pay. Therapists need to examine their feelings here as well, because they could be expressing resentment in the guise of merely doing their job. The exploration should be designed to be neutral but thorough, with supportive measures used where needed as long as both parties persist. Patients' pain is often a fearful deterrent to therapists, and when it is connected to money, even more so, for it is easy to empathize with a financial reverse, especially when the patient's reversal could also be the therapist's. Gutheil (1986) notes the particular reluctance to exploration of beginning therapists when he describes it as "perhaps the most common corruption of the therapeutic process" (p. 186).

Solutions

Although we have awareness, recognition, and understanding, we must still face the issue itself: the patient cannot continue the current fee arrangement. The key question now is what to do about it. The first step is to explore what changes the patient feels she needs to make and to see how these fit in with the overall financial pattern of the therapist's practice. Usually in an ongoing practice there can be sufficient cash flow to have a variety of payment patterns. Thus, some people may pay every week, others every other week, others monthly, etc., so that kind of variation can be acceptable. For example, with the increased number of patients using insurance, a patient may have attempted to pay the entire fee for the month prior to receiving the insurance copayment but found this impossible. Thus, the therapist may agree to wait for that copayment until it is received by the patient. The amount of time this will routinely take can be predetermined with the understanding that if it takes longer, the patient will look into the matter and expedite it.

A larger problem is if the patient cannot pay the existing fee. One option is for the therapist to agree to a lesser fee with a mutually agreed-on plan for the patient to resume paying the original fee, or even to make up the difference for the period of time when the fee had to be reduced. Of course if the therapist uses a sliding fee scale, then in therapy it slides down as well as up, and if a reduction was needed, the scale could accommodate it, at least within the range of the scale. However, even with such a policy therapists tend to think of this approach as a way to set an initial fee with expectations that it will go up, not down, or at the very least will remain the same. Also, in such an arrangement, the patient would not be expected to make up any of the fee reduction, so the income loss would be permanent.

Another arrangement is the deferral of payment without lowering the fee. The patient and therapist agree to suspend payment until some designated time when the patient will be able to pay and then begins paying the previous fee again as well as the unpaid balance. The therapist basically extends credit. Hofling and Rosenbaum (1986) found this a relatively common practice that also proved efficient in securing fees.

Monetary Resistance

These procedures have been discussed by Welt and Herron (1990). Note must be taken that they are at variance with the limit to fee modifications that is probably best articulated by Langs (1982). That approach is consistent in staying with the same fee throughout the therapy and viewing any changes in it as too disruptive to the frame of psychotherapy for effectiveness to be maintained. That changes can be problematic and activate countertransferential reactions is clear, but that fee modifications are of such dire consequence is not so clear, nor is it the most common view among therapists. Lane and Hull, for example, agree that fee changes are significant but state, "We feel that therapists should be realistic and make whatever arrangements are most appropriate and then strive to understand with the patient the transference and countertransference meanings that ensue" (1990, p. 265).

A significant issue in fee reduction is that the therapist will lose money, whether it be temporarily or permanently. Therapists have to be prepared for this possibility in terms of both their feelings and economic situations. When one uses a sliding scale, it appears that some fee is better than none, whereas a fixed fee can mean that none is better than less. Those feelings in turn can be correlated with patient supply, meaning if there are people to replace those who cannot pay the usual fee, then the loss of any patient is not an economic loss since the person gets replaced. However, it is rare that this would happen with such efficiency that no hours would go unfilled. So to take the approach that if a patient cannot pay the usual fee she will have to go elsewhere usually means at least a temporary monetary loss.

When faced with the patient's inability to pay the fee she has been paying, the therapist may elect not to continue the therapy for a variety of reasons, regardless of an economic loss. One possibility is a desire to be rid of the patient, having been unable or unwilling to work out ongoing countertransference and now being presented with a "reality" opportunity. The patient has altered the contract, and so the therapist can feel it is reasonable to make arrangements for the patient to see a more affordable therapist. It is not true that the patient cannot work with anyone else, since therapists die or move while patients are in therapy and many of those patients go on to other therapists. Change in a situation where the therapist wants out is really to the patient's benefit, although it may not at first be experienced that way by the patient if the therapist uses the fee reduction rather than the real issue.

Another possibility is that the therapist is not amenable to the patient's solution to the problem but quickly senses it is the only solution that the patient will accept. The patient wants her own way more than wanting to stay in therapy. For example, a therapist with a fixed fee schedule offers to accept deferred payment, but the patient states that she would not feel comfortable owing the money. Hence, the therapist is left with the choice of lowering the fee or losing her patient. Assuming attempts are made to explore the power struggle and are resisted, the therapist then indicates that the issue is not about the fee but about the patient's intent on having her way. Thus, she lets her go with the hope that ultimately she will see the situation differently. Although therapists want to be sensitive to the needs of their patients, they have to be sensitive to their own needs as well. For example, a therapist who feels comfortable with fixed fees can vary how that works, but she will not feel comfortable with a sliding scale, so it would be a mistake to agree to it. Interwoven with the therapist's discomfort at the patient's proposal is the issue of the meaning of the patient's action. In this case the therapist concludes that the patient is so resistant to understanding that even if she accepted the payment procedure her way, it would not facilitate the therapy. In such a case the financial issue is being raised to sabotage the therapy, regardless of what the therapist does.

A variation on this is a case of a male patient who considered himself very insightful and self-sufficient until his wife suddenly left him and their 10-year-old son. This crisis brought him into therapy with a woman therapist, and he made it clear that he was quite uncomfortable about being in therapy, although his overall emotional distress was obvious. At this point he stated that he needed help, but he also indicated potential financial problems with the fee. He did not ask for a reduction, but he cited the cost of child care, uncertainty about how his insurance coverage would work, the possibility that he might not be financially productive (he was self-employed) because he would have to take time to be with his son, which also might interfere with when and how often he could come to therapy, and similar probable resistances. Thus, there was plenty of evidence to suggest this would be a difficult patient, but his actual financial circumstance (as opposed to a potential future one) appeared adequate for him to pay the fee regularly.

The therapist was clear about her reluctance from a dynamic point of view and discussed her reservations with the patient, and he seemed to understand. However, he did cancel sessions and would resist the idea of the meaning of his cancellations, and he quickly developed a financial problem that resulted in a request on his part to come every other week rather than weekly. The development of the problem was explored, but the reality of it was difficult to ascertain, except that the patient foresaw an end to it within a 3-month period. The therapist indicated that she felt the decreased frequency of therapy would be harmful and offered to take half the fee each week until the completion of the 3 months, at which time he could pay her the balance. The patient explained that he was reluctant to do this because he was not the type of person who owed people money, and beyond that he realized now how dependent he had been on his wife. With the proposed arrangement he would also be dependent on the therapist. However, after further discussion, he agreed to her proposal. However, he also switched insurance carriers during this time, and there was considerable confusion, forms to be filled out, and phone calls for the therapist to make, that had an annoying aspect. Beyond that there seemed an implied threat that unless the insurance issue got worked out, the fee would be in jeopardy. At the same time, the man was polite, considerate, and apologetic about having to burden the therapist with these details.

At the end of the 3-month period, the patient indeed paid the therapist what was owed, and all insurance payments had come as well. However, the copayments were not as large as the patient had anticipated, so he wanted once again to come every other week because of financial hardship. Now this was a patient who was quite verbal, struggling with considerable damage to his self-esteem, and feeling depressed and anxious, yet with an eagerness to talk during the sessions. The therapist reiterated her impression that every other week was insufficient, but she decided to go along with the patient's plan in the hope that he would himself discover the need for weekly sessions. Furthermore, she could discern that his financial difficulties were primarily the result of how he was managing his money rather than an inability to have sufficient funds to pay the weekly fee.

From her point of view, they "limped along" for a number of months. When in sessions he was quite productive but was able to keep emotional distance from issues and from the therapist because of the lessened frequency. Also, she was now clearly suffering a financial loss and had restricted her time by tying up a particular session every other week, which was something she would not have done if those had been the conditions under which the patient had wanted to start therapy.

The patient's psychic distress increased, so the therapist made another attempt to increase the frequency and get a commitment to the therapy. She made it clear she did not see the money as having to be a problem and used a number of examples as illustrations, and she indicated she understood the patient felt he had been betrayed, thus limiting his own willingness to commit himself. However, he needed to do so for the therapy to be effective, and she suggested a trial period of returning to weekly sessions during which the patient could decide to commit or stop. The patient agreed to her reasoning and the trial period but still hedged about potential money problems. Nonetheless, they went through the time, during which there were a couple of cancellations based on child-care problems and considerable talk about money concerns, although the fees were paid promptly and without direct complaint. In addition, the patient was feeling much better, which was encouraging to the therapist in one way, yet a warning to her in another. He was learning to cope with his current situation, but would he be willing to experience the anxiety that could arise with continued therapeutic exploration?

His therapist doubted it, so she was not surprised when at the end of the trial period the patient said he was going to stop. His stated reason, however, was again that he could not afford the therapy. His therapist felt she had to attempt to dispel that, and she did; at this point, the patient rather quickly agreed that he was choosing not to afford it because he felt good enough, and he really wanted to spend his time and money elsewhere. He was very positive about the therapist and the therapy, including future potential benefits, but he had other priorities. Sessions every other week still had some appeal for him, but the therapist would not agree, so they terminated.

This patient had more insight than the one in the previous example, but both patients used money to retard therapy. In both instances the therapists worked on both the motivational and practical aspects and had some success but ultimately decided that termination was the most therapeutic course.

Therapists' Flexibility

A key element in dealing with a patient who becomes unable to pay the fee is a willingness by the patient to be interested in solutions. When that is missing, then the therapy is going to be seriously interfered with, regardless of what the therapist does. Thus, there will be some patients who desire to use the issue of money to end therapy, and confrontation, exploration, free therapy, etc., will not help. They want a disaster, and they will insure its scope encompasses their therapy.

However, there is another group who wants to cope with the disaster and tries to but needs to have some relief from the financial obligations to the therapist. Thus, we return to the possibilities of what is palatable to patient and therapist alike, with the understanding that both parties want the therapy to continue. It is our belief and experience that therapists generally make provisions for patients in these circumstances, and we base this on the popularity of sliding-scale fee policies as well as the number of therapists providing some low-cost or free service (Welt & Herron, 1990). At the same time there are limits to what therapists will do based on their feelings about money and about particular patients, their own economic needs, and their self-images.

The patient who is unable to pay the fee represents the downside of practice for most therapists, and that has to be anticipated. Cash flow is generally not steady, nor is income guaranteed to be consistent, and independent practitioners have to be willing to live with varying degrees of these fluctuations. Using a sliding scale does allow the therapist to shift downward and still maintain a consistent fee policy. However, too many downward shifts, and income is significantly decreased. Hence, each therapist needs to establish "comfort zones" beyond which the therapist cannot go because therapy cannot be effective if the therapist is perpetually resentful of the patient. So situations could occur where, regardless of the fee policy, the therapist would have to indicate to the patient that their work together was ending because the patient could not pay the fee needed by the therapist.

This is difficult to contemplate, no less to do, because we are discussing an existing relationship with commitments on both sides and with therapists very invested in being seen as helpers. Dropping a patient who is already suffering because somebody else rejected her, such as an employer, really makes the point that patients are not purely helpers but *paid* helpers. Yet that is the reality in a capitalistic society with a market economy such as ours, although it is tempered by socialistic elements. Thus, a therapist does not have to deprive a nonpaying patient of therapy, for services are available, but the therapist deprives the patient of therapy with herself. This limits choice, limits quality of care, and makes therapists feel guilty. As a result, very few of them do it.

Instead, therapists often take the hit, at least for a while. Some therapists even feel good about fee reduction because it emphasizes their apparent selflessness, whereas others may find it attractive because they doubted their worth anyway, and this scenario falls more into line with lessened expectations. However, most therapists will not feel positively if such practice starts to appear excessive, which must be a subjectively determined decision. They then may as discreetly as possible convince the patient she is "cured" or needs less therapy or use some other rationalization to get rid of the patient without letting on, probably even to themselves, what they are really doing. It must be reiterated that the majority of therapists have flexible fee policies in regard to ongoing patients, so that most patients do not have to worry about being terminated. However, it is still preferable to get paid as expected and display one's goodness via effective results than to have to make monetary modifications. Thus, there is the probability of some countertransferential anger when the terms of the contract are altered by the patient in some way that is not the therapist's preference.

As with all countertransference, ideally this would get worked out and not be reflected in the therapist's behavior. However, this type of countertransference tends to be persistent because the patient stimulus is an ongoing one. Although the therapist agrees to a particular fee arrangement, such as a reduction, every time the fee is paid there is a reminder that it is less than before. This reminder will be present in any of the modifications, such as delayed payments, or suspension of payments, so it is probably something that will have to be reworked, and the patient may suffer some resentment in the process.

> Harmful countertransferences are problems with changeable fees, fees that are too low, or fees not paid in a timely fashion. Untoward aggression against the patient in response to the hurtful (to the therapist) fee variation is common, even if the variations have been permitted or encouraged by the therapist. (Raney, 1986, p. 98)

The possibility of the patient having feelings of excessive dependency, gratitude, reluctance to express anger, and other transferential manifestations is also strong. Akin to the countertransference, the reminder will also be there as long as the patient-initiated change exists, so it is more difficult to analyze such transference to resolution.

These problems all require recognition on the part of the therapist. At least that way chances are increased that the therapy will remain effective. Most psychotherapists are going to encounter these problems from time to time and are going to make changes. When making them, however, patients ought to be made aware that the type of difficulties described may arise, and that time and effort will have to be spent on them. It is easier not to have to do that, although such changes at times produce useful material.

The therapist is really saying he or she will work better if the financial arrangements are as desired by the therapist, since the focus can then be primarily on the transference. However, if therapists really believe that any alteration of the fee structure is excessively disruptive, as a minority seem to feel, then of course therapists should not raise fees themselves, although a majority do. Thus the minority viewpoint would be that once the fee is set, neither party can alter it without serious problems in the analytic process. In contrast, the majority view is that problems may well occur but they can usually be worked out. However, they are likely to be greater if the fee is lowered at the patient's request than if it is raised at the request of the therapist. While a bit lopsided, it is nonetheless real because there is less likelihood of interfering countertransference. Some still remains, so the idea that it is easier if, for any specific therapist–patient dyad the fee is not altered, would be true. Nonetheless, economic circumstances will usually result in changes initiated by patients and therapists, particularly over the course of long-term therapy.

This brings us again to the question, what if the therapist does not want to make a change that is going to lower income? The therapist may need the money, already having too many low fee patients, or the therapist may feel it is antitherapeutic, or the therapist's self-esteem may require a certain monetary return from work. In all of these instances therapists would rather wait for a full-fee patient than continue with one who can no longer pay the fee. The therapist has the responsibility to aid the patient in obtaining therapy elsewhere at an affordable rate. Beyond that, she needs to tell the patient why the discontinuance is going to happen. Therapists are not prone to do this, often finding other ways, including their own discomfort, to continue or terminate. However, unless therapists are comfortable enough with fee modifications, they should not make them, and they should always explain their reasoning.

We favor making accommodations within limits, but situations can change, and it is necessary to consider the position of those therapists who do not. In such cases, the patient could be told that it would not be an effective arrangement, that the therapist could not work that way for any or all of the reasons that have been described. The therapist would spend some time working out the patient's reaction to that decision, but ultimately, and in a relatively short time, there could be termination.

Such a stance emphasizes the economics of the transaction and the meanings of money for both therapist and patient. At this point there is a strong desire to take back the words just written, to say a therapist once committed is always committed, and certainly money would not stand in the way, but money could and does. Therapists are paid providers, bound by both theoretical convictions and economic realities as to the effectiveness of their work. This is a reality that, when it arises, has to be faced by therapists and patients.

FOR RICHER

As far as is known, there are not any studies on this issue, but from personal experience, it became apparent that most patients who stayed in therapy until mutually agreeable therapist–patient terminations tended to get richer over the course of psychotherapy. This hypothesis was checked out informally with a number of colleagues, and they reported similar results. There is a logic to this in that improvement tends to coincide with success in life, and that usually includes material success. Certainly not always, but rather frequently, one of the goals in psychotherapy is for the patients to improve their standard of living, and over the time spent in therapy, that indeed happens. Also, it has usually begun to happen in a significant way after some time in therapy but before an agreed-on termination date.

This development has its own set of assets and liabilities for both patients and therapists. On the positive side for patients, it can provide a tangible return for their investment, it can make the fee less of a burden and an issue, and if they want to expand their therapeutic experience in terms of duration and/or frequency, that is a greater possibility. In the same vein, for the therapist, payment can become less of an issue and certainly less connected to reality if posed as a resistance, and it is possible to develop treatment plans that can be more open-ended without as much concern for their cost. If a therapist experiences guilt or discomfort about a patient's ability to pay whatever is being charged, these feelings can be more easily alleviated.

On the negative side, patients can equate financial gains with total psychic improvement, or at least more psychological gain than is congruent with the therapist's view, and thus want to end their therapy before they have derived maximum benefits. The proposed termination is not premature in the usual sense, but it is a type of "shortchanging" that patients could do to themselves only to discover subsequently that problems remain. In addition, there are plenty of books written about the problems of having money once one has acquired it. Yet if the therapist disputes the patient's contention of sufficiency, then the patient may see the therapist as wanting to exploit the patient's new financial condition. A similar feeling might appear if the therapist is raising the possibility of more sessions per week. A related concern is that if the therapist is using a sliding scale, the patient may try to conceal financial gain for as long as possible to retain what is now a "bargain rate." The temptation exists to be deceptive and hostile if the patient is so inclined, either by character or via the transference.

Depending on what money means to patients, they may use the increase in it to display a variety of feelings to the therapist. One patient who inherited a considerable sum became insecure because she now worried about the loss of it and, if she considered spending any of the principal, immediately saw herself as having less money, although she would have still more than before the inheritance.

Olsson (1986) and Warner (1991) have discussed the possibility of patients who are particularly rich being contemptuous or condescending or controlling in regard to therapists. Thus, as the patient acquires more money, she may equate this with more power in therapy and want to engage in that type of struggle with the therapist as an expression of new-found psychic riches. This can be useful as an area for exploration, but if it hardens into a resistance to any interpretation, then therapy can become stalemated. Sometimes this power struggle may take the form of the patient wanting to be good to the therapist, such as suggesting a higher fee than the therapist wants, or passing along stock tips or investment opportunities, or excessive gift giving. This side of the coin appears more pleasant, yet it too requires exploration and can lead to apparently intractable resistance.

A countertransferential problem for therapists may be that they now see these patients in a new light. Beginning therapists in particular may envy the "rich" patients, or wish to merge with them and see them as really having the answer, with the result that therapy gets misdirected and distorted. Another possibility is therapist contempt, resulting from the patient still having problems despite wealth, thus turning the patient into a "sicker" person than she was perceived to be prior to the monetary advancement. There also may be a temptation to use financial information provided directly or inadvertently. More than one therapist has already made the papers because of insider trading due to using such privileged information.

A common problem is that as patients acquire more money they want to do things with it other than spend it on therapy. This is understandable, but it constitutes a problem because it can happen before the patient, in the therapist's view, ought to shift priorities. Also sometimes because patients use money to do many significant things, such as buy a house, they incur greater debt than anticipated, and their priorities get shifted without that having been their intention. Thus, many home buyers are not experts at the use of financial instruments, take variable rate mortgages because of a low initial monthly fee, only to find their rate is pegged to some index that seems to rise every year. The end result is they are in financial trouble.

Thus it is possible that just as with patients who encounter financial difficulties, patients who get richer while in therapy may also decrease therapists' incomes by decreasing the frequency or duration of treatment. However, it appears that patients get richer in therapy more often than they get poorer, which should offer some solace in terms of income security, and usually those who get richer opt to decrease therapy less often than those who become poor, which should further alleviate worry.

Still, a change in therapist incomes happens, and it is necessary to be prepared to deal with the changes. The more common issue of working with the problem of patients having less money as they are in therapy has been discussed at length. The problem of patients becoming richer has to be approached somewhat differently, since the therapist is not being asked by the patient to do something to keep her in therapy. Of course the meaning of the patient having more money needs to be explored, as does the countertransference, but the issue may come down to a dispute between patient and therapist as to continuance. Of course if the therapist believes continuance is the best course, then regardless of being perceived as exploitative or greedy, or some other negative, the opinion needs to be given. However, it is the patient's prerogative and if she chooses to spend her money elsewhere, let the therapist wish the patient well. If one is going to lose a patient prior to the person reaching a certain potential for psychic development, it is at least comforting to know that the patient is satisfied in one or more ways. Patients will stop therapy when, from their point of view, it is no longer cost effective. Thus, what is ideal from the therapist's viewpoint is often not the psychic reality acceptable and sought after by the patient. It is the latter with which therapists need to learn to live, with only gentle discomfort.

THERAPISTS' FINANCES

There has been a marked increase in the number of people entering private practice and a marked increase on the part of third-party payers, who facilitated the first increase, to restrict the income of the psychotherapists. Naturally this has made many therapists feel insecure, and since institutional positions are not that financially rewarding, and so not a desired alternative, marketing strategies for private practice are proliferating. A good example of this is the chapter "Techniques for Expansion" by Morrison (1990) in *The Encyclopedic Handbook of Private Practice*, edited by E. A. Margenau. Morrison's chapter and articles akin to it (Zemlich, 1983) make it clear that a psychotherapeutic practice has an ever-increasing number of possible insecurities.

Thus, reaction to the possibilities raised in this chapter of lowered or lost income will be tempered by the financial situation of the therapist. If the therapist is financially secure, which of course has to be a personalized definition, then potential and real losses of income based on the situations described will be easier to deal with from a more objective therapeutic stance. If the therapist is struggling financially, then there is more probability of an exaggerated monetary focus, either in the direction of exploitation of the patient or a reaction formation resulting in exploitation of the therapist and continuing or further financial problems. Essentially the message is that psychotherapists ought to get and keep their financial houses in order so that they can work effectively with the money issues that are really such a basic component of this type of service provision. This means therapists will enter into a variety of financial arrangements that are necessary for their security. If these are ethical and legal, then they become a component in the successful therapeutic protocol of those therapists.

Chapter 6

PAYING TO BE HEARD

I n Chapter 3 we described the philosophy of service that is appropriate for psychotherapy, namely, that it is a professional relationship in which the psychotherapist provides services for a fee. We also indicated that this poses problems for both therapists and patients. Chapter 4 considered how the fee can operate as both an economic and emotional barrier for some patients, and in Chapter 5 we described fee issues that arise when there are changes in patients' economic situations during the course of therapy. Now we consider how patients' feelings and perceptions of the therapeutic relationship affect the ways they work with the process of payment. These are categorized as deals, complaints, and limits, with, as usual, some overlap.

DEALS

Many patients have a relatively good grasp of their ability to pay for therapy as well as their interest in and need for it. This is accompanied by a relatively accurate expectation of fee arrangements, so that the deal they agree to is the one proposed by the therapist. This agreement does not eliminate ambivalence, or periodic resistances using the fee. In fact, since resistance is guaranteed to occur and recur throughout therapy (Blum, 1985), so will fee problems as a manifestation of the resistance. These do not have to be a source of anxiety for the therapist but instead can be used as interpretive opportunities. Furthermore, because the patient has agreed to the therapist's contract and understands it, a set payment will usually be in place without apparent difficulty on the patient's part.

The resistance will appear in deviations from the pattern and, if pointed out, will generally be accepted by patients as material for exploration.

These deviations usually are in the direction of hostility toward the therapist and include, but are not limited to, forgetting payment, underpaying, misunderstanding cancellation policies, losing bills, or having to write checks after the session time has elapsed (Welt & Herron, 1990). These are tests of therapists' tolerance, durability, and sensitivity as well as opportunities for patients to be oppositional and to get a little bit more for their money than was in the initial agreement. It is important for patients to be able from time to time to check out what kind of parents they have in their therapists, as well as for therapists to allow these opportunities to exist. Since they are not constant, they should not be a prime source of irritation for therapists, but they do bear notice and exploration, and then patients expect that as well.

An example is a patient who customarily paid her bill monthly at the last session of the month. In one month, ending on a Friday, the patient indicated to the therapist that she would pay the bill on Monday. She explained that she had been distracted the past few days and was uncertain about her finances but would have everything in place by Monday. The therapist responded on an apparent reality level by stating that she was not going to deposit the money until Monday anyway, so if the patient would like to follow the usual pattern, it would not have any different effect on the patient's finances than if the patient paid on Monday.

This is the therapist's way of opening up the issue of the meaning of the patient's variation, which is a withholding, even though in reality it was not going to affect the therapist's use of the money. Of course the patient did not know that until the therapist indicated it as a query about the patient's intentionality. The patient declined the therapist's offer, stating that it would make her too uncomfortable to pay it now, regardless of what the therapist would do. The therapist could drop it at that point, getting back to it in the future, or keep exploring, depending on her impression of what would clinically be most effective.

The matter was deferred until Monday, when it was revealed that the patient's holding back was primarily because of a mistrust of herself, an acknowledgment that she should be giving the therapist her due without restrictions but could not because she had failed to be as attentive to her finances as she felt was necessary. The therapist's presentation of the situation so that it would not matter was not accepted by the patient because it did not change her sense of inadequacy, an issue then open to further exploration.

Sometimes the fee resistance goes in a direction that does not appear to be depriving to therapists, such as overpayment, or prepayment. These are still changes in the original contract, and whether or not the therapist accepts them, their meaning again needs to be explored. They are also transference signs, testing the therapist in still other ways. Perhaps the patient is wondering if these changes would be noticed, is setting up possibilities for therapists to accept contractual variations that might apparently benefit the therapist, or maybe she is expecting gratitude for such behavior. On the practical level therapists can refund overpayment, or if bills are paid monthly and the overpayment is one session, it can easily be credited to the next month's bill. The point, of course, is that something went on with the fee that was not contracted for, something aimed at ostensibly benefiting the therapist or, put another way, manipulating the parent's favor.

The use of cash is another example. It is a popular conception (we hope, misconception) that therapists hide some of their income and that cash payments help them do this and will generally be so used. Again, the issue of interest is the patient's motivation in making a cash payment.

Now some of these fee-flexing approaches can be ruled out by specifications in the therapist–patient contract, but that will not rule out attempts by patients to use them. Furthermore, contract flexibility can be clinically useful, and too much detail in the beginning may not be comprehended by the patient. The therapist can take care of some of this when it occurs, so obsessive contracting probably is not helpful between therapist and patient (Herron & Rouslin, 1984). Also, the type of patients we have been describing are attempting, most of the time, to follow the therapist's procedures. Thus, it is important that these not be viewed by patients as exploiting of either party. If, for example, the contract is seen as excessively rigid, the very adherence to it may include the patient's feeling that he cannot question it in any way. At the same time, if it is so loose that patients essentially do it their way only, it is hard for patients to respect the therapists. Most patients expect a reasonable deal but can get into unreasonable ones, particularly if tilted in their favor. It is the therapist's responsibility to make sure the contract is indeed reasonable, fair, and appropriate.

There are also patients who are looking to make a deal that consciously meets some distorted motive of theirs. The most obvious is to take advantage of their belief that therapists' routinely lower fees if convinced their prospective patients are poor. So, although they can afford more, they nonetheless try to get services for less, a tendency not limited to therapy. They play on therapist guilt, which can be extensive and easily aroused (Krueger, 1986a), but they cheat themselves, because they bury an issue that is a characterological problem. Therapists can usually avoid this if they are willing to explore the patients' financial situation, but unfortunately such willingness is not that prevalent (Jacobs, 1986).

A variation on this type of patient is the one who offers therapists deals that can benefit both of them. These are deals that corrupt the therapist (and the therapy as well, but both parties unconsciously agree to overlook them). These customarily involve defrauding some third party, such as insurance carriers or the IRS, but they are bad deals regardless of what justification the parties put into place.

Then there are patients who unconsciously tap into those needs of therapists that cause them to offer unusual fee arrangements. Thus, a therapist may decide on a rather superficial basis that a patient cannot afford the usual fee but then feel the patient is obligated to the therapist because of a "break" that the patient did not consciously request. Patients who are attractive to therapists can also fall into this category (Goldstein, 1971). They could be sexually attractive or be intriguing in some other manner. Although this is not a planned approach on the patient's part, some have had similar experiences in the past, so awareness is at least preconscious. Others are victims, and this means patients are wise to explore whether they are being given unrequested deals and, if so, what are the motivations and feelings of the therapists. Because the relationship is so important in psychotherapy, any deal needs exploration, including legitimately being a low-cost patient. The patient needs to be as certain as possible that he or she will get the therapist's best effort. Thus, unless one really needs a deal on the fee, it is safer to go with the usual fee because it increases the possibility of good service.

Misunderstanding of the therapeutic relationship and of the way in which therapy is structured to help people contributes to the problem. Therapy is designed as an unusual helping business. The unusual part is the tremendous focus on the patient in a dyadic relationship as well as the fact that therapists have a special interest in others for which they are not getting paid in money. The business part is also definitely there based on therapists' abilities to use learned skills, and patients are expected to pay for that, with therapists assigning the value to it. Assuming that the value is reasonable, and in a market economy that is readily determined, then the business runs best for all concerned when it runs at a profit. Patients will really cut the best deal for themselves if they consider therapists' needs to profit economically from what they do.

COMPLAINTS

The mixed environment of psychotherapy does provide grounds for a variety of dissatisfactions from patients. The most obvious center on what is being received for the money being paid. These types of questions vary in frequency and antagonism based to a large degree on how willing therapists have been initially to explain the therapy process and its progression. Limited explanation, or persistently returning the queries to patients, can certainly promote complaints. However, even with detailed explanation, complaints still occur and require a response.

Patients are generally looking for dramatic and rapid changes that are going to endure, but because of the lengthy change process that appears to be the fate of most people (Koss & Butcher, 1986), psychotherapy will not work that way. Even if one opts for short-term treatments, including therapy as brief as a single session (Bloom, 1984), this is hardly a guarantee of lasting change. Whether in or out of psychotherapy, change takes continual work, and people often blame the need for that on the "limited effectiveness of psychotherapy," whether they tried it briefly or spent years in therapy.

Of course the complaints are more likely to appear in long-term work because the overall cost is greater during the time spent in therapy. Sometimes these come from frustration at being unable to effect self-change, sometimes from a desire to be difficult, sometimes from doubts engendered by others, and sometimes from insecurity about relationships, as well as many other sources including a lack of competence by therapists. Therapists need to respond to complaints about progress and the value of therapy by recognizing that such complaining is understandable.

The first step in gaining understanding for both patients and therapists is to discover the reasons for patients' discontent. It is important for therapists to be open to complaints and not write them off as resistances to be disposed of as quickly as possible. For example, a patient may indicate that he has had enough of therapy because it is too expensive for what he is getting out of it, and he prefers to spend his money on other things, as well as believing he can get along well enough without it. This is a question of priorities that requires exploration before the therapist can render an informed opinion, though ultimately such an opinion is due the patient because the therapist is a paid expert.

The exploration would involve learning what the patient has expected to get for his money, how well he understood what therapy was designed to do, his impression of the therapist's competence, his motivation, interest, and effort, what he thinks he has gotten thus far, and why the issue is arising at this particular time. Accompanying this will be the therapist's impressions of what the patient has gained from therapy, what he could gain, and how well he will get along without it. Then the therapist ought to provide as objective an opinion as possible, keeping in mind his own contributions to the patients' current stance.

Now psychotherapy can be a life-or-death process, but it is not usually either that definitive or dramatic. It is much more about quality of life than existence. Hence, it is rare that a therapist could tell a patient that he must be in it, and yet, it is also rare, because of its educative emphasis, that a therapist assure a patient that he might be better off without it. However, the qualifier is any patient's interest in continuing to learn, particularly in the context of the paid therapy process. Clearly, learning takes place without therapy, as does change. So, the final answer is the consumer's. After looking at all the issues involved, does he want to continue using his money this way?

It is important that patients feel free to raise questions about the value of the therapy and that therapists feel free to accommodate changing priorities for patients. If therapists believe a patient is at risk without therapy, then they should make that clear. Also, some patients use this type of questioning as a way of avoiding the best possibilities of therapy because the relationship is making them uncomfortable, resistances their therapists should attempt to work with. However, it is important that therapists be open to people flying solo, learning on their own, just as teachers know and expect their students to graduate and still keep learning. One could be in therapy, or school, forever and, assuming appropriate learning conditions, always derive benefit. But it could be argued that this might foster excessive dependency and prevent appropriate autonomy. However, since the focus here is the fee, it should be kept in mind that people do not want to keep paying for something they can get without a fee. Hence, therapists have to judge if that point has been reached, and if it has, then the business is over with those particular patients.

Therapists can certainly be pulled in opposite directions about the value question. Theoretical opinions are one variable, and personal feelings are another. In regard to the former, beliefs about necessary duration of treatment will clearly affect reactions to patients' complaints about time and accompanying cost. These should be explained to the patient in a complete way, including the fact that there are contrasting opinions (Phillips, 1988). The latter problem of subjectivity is more difficult because it is less obvious, for it is certainly possible for therapists to conceal their feelings about patients yet have these feelings stimulated by complaints, and act in accord with them. Since a patient, and a therapist as well, could be unaware of the motivation for a therapist's response, a major source of distortion could enter into the therapy. If a therapist does not like the patient enough, then he may be too quick to agree that therapy is no longer worth it for the patient. In contrast, if the therapist likes the patient too much, he may reduce the fee to try to keep the patient around. These are counter-transference reactions that can slip by under the guise of being therapeutic, so therapists need to watch out for them (Gorkin, 1987).

Then there is the basic issue for the therapist of the potential loss of income that is at least implied when any patient questions the value of therapy. This is associated with one's opinion abut the patient's questioning and feelings about him. But even if a therapist thinks the patient can get along relatively well without therapy, or considers the patient an irritant, if the patient leaves, so does the fee. It is clear that ethical considerations must prevail here regardless of the therapist's economic needs, but it is useful for all therapists to deal with disturbing feelings that could well appear in reaction to the monetary loss.

It is the patient's opinion about the value of therapy that is the deciding factor, and in that respect therapists should not attempt undue influence. At the same time, patients do expect a response to their comments about the value of the therapy for them. Also, patients and therapists do not necessarily agree to the value, and although the value decision will ultimately be made by the patients, the best decision is made when the therapists' input has been made available as well.

The patient then has to evaluate the input. It is certainly appropriate to raise questions abut the therapist's reasoning if the patient has them. The question of value certainly goes beyond the fee, but the fee is an obvious focal point for legitimate concerns, resistance, transference, and countertransference, and for that reason, it can be utilized as a therapeutic opportunity.

There is a second type of complaint that many patients feel and at least some voice. This is not about how much therapy is worth but revolves around doubt about the value of the relationship between patient and therapist because it is perceived as based essentially on money. For example, a patient may ask, "Would you see me if I could not pay you?" What we are addressing here is a hypothetical question asked even though the patient can afford the fee. The patient wants to know what is valued more by the therapist, the fee or the patient.

This can be a disturbing question for both patient and therapist, yet it can be very useful because it provides an opportunity to clarify the relationship. The therapist provides a service in which the patient–therapist relationship is an integral part, but the therapist is not being paid to like the patient. The relationship begins because both parties agree to certain ground rules, and the fee is one of them. The fit between patient and therapist involves a certain type of caring, affection, and concern on the therapist's part, but it does not require, or even imply, a social interest in the patient outside the therapy. It is easy enough for patients to get confused about this because of their projections and because of a therapeutic situation that encourages free verbal expression of feelings. Boundaries develop fluidity with patient expectations increasing the patient's belief that fantasy can be translated into reality. Also, therapist countertransferential responses, such as seductiveness, can distort and contribute to such expectations. However, the fee emphasizes the boundary, so the patient wants to know if that can be removed.

The reasons for wanting to know this have to be explored. Often, in the exploration the question answers itself by turning out not to be the question. In one sense it is a false dichotomy because the therapist likes or dislikes the patient for many reasons, and the fee is merely one of them and often not a major one. At the same time, the therapist wants the fee, and it is an expected part of the relationship. In fact, it is usually one of its defining characteristics, facilitating its professional character and protecting the patient from undesirable transformations. When the fee is directly absent or limited in some way for the therapist, the patient is more at risk for harmful countertransferential manifestations. Therapists may like particular patients a great deal yet not be motivated to do therapy with them, instead preferring some other type of "special relationship" that is not in the original contract.

Some patients may be looking for that from the start, whereas others decide they want it as the therapy progresses. Both groups may feel that payment guarantees love, and once that is in place, that is more important than and different from the therapeutic relationship. Thus, they want to know that the therapist feels the same way and would remove the fee as a symbol of this (Meyers, 1986).

These patients are involved in reenactments of previous relationships where a number of possible scenarios took place, all ultimately resulting in deprivation. The intensity of early object attachments and examples of these suggested by Fairbairn (1952), such as the gratifying, enticing, or depriving mother, and the accompanying ideal, exciting, and rejecting object, illustrate common repetitive patterns. The therapy situation has fostered fantasy to the point that the patient sees the potential relationship with the therapist as the answer to the patient's interpersonal problems. This is designed to be a transitional stage from which the patient will move on to other significant relationships that can meet his relational needs. As long as the patient understands the situation and is open to having it interpreted, the original question about "fee or me" is not particularly guilt provoking to the therapist, nor does it tend to become a resistance or, ultimately, even a question.

However, because therapists can get caught in the patients' apparent dichotomizing, the question is not always handled appropriately. One example involves a woman who throughout her therapy commented to the therapist that he was indeed her friend and that she felt closer to him than to anyone else. The positive transference was useful in establishing and maintaining a relationship, and the patient was able to improve her relationships with others significantly. However, as termination approached, the patient's understanding of the boundaries of the therapeutic relationship was not sufficiently delineated, and apparently neither was the therapist's.

Gorkin (1987) has suggested that throughout the course of therapy the patient will have some interest in knowing the therapist as a real person, and the therapist may have a corresponding wish to be so known, a wish that will increase as the therapy comes to an end. In the above case the patient had worked out the issue of the therapist's identity so that he was neither her "best" nor "only" friend, but she wanted to keep him as "a friend." She owned a sailboat and invited him to go for a sail with her and her family at a date to be determined, but after termination. He did not overtly respond to this at first, assuming it was a wish that she did not expect him to really fulfill. However, a few weeks after her last session she called with an invitation and wanted to settle on a time. In essence she had paid her money, put in her time not quite being in the type of relationship she wanted, and now that was over, and she felt free, as well as having earned the right, to change things.

Several things got in the way for the therapist at that point. He wanted her to continue to think of him as her friend, rather than a paid provider toward whom she had felt friendly, among other feelings, yet he did not consider it appropriate, nor wish, to be her social friend. He told her he would not be able to go sailing because that activity caused him to experience symptoms of motion sickness, which in fact was true. She tried to convince him that this would not occur, but he held fast. Sensing she was disappointed and not wanting her to think that since she was no longer a paying customer he had lost interest in her, he said he would not mind taking a look at the boat some time. She accepted that without even asking for a time, and he felt she was clearly disillusioned as to the nature of their past relationship, which he regretted. Yet the real regret belonged to the lack of proper clarification in the first place, a clarification that the patient was paying for and one that the therapist did not quite get in place.

It is clear that patients want an empathic response to their needs, and that at times they will view the fee as an obstacle to this. The empathic expectation, however, exceeds the range of proper therapist responsiveness, and this is part of the transference. Disillusionment undoubtedly will occur as the patient becomes more reality based. The therapist wants a return for his work, and nothing else the patient can offer, or ask for, assuming there are no extenuating economic circumstances, is going to replace the fee. It is up to the therapist to make that clear despite the probability that any patient may not like it at times and may use the fee as a mechanism for questioning the sincerity of the therapist's interest in, and concern for, the patient.

LIMITS

The fee has utility as a boundary for the therapeutic relationship, yet the cost of therapy can restrict entrance into or continuation of therapy. It is the latter that prospective patients now, more than in the past, raise as a potential restriction for therapists. In essence, more patients arrive with predetermined plans as to how much time, effort, and money they are going to spend in therapy. They leave the specific methodology up to the therapist, but they expect the therapist to shape the treatment to the patient's planned limits.

Two trends contribute to this. One is a holdover from the past, described as "money illiteracy" (Béland & Cronin, 1986), which results in ambivalent uses of money colored by guilt and apprehension. This is combined with the increase in managed mental health care. Both of these push patients in the direction of what appears as limited therapy, the limits often being defined in advance of meeting the therapist. That patients indeed may expect to have these limits met is noted by the fact that therapists are reported, at least in some managed-care settings, to have changed the way they previously worked (Richardson & Austad, 1991). Thus, patients are likely to define their economic possibilities for therapy in terms of whatever their insurance covers or what they feel they can spend a week or predecide that they do not want this to take too long or that all the time they are willing to spend in therapy is once a week or once every other week. Given guilt about having and spending money, as well as the idea stressed by the managed care system that therapy has been too lengthy and expensive in the past and that therapists can do the same job faster than they have been doing it, it is understandable that patients' expectations are now formed for rapid, relatively inexpensive solutions.

What is going to happen to these expectations? A variety of solutions exist, which we will look at in more detail in the next chapter, where the focus is on therapists' definitions of their jobs. Although we may have managed mental health care, we still are attuned to the need for accountability, for the development of appropriate, ethical practice standards, quality care, and reasonable pricing.

It is also clear that the job of working with consumer expectations belongs to therapists who must educate consumers as to what is possible and to what degree the possibilities are likely to be effective. Some of what consumers are asking for is possible and has been in place anyway. Although it has become politically correct to criticize therapists as a group for being addicted to lengthy therapy (Shueman, 1989), the average number of sessions patients tend to stay in therapy is certainly not lengthy (Phillips, 1985), and the largest single theoretical orientation tends to be eclectic in nature (Wogan & Norcross, 1985), suggesting considerable flexibility in treatment procedures. Psychotherapists can only do what patients are willing to do. Mainly, that has been relatively brief and eclectic therapy, but all possibilities still ought to be discussed.

PART III

THERAPISTS' ATTITUDES ABOUT FEES

N ow our focus shifts to the therapists, with Chapter 7 being the flip side of the patient–therapist coin. Here, the therapist has to come to terms with her role and clarify the professional nature of the therapist–patient relationship that can be delineated within the symbolic boundaries provided by the fee. In essence, the fee can represent the definitive "safe harbor" for all participants in the therapy process because it is a repetitive, obvious, tangible container for the relationship.

Thus, the fee has the invaluable potential for helping therapists and patients understand the therapeutic boundaries of psychotherapy. This point can and should be made from the start of any psychotherapy, as illustrated in Chapter 8. Here we stress the importance of the beginning stages of therapy for handling payment issues. First, we talk about the ability of the therapist to identify with the role of paid professional service provider. The issue of valuing relationships and the costs of relationships are noted, with the point being made that the monetary aspects of all relationships can indeed be integrated without somehow damaging the relationship. Setting fees is considered next, taking into account possibilities for exploitation of patients and therapists. We discuss initial negotiations, expectations of patients, and then conclude by stressing the therapeutic value of prompt discussion and establishment of fee policies.

Chapter 9 describes the assets and liabilities of possible fee policies, using the two general categories of flexible and fixed fee schedules. Beginning with flexible fees, consideration is given to institutional and private settings, the therapist's image, and fee negotiations, including hidden dangers as well as ways to be flexible effectively. Then fixed fees are looked at, first reviewing the advantages, then the disadvantages. This is followed by an overview that takes into account the role of tradition, practicality, and subjective issues in determining fee policies. The special roles of third-party payment and managed health care are described, which leads to a discussion of therapists' motives. Then we consider the details of the therapy contract and describe various service packages with emphasis given to the availability model. The chapter concludes with a description of the ethical and legal concerns involved in fee arrangements.

Chapter 7

PAID CARETAKERS

I n the preceding chapter we emphasized patients' distortions of the therapist's role, with particular emphasis on the use of the fee. In doing so, we also considered the impact on therapists, their responses, and their problems, although our spotlight was primarily on patients with their expectations and misunderstandings of how fees and relationships coalesce in the therapy process. After having indicated what may be expected from patients around fee issues, we now shift to what may be expected from therapists, using the same three categories of deals, complaints, and limits.

DEALS

Psychotherapists customarily structure the contracts with their patients and in doing so introduce both rational and irrational possibilities (Herron & Rouslin, 1984). The proposed arrangements, the deals, are motivated by tradition, legal and ethical considerations, and personal feelings. The first two components are fairly easy to learn and put in place for therapists, although some variations are possible based on interpretation of these guidelines—but within a narrow range.

For example, many analytic institutes state that for therapy to be considered psychoanalysis the patient must have sessions three times per week, whereas others insist on four, with still others opting for two. Thus, a particular analyst's training and her reaction to it will affect judgments as to the frequency, and in turn cost, of what is required for an analytic patient. In order to respect tradition, and coupled with an interest, belief in, and liking for one's theoretical position, individual therapists may be willing to reduce fees if necessary to assure a certain number of patients in the therapy mode that is especially appealing to the therapist (Gediman, 1990). Therapists view this as doing what is best for themselves and their patients.

Of course this is not the policy with patients who can afford regular fees, but if a patient has economic problems and is willing to follow the therapist's prescription, and the therapist has a need for such a patient, then the therapist is likely to offer a fee reduction. However, two problems come along with this type of arrangement, which are related. One is that the therapist may resent the therapy if it continues for too long a period of time ("too long" varying with individual therapists) and/or becomes the case for too many patients. The other problem is the need to make up the fee differential elsewhere, such as with more affluent patients, or patients who will pay the asked-for fee but cannot adhere to all the therapist's usual procedures. For example, they may require more or less activity on the therapist's part, or other variations that push the therapist in an eclectic direction and require compromise. These variations have a clinical base but, from the therapist's point of view, are not ideal, and can also result in resentment and frustration.

A legal issue that can be played with a bit is the question of the real fee in respect to insurance coverage. Therapists are required to bill for what they really charge, meaning what they expect to get paid by the patient. If the patients do not pay them, then those fees may never be collected. In that sense, the balance is "forgiven," though this should not be equated with "forgotten." However, the intent in the billing is to collect what is charged, meaning that is what the patient should pay. A sleight of the mind has at times resulted in the view that it is really all right to get the insurance company to pay a fee desired by the therapist as the real fee by making it appear that the patient is being charged a higher fee. For example, the insurance company pays 80%, and the therapist wants an $80 fee, so she submits bills for $100 per session and tells the patient the difference is forgiven (and forgotten). This approach is based on the justification of presumed injustice by the insurance provider, yet it is illegal, unethical, and corrupts the therapeutic alliance. It is also fairly common, though not carried out from a desire to be either criminal or unethical, but to facilitate a patient being in therapy and as a covert protest against insurance limitations. No matter what the case, it should not be done, for patients will really not benefit from therapy that operates this way.

Actually, surveys of psychotherapists indicate that what is considered good practice tends to be stricter than what is defined in ethical codes (Pope, Tabachnick, & Keith-Spiegel, 1988). Theoretical orientation also has a relationship to the considered appropriateness of procedures, as some issues tend to change over time. For example, in 1977 Kudirka described paying for therapy with goods, namely art, rather than money, whereas barter would now be considered a dubious practice.

Our point here is not so much that patients are likely to get taken by therapists, or that therapist–patient corruption and collusion are blatant and widespread. Such is not the case, and we illustrate in detail in Chapter 9 what the usual fee policies and practices are. However, it is clear that therapists do originate deals as well as make them when originated by patients, but they generally do so within relatively narrow limits based on their interpretation of good practice.

Now, that interpretation is influenced by the third factor we mentioned, personal reasons. Beyond that, however, are deals that distort the interpretations to the point that good practice is abrogated. This is a function of countertransference that has a duality that has not been clearly considered in the literature. The usual way of viewing countertransference is to see it as the therapist's reaction to the patient, which includes one of three possibilities. These are that it represents all the therapist's feelings and attitudes toward the patient, or as the transference of the therapist to the transference of the patient, or as a responsive compliment to the style of the patient (Epstein & Feiner, 1979). In a similar vein, Spitz (1980) provides a broad working definition that sees countertransference as one part of the therapist's relationship to her patient that will have varied manifestations in form and content. It is considered normal, with constructive and destructive possibilities, and is the therapist's transference to the patient.

The component we would add is that there is also a transference to money. This predates the patient and therefore is in place when therapists construct their fee policies. It is essentially a cultural, societal transference that is a derivative reaction to the ambivalent structure delineated for the role of the psychotherapist. It is clear, for example, how therapists express their sexual and aggressive drives in psychotherapy. Boundaries are delineated that are designed to stimulate guilt and punishment if they are crossed. The superego and ego are synchronized in a defined way. Certainly there is some latitude, and derivatives come into play without therapists' awareness, but once these are detected, the rules are rather clear.

In contrast, the proper place of feelings and attitudes about money in the psychotherapist's role is not so clear. Whether one wants to delineate a separate money drive or stay within the libidinal and aggressive drive theories and view money as a component of both of these, there is considerable uncertainty about appropriateness in regard to money.

This uncertainty may result in shifting attitudes and behaviors, depending on roles and interpersonal situations. Hence, of course the therapist's money transference interacts with his or her patient transference. Another possibility is that uncertainty is supposedly resolved with a fixed monetary approach that attempts to transcend situations and individuals and in turn would "lock out" the patient as an influential stimulus, but that undoubtedly leaves a great amount of unconscious material teething on the repression barrier and blocks identification and empathy. The role of paid provider is loaded with countertransferential possibilities that involve transferences to the role concepts, pay, and provision as well as to each patient.

The development of these transferences in the therapist has a psychogenic history that parallels transference origins in patients. These are also repetitions of the past. In one way the patient in therapy is relatively helpless, whereas the therapist is helpful, but this can be reversed when it comes to the fee, because then the therapist needs the help. This shifting helper–helpless possibility raises questions about the ego-ideal for any person functioning as a psychotherapist.

Spitz (1980) describes two types of relationships that occur between therapist and patient. The first he calls *anaclitic*, meaning leaning onto, which involves the apparent attitude of the patient, and the second *diatrophic*, a maintaining attitude that is the therapist's. In the normal course of development the latter follows the former, just as in the course of therapy, the patient would essentially follow the same progression in becoming self-sufficient. However, the therapist is also subject to the same basic developmental patterns. For therapists there are also stimulations of both anaclitic and diatrophic feelings with impulses to action within the therapy, and the fee is a target.

In developing standard fee arrangements, therapists need to take into account their own anaclitic–diatrophic balance. Spitz (1980) charts the course of development with the original anaclitic relationship of child to parent and the child's relative helplessness. This fades into a diatrophic relationship as parental identification fantasies begin and eventually result in socialization with anaclitic relations more in the area of fantasy.

Within therapy, all of this is designed to be relived verbally and in fantasy rather than in action as therapist and patient relate. Also, the anaclitic–diatrophic balance between patient and therapist is clearly tilted, yet it is in regard to the fee that the therapist may experience reversal, denial, reaction formation, and in a host of defenses aimed at keeping her balance in accord with the ego-ideal of psychotherapist.

The role is as a paid provider, and psychotherapy is a helping business. The question remains, how "businesslike" is any particular psychotherapist supposed to be? As the helper in the diatrophic parental mode, it is congruent to expect the patient to be responsible, and the fee structure is consistent with this. Yet, it is unrealistic to tailor that structure solely to the wishes of patients, since the anaclitic needs of therapists also have to be met by the fee. Furthermore, psychotherapists have ethical obligations to serve others, including those who have limited resources, and to serve them as well as those who are more affluent. So, in making peace with their greed and keeping it in a healthy place as part of an essentially constructive narcissism (Welt & Herron, 1990), therapists strike deals with themselves as to the deals they will do with patients.

These are rarely perfect deals, but they should be good enough. Therapists need to feel they are good people performing useful services as well as successful people, economically and professionally. In creating fee arrangements, it is important to recognize that the economic return is set within a framework of time worked and the money supply of patients who will be the payers. This has to be realistically appraised, with fees set accordingly. Each therapist has her therapeutic ego-ideal, and assuming it has enough ego to contain the ideal, and enough ideal to contain the id without ego deprivation, then the goal has been achieved. The therapist originates the fee arrangements, even if the patient somehow starts the specifics, so any deal proposed by the patient is weighed in light of the therapeutic ego-ideal and accepted or rejected accordingly. This is how it ought to work. Other possibilities may occur along with their associated pitfalls to doing effective psychotherapy. We will also add that the therapeutic ego-ideal is not fixed for life and that reappraisals are definitely appropriate.

COMPLAINTS

From everything we have said thus far about patients' feelings toward fees, it should be clear that therapists can expect comments and complaints about the cost of therapy. That does not mean that psychotherapists want to hear such complaints, since they emphasize the business part of therapy, which therapists prefer to downplay. Also, these comments often make therapists feel they should do something besides listening or interpreting, that they should reduce the cost to patients. We discussed in Chapter 4 the fact that the fee can be an obstacle to therapy, and in Chapter 5 we looked at fee adjustments that may be required during the course of therapy because of patients' changing financial circumstances. In Chapter 8 we describe appropriate ways to begin the therapy that reduce problems connected to neglecting the financing of the therapy. In this chapter our focus is on therapists' reactions to patients making an issue of the fee whenever they choose to do it.

Financial problems are familiar in their various forms for most people, including therapists. Hence, in raising them in regard to the therapy, patients are not automatically looking for an action. Patients raise such issues for many reasons. However, if therapists feel guilty about charging for their services, then this reaction is stimulated by any complaints that appear at all reasonable. Whereas there is increasing documentation of the importance of empathy (Jordan, Kaplan, Miller, Stiver, & Surrey, 1991), what therapists may think of as an empathic response is really a response to the therapists' world that is threatened by the patient. This may be happening in two ways. There is the possibility of monetary loss if the patient decides therapy is too expensive to continue and the possibility of damage to the therapist's helping image. As the therapist hears the patient's plight and begins to enter the patient's world, she shifts the patient's difficulty into what it is going to be like for the therapist if the patient chooses to leave. The therapist ends up wanting empathy from the patient in regard to the therapist's need for the fee, and of course this type of therapist transferential projection obscures whatever the patient is really trying to say when using the fee as a focal point.

Therapists would prefer that patients accept their fee arrangements as a necessary part of the therapy process and that they have an empathic understanding for the business end, which requires little or no discussion. The wish is to keep the helping image untarnished, although in the presence of transference, this is particularly unrealistic. Even if many therapists retain their ambivalence about money, the fee as an issue does not have to be viewed as the fee as a threat.

Instead, it can be expected as a transferential response and as a resistance, both opportunities for exploration and interpretation. The therapist's initial task is to figure out the reason for the patient's bringing up any concern about the fee and in doing so to sort out the realities and the resistances. Patients may develop financial problems, and therapists have to have contingencies for working with these problems to insure any needed continuation of therapy. At the same time, it is also clear that the fee is an "easy resistance" for patients, particularly since it can be connected to reality and because it is difficult, in many instances, for the therapist to untangle the real from the projected.

However, even when that difficulty arises, the possibility remains of exploring how a patient developed financial problems. In that process the resistance aspect is usually clarified as the implications of the monetary situation for therapy tend to be revealed. For example, a patient began a session by stating that she was having financial difficulties. The therapist asked about what they were and how they had come about. As he began his inquiry, he did wonder if this was her way of indicating that she was going to have a problem paying her fee. He felt some annoyance that this might be the case because this was a chronic problem with her and often did operate as a resistance, and he felt concern that she was caught in a destructive repetition, and he was curious as to what was triggering the repetition. Indeed, it developed that she was going to be able to pay only part of the fee as scheduled, though she explained how she would pay the rest at a later date. In their ensuing discussion it became clear that she was testing the therapist in a way that she tested many people, namely, by putting her immediate needs ahead of theirs and expecting them to accept that without rancor. Of course some people did resent it, many in fact, but she responded to them with hostility rather than apology. Certainly the therapist would hve preferred to be paid as scheduled, but he was able to use her delayed payment as a way to explore her feelings of deprivation and subsequent entitlement and their interpersonal consequences.

She did raise the question of whether there were feelings of annoyance on his part, and he responded by asking for her impression of his feelings. She granted that he might have such feelings, but she felt that he should understand her situation because he was the therapist and added that he had more money than she did anyway, so he could afford to wait. Her reply struck at the two key problems we have mentioned, namely, the therapist as helper, who because of that role "should understand," and the therapist's interest in money, implied in this case to be significant.

These comments could have been experienced by the therapist as threatening because they imply that if the therapist was annoyed that the patient failed in her responsibility to pay him, the therapist would in turn be failing at his job of understanding her. They also imply that the therapist was rich, whereas she was poor and so privileged in their relationship to take advantage of the therapist. However, although the therapist was not even close to rich and was treating the patient for a reduced fee, he did not become defensive. Instead, he used her comments as a way to explore further their relationship and her transference, which took them into issues other than money.

The example brings up another question about money, namely, how responsible can therapists expect patients to be about monetary arrangements? In much of the therapy therapists appear as parental figures and patients as children at different developmental levels working toward maturation. Therapists need a certain tolerance range for their feelings around the fee, or the affective reactions will be inappropriate. Therapy is not constructed for therapists and patients to reverse roles in displaying affect. So, although patients take care of therapists in one way by paying fees, therapists should expect certain irresponsibilities as transference and resistance manifestations. The constancy of the therapist returns her to the therapist-patient contract, whereas flexibility allows for understanding, exploration, and, if appropriate, modification.

Although patients' complaints about cost and the dollar value of therapy are unpleasant for therapists, they pale in noxiousness relative to the allegation of charging as opposed to caring. Therapists often have trouble with this because they have not resolved the issue for themselves, so they either hope patients do not bring it up or try to find ways to mitigate any such perception.

Thus, there is the description by Zaraleya in 1979 of an educational mode for doing therapy, about which she comments: "The question: How

can you love me and charge me? arises seldom with this semester approach"
(p. 46).

The countertransference to that question, and any of its similar variations, is still around. It can be a useful complaint because along with other fee issues, and probably more than any others, it highlights the therapist's role. The boundaries are drawn, and the therapists' humanity is declared visible in their desire, even demand, certainly need, that they be paid for their services.

Of course their services are not love, or intimacy, or friendship, or any of the roles patients may assign to them transferentially. That does not rule out therapists having such feelings and even finding out ways to display them, but such feelings by therapists are not what they get paid for. They get paid for special skills that are designed to help people change their lives in little and big ways. Certainly feelings are involved, and the relationships that occur can be very special, yet they are definitely circumscribed. Considerable time, effort, and wisdom have been spent, and continue to be spent, on defining the ingredients of psychotherapy and the elements of good practice, and of course the disciplines involved have developed their ethical codes. Understandably, gray areas remain, and it is unlikely to become a precision process, but enough is known for therapists to be able to tell patients what roles are appropriate in the process.

Spitz (1980) commented, "Analysis has to be carried out in abstinence, said Freud; I may add, abstinence of the patient and abstinence of the analyst" (p. 450).

Now there certainly has been controversy over this "abstinence" concept, particularly in regard to its scope and implications for dependency and autonomy, but those are not our issues here. Instead we use the quote to make the point that the relationship has limits, and both parties to it have limits, and that therapists need to get more comfortable explaining their roles as paid service providers. (Without wandering too far into the evolving meaning of abstinence, we can affirm it has nothing to do with abstaining from paying or taking fees.)

LIMITS

From the therapist's side the therapeutic situation has relatively definite limits, and in turn, what the fee purchases is a professional relationship in contrast to social and, clearly, sexual relationships. It is up to therapists to make these boundaries explicit, and the fee is a useful reminder to therapists as well as patients. Because patients' projections are the content of most psychotherapies, it is easy to see why consumers can get confused, and that increases the need for therapists to be clear and explicit about their professional roles.

Then there are other limits connected to fees that are of increasing interest. For the more than a decade that we have been practicing psychotherapy, fees have been increasing, and that includes both the fees we paid to our analysts as well as the fees we have charged. It has been in the main an inflationary economy, with some recessionary trends but no great depressions. Although goods and services cost more, incomes have also increased so that fees for psychotherapy seem, in essence, average, and because these fees are tied to time, there was a limit on how affluent one could get in the psychotherapy business. The most recent survey by *Psychotherapy Finances* (1991b) has continued to report income growth, but that is a trend that may not continue because of managed mental health care. The growing use of this cost-containment approach means that from an earnings point of view, many, if not most, private practitioners will have to develop ways to cope with it other than total avoidance.

Assuming the care packages stay within ethical and legal guidelines, one solution is simply to join up and accept the probable economic limits. This is most appealing to therapists with hours to fill who also are interested in the type of therapy espoused by these plans, therapy that is generally brief. Another is to move out of the direct practice of psychotherapy to whatever extent necessary to be part of the management. It will be possible for some therapists to increase their incomes this way, but there is a limit to the number of managers. Other possibilities include the reduction of office expenses, which tends to be about 30% of the gross income (*Psychotherapy Finances*, 1991a) and can be attempted in or out of managed care, as well as the reduction of excessive fees, which, although representative of a small minority, represents poor pricing procedure, particularly with all the concern about excessive cost.

Of course there is the issue of what the practitioners will do who want to keep things as they have been. When they notice what is happening, they will complain, but that is not going to be sufficient, nor has it been, because short-term therapy is both popular and funded. Thus, long-term therapists, which automatically includes most psychoanalysts, are particularly affected, as they are slowly beginning to notice. In fact, any therapist who believes that potential consumers really ought to have choices is going to have her problems with managed care.

In the mean time, where will all the analysts go, and what will they do? Some will stay where they are and keep doing what they are doing, but they will have to sell their product more than in the past and will face increasing competition from therapists offering briefer therapies, especially pharmacology. Many analysts are already doing a substantial amount of psychoanalytic psychotherapy that is less costly to the patient than psychoanalysis because it is less frequent. Also, planned short-term psychodynamic psychotherapy (Bauer & Kobos, 1987; Strupp & Binder, 1984) is a possibility and can fit within managed care boundaries.

Considering that the average patient has made brief use of psychotherapy, and the dominant orientation of psychotherapists has been eclectic, is there really an issue in regard to the fate of psychoanalysis? Definitely, particularly if one happens to be an analyst, but it goes beyond that. There is a very lengthy, innovative, and enduring psychoanalytic tradition and influence in the mental health field. Furthermore, psychoanalysis tends to be the second dominant theoretical orientation, so there are a relatively large number of psychoanalytically oriented practitioners. In addition, psychoanalytic practices have been variable, particularly in urban areas where there have also been many analytic training institutes with low-cost clinics. The climate for these practices was favorable; however, that is shifting, and so constructive reactions are needed.

Psychoanalytic theory has very broad-based application and is the most comprehensive explanation of personality development and psychopathology. This gives it many possibilities even when more extensive work with patients is not in favor. A good example of the adaptability and utility of psychoanalysis is illustrated by Gabbard (1990) across pathologies and in diverse settings:

> Our special training and our daily experiences with patients repeatedly convince us of the value of psychoanalysis and other long-term treatments. We must not abandon this belief, but neither can we expect it to automatically endure in these times of great change. A clear assessment of reality and a prepared, flexible adaptation to it are basic parts of our daily "prescriptions." Now we must take this medicine ourselves. (McGrath, 1986, p. 256)

Thus, environmental change is bringing increased recognition on the part of mental health practitioners that they are indeed paid providers because the source and size of the pay are being questioned. In adapting to this new order there are indeed possibilities for self-recognition and role explanation to patients so that economic issues can emerge as a regular part of the therapeutic process. In the next chapter we discuss ways in which that emergence can and should occur in the initial phase of psychotherapy.

Chapter 8

STARTING ON
THE RIGHT FOOT

A crucial and delicate time in working out money matters between therapist and patient is the start of therapy. If the issue is handled well then, a number of subsequent potential difficulties will never occur. However, the initial steps taken about the fee are in service of relative assistance to the whole process rather than a guarantee of no future troubles. Money is too important an issue for the fee to be put securely in its place in the first few sessions. Anyway, its place is likely to move more than once before the course of therapy is concluded. Still, the opening moves are particularly significant, and when handled ineffectively, they are very likely to promote future problems. If odds were to be taken on the success of any therapeutic endeavor, it would be wise to bet on the therapist who took care of the financial aspects efficiently and openly. The beginning of therapy is the first opportunity to see if indeed the key fits in the lock and whether the door to the person's life secrets will actually be opened.

Despite continual advice over the years for therapists to be frank and open in discussing fees, therapists remain uncomfortable with doing this and in fact often do not (Jacobs, 1986; Welt & Herron, 1990). In any case, they expect, hope, and wish to be paid certain amounts at certain times, but they want a way to get this across to the patient without being too "obvious" about it. It is as though they want the patient to enter the situation with an awareness of exactly how a particular therapist wants the fee paying taken care of and then act accordingly throughout the therapy. This type of hallucinatory wish fulfillment usually gets discarded, and therapists develop some methods of fee setting aimed at alleviating their own discomfort, though these are frequently not that effective for patient or therapist.

For example, Harari (1990) states:

Questions of financial responsibility for missed appointments, lateness, vacation and legal holidays need to be clearly articulated in advance. I find, however, it to be too oppressive to deal with all contingencies beforehand and leave some to be dealt with when particular events arise. At such times, I generally set policy for the next occasion and do not require that the single instance be paid for. (p. 245)

The reaction to this has to be puzzlement. "Too oppressive" for whom and why? If the therapist took the time to explain in advance, he would have a reason to get paid. He would also know more about the patient, who in turn would not have to wonder why it had not been explained originally. Most patients have plenty of trouble about money to begin with, so it does not help if the therapist has it as well—and shows it.

THERAPISTS' VALUE

Therapists generally consider themselves capable of establishing diagnostic impressions, formulating treatment plans, providing explanations to patients of what the problems are and what can be done about them, and then carrying out the treatment. A description has already been given of how the therapy process can be explicated for psychoanalytic work; Caroff (1990) also has a very lucid description of psychosocial therapy. Weiner (1986) provides a useful delineation of therapies into three types—repressive, supportive, and evocative—which is akin to the supportive-expressive continuum described by Gabbard (1990). The point of mentioning these examples is that they symbolize the fact that therapists have definite bodies of knowledge and specific skills that they can describe in considerable detail and for which they expect to be paid. There is a definite philosophy of payment, so therapists need to be comfortable with that idea. If not, they will frequently question their own value and the value of the whole enterprise, with resultant difficulties about the fee as well as other distortions in the therapy.

Thus, the ability to be comfortable in the role rests on the ability to identify with the role as we have described it, namely, as a professional service provider. This by no means indicates that therapists have a generally accepted technical mold or even agree to the balance of science and art that is involved. However, it does mean that whatever psychotherapists do, they value it in monetary terms. Of course they could "give it away," as is the case in any service situation, but if that were to happen, it would no longer be a profession in terms of a way to make a living. The situation for psychotherapists should be that they believe in the dollar value of their services.

Because of the relationship that is involved, the discomfort with charging people is increased. Even in short-term work, qualities of empathy, respect, and genuine attempts at understanding are emphasized. Psychotherapists are generally depicted, when not being satirized, as caring, concerned people who like their patients. It is an image that therapists and patients both favor, and it is generally true. However, it creates emotional static around discussions of financial arrangements between therapists and patients.

For example, Schoenewolf (1990) described an intriguing exchange between himself and a woman patient in which he logically attempted to convince her that he cared about her regardless of the fee. His logic was quite appealing, but she remained unconvinced. He noted her defensiveness about taking any other view and ultimately got her to work with the resistance. However, an interesting feature of the dialogue was that it led him to explore how much he was in it for the money and concluded that that certainly had helped his caring. Yet his conclusion seems based on still another distortion about therapeutic relationships. He decided that because she was not somebody he would have wanted as a friend, monetary motivation played a larger role. In his case he may have been right, but liking patients a limited amount, not wanting to spend that much time with them, and/or not wanting them as friends, does not mean the therapist has no feelings for her patients. The idea is that patients interest therapists, for whatever reasons, many of which do not have automatic ties with money. In one sense therapists are always in it for the money, but only to an extent. Fees are not determined based on how much one does or does not like a patient. The patient described by Schoenewolf (1990) actually sounds challenging, so that aspect could motivate the therapist more than the money. Besides, therapists have a pride in their work that helps them care about all patients. Of course Schoenwolf knows better than we do what his feelings were, and we certainly can agree that business can intrude.

Nonetheless, the intrusion can be considerably less than therapists seem to worry about, if indeed the therapeutic relationship is properly understood by therapists. Unfortunately it often is not, although that's not for lack of trying. An additional problem is that many therapists, probably including ourselves, learn the role well enough and try to impart it to others, but they have trouble practicing it. It takes continual work because of the struggling aspects of therapy, that is, struggle with the patient, with oneself, with one's own image, mood, and vulnerabilities.

The work of Goldberg (1986) is an example of the above. He makes useful distinctions between operational and personal skills in the therapeutic role, shows a lot of insight into the reasons that people become therapists and how those reasons affect their practices, has a realistic view of therapeutic struggles, is a seasoned practitioner, yet leaves the reader potentially confused as to the role of the therapist. It is as though he understands it as well as anybody else, probably better than many, but he does not quite like what he understands, so he keeps it fuzzy. The notion of paid provider is downplayed. Of course people who are even more definitive than he is, let us say those stressing operational skills, do not talk very much about learning how to make sure the therapist gets paid appropriately.

Jacobs (1986) represents a refreshing contrast to those who have the more prevalent tendency to keep the issue in the background. In addition to his commendable openness, he touches on an aspect of the fee arrangement that is rarely mentioned yet is a major element in understanding and accepting the therapist's role. He notes the "cost of emotional relationships and the price to be paid for involvement" (Jacobs, 1986, p. 123). Thus, it is not just that the patient must pay a fee because the therapist needs it to make a living. Rather, because it is a relationship, therapy has a cost, an inherent part of relating. One does not have an intimate relationship in particular without paying something for it, even if it is not money. Actually, though many times it is money that must be spent, as it must be spent in being married or rearing children, the expenditure is not seen as deprecating the relationship. Relationships cost the people involved something to have them, because the other member is never selfless. Relationships are developed to get something from another person as well as to give, and the balance is a variable, but both parts are there or usually the relationship ends.

Now it is certainly true that money has the reputation of somehow tarnishing a relationship, but a relationship is not necessarily purified if money is absent from any significant exchanges between the people involved. Money plus love is just fine in marriage, for example, and it is common enough for lack of money to be equated with lack of love to contradict the above assumption. The many uses and meanings of money are apparent in relationships, yet it is clear that one can like or love another and receive money from, or give money to, that person. There is no reason that psychotherapy needs to be made exempt from that fact (Nickerson, 1991).

The variation is that in certain intimate relationships money is given and taken because of the love, whereas in psychotherapy the money is given and taken because of the skill of the therapist, with the relationship being part of the display of the skill. The therapist is not getting paid to love the patient, nor is the patient paying the money out of love for the therapist, even if those feelings exist. Still, because there is a relationship, both people want something out of it, and one of the things the therapist wants is money. There is no good reason to keep that a secret, nor is it incompatible with caring for the patient. How much the therapist likes a particualr patient has to do with the fit between them. Money could be used as part of that fit by either party, but it does not have to be. Assuming there are no unusual fee arrangements, liking is a separate issue, and therapists need to remember that. Therapists are paid to help people, and the job is different based on how one feels about the person. Some patients are in therapy precisely because they are not generally liked. Their therapists may unsurprisingly also find them hard to like, which may be an appealing challenge to some therapists and an irritant to others, but the fee is not designed to change that. If it does, then something is amiss in the therapist's role. Fees are based on competence. If that is missing, there should be no fee for there is no therapy.

> It is in the establishment of the fee, its payment, and its receipt that the mutual nature of the therapeutic setting is often most clear and takes its most concrete form. The patient needs the skills of the therapist. . . . The therapist needs to be reimbursed for his skills. . . . (Jacobs, 1986, p. 123)

SETTING THE FEE

Assuming the therapist has accepted the role of paid service provider and is comfortable with the idea that the fee is integrated into the relationship, then the therapist has to discuss fee arrangements with each patient. This means the therapist has to decide on how much she is going to charge. Private practice is the best example of this because in other settings guidelines are already established. In one's own practice, it is a more personal decision (Citron-Bagget & Kempler, 1991), with some constraints based on the market, but the basic idea is to be paid what each therapist feels she needs. Exploitation of the self or the patient needs to be mentioned because although we do not know therapists who set out with this in mind, it can happen.

Patient Exploitation

It seems appropriate that therapists base their fees on standards of competence, with their needs adjusted accordingly. However, these standards are not as established as one would like, and consumers are not well attuned to the different possibilities. Thus, beyond licensure, credentials such as a diplomate and postdoctoral training are credentials within specialties, and coupled with experience, should be taken into account in determining personal value and the fee. They usually are used this way by people who have them, but beginning practitioners may simply set their fee at the "going rate" for psychotherapy. Without proper external and internal quality control, the consumer then can be exploited. One of our suggestions in regard to insurance reimbursement is that the competence standard be taken into account, which would help avoid this type of exploitation. Consumer education by the various professional organizations would also be useful.

Many beginning practitioners recognize the discrepancy in competence between themselves and the more seasoned practitioners and reflect it in their fees. If they are in therapy themselves with a more experienced person, which is usually the case, they will use the "usual fee" of their therapist (and his fee policies) as the norm and keep their fees below this. However, for the small group of beginners who charge at the market from the start, this is a policy needing reconsideration.

Another possibility is that the personalities of certain patients set them up as possible victims for any unconscious tendencies therapists may have to take financial advantage of patients. In the beginning stages, this could appear in the form of agreeing to a higher fee than the patient can afford out of a desire to please the therapist, who in turn accepts it without a thorough investigation. A different possibility is overpaying the therapist, who then may "forget" to credit or refund the extra amount while the patient apparently "forgets" as well. These types of possible manipulation are apparent in masochistic, passive, dependent patients, who also may have trouble in the termination stage and may want "questionable" extra sessions as well along the way. They can be seductive in their apparent willingness to please, so therapists' awareness may be dulled. Making a mistake in terms of getting more of a fee than is appropriate can certainly happen, but it should be guarded against and, if noticed, overtly corrected with a discussion of what appears to be happening. The other side of the surface presentation is hostility, so that these patients may be consciously (or unconsciously) testing their therapists to see if cheating is going to occur. Although these patients could even stay in therapy for a long time and seem not to notice what is happening, they may be well aware of it and use it to fuel resentment and a paranoid position that limits their ultimate progress.

Once discovered and explored, the therapist should be willing to admit, if the point is raised, that she may indeed have wanted the extra money, because for this type of error to occur, both therapist and patient have to have participated. Therapists' reluctance to face such an admission will limit both discovery and exploration.

The opposite type of patient, namely, one who is obviously difficult and annoying, also may invite some exploitation. The therapist's initial reaction may be that she does not care whether she sees this patient again or may even hope she does not. Thus, there may be the temptation to charge such a patient as much as possible. A variation on this is the patient who simply refuses to pay attention to her funds; that patient is always confused about the status of her bill, and annoys the therapist to the point of overcharging, which really would go undetected by the patient because of the accustomed monetary confusion. Although it is a bit of a task to keep discussing the tendency of these patients to avoid knowing their monetary status and also to keep monitoring it carefully, this may have to be done.

Once the therapist accepts the idea that the fee has considerable potential for therapeutic development, then it should be clear that it cannot be neglected. This means from the start that the therapist has in place an appropriate attitude that will keep her alert to what is happening with the fee from both sides and will provide a path to open discussion.

Therapist Exploitation

A more frequent problem, however, is undervaluing the services so that therapists often end up with patients paying whatever (within a certain range) they want to pay rather than what therapists want and feel they deserve. Now, ego payment, that is, fees dictated by the realities of what people are willing to pay, the supply of available patients, the type of therapy required, and the competition as well as the therapist's existing state of self-esteem, is often not the same as ego-ideal payment where one definitely gets what is felt to be deserved. The realities have to be recognized without excessive tugs from the ego-ideal. Many times an idealized fee is established in a therapist's mind, mentioned to colleagues and patients as "my usual fee," but rarely if ever expected or collected. Doubts about competencies, distortions of the therapist's role along with an unwillingness to really talk about fees and negotiate, cause the therapist to feel exploited by the patient.

Exploitation of either party is no way to start the therapeutic relationship. The therapist should view the realities, decide her fee policies accordingly, and learn to be comfortable with putting them into practice. The flexibility of the fee policies is something we discuss in the next chapter, but initially it is important to have a fee policy and whatever that may be to set it in motion.

Initial Negotiations

Jacobs (1986) indicates the importance of fee negotiations as an early opportunity to explore the patient's psychodynamics and to establish the best conditions under which the therapy can proceed. The fee issue should be raised as promptly as possible given the patient's presenting state. Therapists who are invested in delaying any money discussions will tend to use the patient's condition in each session as an opportunity to delay, but since the money topic offers a very useful way to discover more about the patient's difficulties, the delay is costly to both parties.

The first contact with any patient is usually at some distance, often over the phone or through a referral source who indicates someone is considering therapy and asks about therapist availability. At that point the therapist has an initial and easy opportunity to say to the patient directly, or the referral source who can inform the patient in advance, the fee for the initial session will be __ dollars. This way both the therapist and patient are committed to at least one meeting for a predetermined fee that they both know about in advance. Anybody who contacts you initially, even if she is in extreme distress, still needs to know details such as the location of your office, the time of the appointment. Hence, there is nothing extraordinary about including the cost as an informational detail (other than that many therapists do not do it). The fact of the fee will rule out a number of people who either cannot or will not pay it even once. Some patients do inquire about it themselves if the therapist has not provided the information. If the prospective patient leads off with the fee then that is usually indicative of "fee shopping," rather than an interest in quality, or a particular therapist. But if the therapist has not provided the information, then the patient's asking before appointment arrangements are concluded is quite appropriate. Many patients do not, however, being just as interested in avoidance as their prospective avoidant therapist.

Thus, the fee can be an appropriate screening device to save time and effort for both parties. However, if the therapist does not want to deter any possible patients because of the fee, she can indicate that the fee policy is a negotiable one to be discussed at the first session. If the therapist wants to screen out patients who cannot or will not pay some minimum fee, then a particular fee range can be described. Some therapists do not charge a fee for an initial consultation, and some of these charge it retroactively, that is, only if the person continues with them. Whatever the possible fee arrangement, the patient needs to be told in advance, so that when the parties meet for the first time, there is a general awareness both of the fee and how it will be determined for that session.

Sometimes sufficient information can be obtained in one session to make a decision as to continuance. If that decision is positive, then the details of the financial arrangements need to be explored. Usually it takes more than one session to do this, however, so for purposes of this discussion, we will allot three sessions for both parties to decide whether it is worthwhile to enter into a course of therapy. During that "diagnostic" time, the purpose of those sessions should be explained as well as their cost. Again, whatever variety of fee structure the therapist utilizes will have to be delineated during this time. If the therapy is to be undertaken, then by the end of the third session most of the contingencies should have been discussed.

Of course it is probable that not all possibilities can be anticipated or that some are so remote that it is pedantic rather than therapeutic to mention them. For example, if the patient is on the way to a scheduled appointment and is injured in an accident and so cannot get there, does the patient owe the therapist for that session? Indeed, if the patient is killed in this accident, does the estate owe the therapist the fee? Sometimes such things happen, but these are not the kind of events either party is customarily anticipating (unless of course the patient has a phobia about such possibilities, or the therapist is someone who really should be avoided at all costs).

Also, it is probable that patients will "forget" some of the details, such as payment policies, cancellations, or vacations, so some of the information will have to be repeated when the issue arises. If therapists make such discussions routine at the inception of therapy, then there will be no question as to the source of the resistance. Furthermore, at the time of the first presentation of the information, it is helpful to encourage the exprssion of patients' feelings about the fee because then they will be less likely to forget that the subject indeed had previously been talked about.

Jacobs (1986) is a proponent of a detailed discussion of the patient's financial circumstances, although he indicates that this should certainly be carried out tactfully. He is well aware that such discussion is not easy for therapists to consider, no less carry out, but he provides a good model for establishing a safe monetary environment for patient and therapist.

> As one tries to do this, it quickly becomes apparent that some patients tend to underestimate or overestimate what they feel they can afford. A frank discussion of their income and how they apportion it, before a fee is determined, is often helpful not only in setting a reasonable fee, but in being able to begin the exploration of any neurotic distortions about money and the fee that may reveal themselves in the discussion. It is important, for instance, to discuss not only the amount of income, savings, and insurance a patient may have, but the role of these assets in the patient's thinking about himself and his treatment. . . . should provide the therapist important information about the way in which the patient organizes and views himself in relation to others, as well as to his own impulses. (Jacobs, 1986, pp. 124–125)

How much does the therapist need to know? Obviously the patient has many issues besides the fee, so although the therapist needs certain information and should expect the patient to be open about money matters throughout the course of therapy, fee negotiations are not an IRS audit.

Basically, the therapist needs to know at the start if the patient can afford the therapeutic plan the therapist considers best for the patient, and if not that, what other arrangements might be worked out. If the fee is to be negotiated, the therapist probably needs more details to be assured that it is equitable to the therapist than if the fee is fixed. If insurance is to be used, the therapist needs to know the details. Sometimes patients are vague about this, stating they "think" they have coverage, or they "think" the payment is a certain amount. This matter should be clarified quickly, and the therapist should be clear that the continuance of insurance coverage may require the therapist to divulge information about the treatment to the insurance company. It is useful for therapists to be familiar with the payment policies of the insurance carriers used by their patients so discussions about insurance coverage can be realistic.

In addition to the amount of the fee, the therapist should also spell out the totality of her fee policy. When does the therapist expect to get paid? At each session or monthly? Does the therapist routinely present a bill or only when the patient has indicated it is needed for some purpose, such as insurance coverage? Does the therapist expect the patient to pay her directly, or will the therapist accept direct payment from the insurance company? What is the therapist's policy in regard to payment for missed sessions, cancellations, vacations, changes in appointment times, temporary or lengthy absences from therapy, sessions missed because of the therapist's unavailability, lateness by the patient, or lateness by the therapist?

These possibilities are mentioned because therapists have policies about all of them. For example, most therapists charge for missed sessions, but the policy varies on cancellations, and relatively few therapists insist that patients take vacations at the same time as the therapist or pay for the sessions. Some therapists make up sessions they missed because they were unavailable, for example, they went to a professional conference, whereas others consider those as representing income they gave up voluntarily because they wanted to do something other than therapy at the time.

The advantages and disadvantages of different fee arrangements are covered in detail in the next chapter. Our point here is that whatever the fee arrangements, they need to be presented clearly to the patient as early as appropriate in the course of therapy. Also, as much as it is possible, therapists should indicate how flexible they will be. Patients' lives change, as exemplified by their financial circumstances. Other events occur that also affect the routine of therapy, such as a job change with different hours of availability, or illness, or giving birth, so that patients may need changes in the original contract. Therapists may consider pointing out to patients that initial arrangements pertain to the foreseeable future. In other words, if something unanticipated comes up, it will be discussed and possible resolutions will be explored. In addition, if therapists raise their fees routinely with ongoing patients, then the usual time frame for escalations as well as the amount should be indicated.

What we have been describing may sound like too much to even attempt in the early sessions. Some of it can be presented in a general way, with one or two examples to make the point. Of course what is presented depends on the fee policies of each therapist, so these subjects really need not be discussed exhaustively. Our point is the necessity and value of being clear and explicit about fees early in the process.

Fee policies for long-term as compared to short-term therapists may vary in focus. A lot of problems are more likely to occur given more time, so some fee policies will not even come into consideration in short-term therapy. For example, it is not necessary to explain to a patient the therapist's vacation plans 6 months from their starting therapy if the therapy is, by design, only going to last for 3 months. Total cost is going to be less, as is total time consumed, so short-term patients can feel easier about paying higher fees and coming at less convenient (for them) times. However, there still are fee concerns, and issues such as lateness and cancellations may assume proportionally more significance because of the briefer time frame. Also, there is the possibility of the necessity for extending the time frame, a possibility that, even though it may have been explained at the start, may be met with strong resistance if the need occurs.

Short-term work presents the problem of not allotting that much time to explain and reexplain fee policies. It is more likely that if the therapist makes an exclusionary error there will be less opportunity to correct it. Hence, it is particularly incumbent on the therapist to assure mutual understanding of the specifics unless therapists want to assume that they will take the loss if the patient misunderstands, which generally tends to be the case in long-term work as well, although repeated or persistent misunderstandings are more likely there. As an offset, if therapists have initially explained the fee situation explicitly and have received patients' agreements, then it is more likely for misunderstandings to be voluntarily resolved by patients after explanation in the original terms. Difficulties are more likely to arise when the therapist was too vague or too general in the first place.

PATIENTS' EXPECTATIONS

Patients expect to pay a fee, and they usually have a relatively accurate idea of what therapists' fees are likely to be in various geographic locations. Furthermore, they tie in their perceived status of the therapist, so, for example, they expect a psychiatrist to charge a higher fee than a social worker, which expectation is indeed usually accurate. The patients' expectations can be helpful to therapists in providing an avenue for therapists to explore the issues including appropriateness of the established fees. However, patients may not be eager to discuss fee arrangements or explore their financial situations. Patients may be less fee-avoidant than therapists, but they are still avoidant, so if therapists want to delay or be vague, particularly as to when and how payment will occur, they will often get cooperation in their hesitant stance.

Patients also vary a great deal in their sophistication about fee policies. Usually they are prone to pay as low a fee as seems appropriate for quality service, but they are unsure as to how that can be effected. A sliding fee scale gives them some idea, whereas the fixed fee enables them to make a basic decision as to whether they are willing to pay it even if they did not get to negotiate fee amounts with the therapist in terms of income evaluation. In the case of a fixed fee, the patients actually negotiate with themselves as to affordability.

Also, many patients expect therapy to be relatively short-term. They make comments such as, "I don't want to be in therapy as long as ___ ," naming some person whom they know and view as having been in therapy too long. Or, if informed that the process may be lengthy, they may state, "Well, I don't want to be in therapy for the rest of my life." Certainly that is not the therapist's expectation either, but the patient needs to know the open-ended possibilities of longer-term therapy in order to estimate cost.

With the media emphasis on short-term work as well as the increase in restricted insurance coverage, patients are now more likely to expect briefer work and so less total cost. Thus, the burden is increased for therapists who offer longer therapeutic strategies unless the frequency of contact is limited. Overall, patients now appear to expect relatively limited contact with therapists, even if the contact is over some duration, as a few years. This trend does make psychoanalytic therapies harder to market. However, by being aware of probable patient expectations and anticipated costs, therapists can be better prepared to explain the potential value of a particular service. Such elaboration and justification of costs are quite useful and germane to the therapeutic process because they assist patients to clarify their goals and motivations. Such exploration includes the reasoning involved in all the therapist's fee policies, such as time of payment, cancellations, frequency of sessions, and probable length of treatment.

Although sliding fee scales have been the most common approach among psychotherapists, patients frequently do not expect this. Their experience is based on other health care providers who most often charge fixed fees, such as physicians and dentists, and who are grouped more into categories of expense based on what the fixed fees are. Thus, the flexibility in therapy fees may cause patients to give the therapist less than what is fair based on income or, less likely, to pay the top of the scale out of a desire to accommodate or be favored, or possible embarrassment at seeming poor. This again emphasizes the therapist's responsibility to explore the reality of the fee. This responsibility is more obvious with flexible fees, but it is also there with fixed fees because it is of no value for patients to begin something they will continually resent and probably be unable to complete if they cannot afford it.

Then there are some patients who expect to haggle, and they will do it regardless of how flexible the therapist tries to be, so with these patients boundaries have to be established and reestablished if the patient continues in therapy. If this is not done, the therapist will find the patient continually wanting to change fee policies to the detriment of the therapist. This attitude on the patient's part, if detected in the screening sessions, is something that could certainly deter a therapist from wanting to work with the patient. At the same time, the attitude is reflective of the patient's difficulties, so it is actually an indication of the need for treatment. Thus, this type of patient is possible despite the relatively obvious resistance, but the therapy relationship does require the clear setting of fee boundaries early in the process as well as reminders about the structure and repeated exploration of the meaning of the relatively continual attempt to tamper with the fee. Such patients are a minority, and when they do appear, they make apparent how much of an issue the fee can be, right from the start.

Most patients, in contrast, will only offer clues to their feelings about monetary matters, with details emerging as therapy proceeds. It is useful to provide as many early opportunities as possible to make these discoveries, so that in the process of establishing the fee, questions can be posed as to what the patients expected and how the proposed arrangement fits in with these expectations such as being taken care of, or taken advantage of, or being treated fairly. This also provides an opportunity to discover patients' views of therapists' monetary needs, interests, and attitudes, which in turn will bear relevance to the development of transference and countertransference.

CONCLUSION

Prompt discussion and establishment of fee policies between therapists and patients facilitate an ongoing therapeutic process. Although fees are a delicate issue for all parties, there is a great deal to be lost if they are not discussed and agreed on in the beginning stage of therapy. Patients' general awareness that there will be a fee provides an obvious avenue for therapists' to initiate discussion. Unwillingness to do so is a disservice to patients and therapists alike, creating unnecessary opportunities for resistances and transferential distortions on both sides.

In contrast, frank discussion about money matters sets a tone of openness and ease, and also structures the relationship. It is clear that there is a mutuality to the relationship in the therapist's need and desire to be paid and the fact that the therapist respects the patient's capacity for responsibility. This approach also provides a model for the patient to talk about everything since money is an issue so frequently cloaked in taboos. Thus, afraid or not, the therapist should discuss such an issue, indicating that it can be done, that the patient is expected to do so as well, and that the therapist will not be devastated or retaliate in response to whatever the patient talks about. By talking about money in an appropriate manner, the therapist also gives money its due as an important factor in people's lives, thus neither exaggerating nor denying its importance. The groundwork is laid for the growth of a productive therapeutic relationship in which both parties can, from an economic point of view, realistically afford to be there.

Also, discussing money matters provides useful information about the patient's attitudes and feelings. It is an early entryway to psychodynamic understanding. Of course it is quite probable that part of any patient's reaction may be anxiety, resulting in "not hearing" or "not understanding" some aspects of fee policies. Therapists can expect to repeat some of the agreement and need to exercise their discretion in the manner of enactment when some part of the contract is distorted by the patient. However, if the therapist puts the structure into place at the start rather than subsequently, resistances to it are more quickly and easily resolved.

Of course we recognize that all this will be effective only if two events take place. The first is the patient's ability and willingness to pay the fee and adhere to fee policies. Of course, if that is missing, then early screening is very helpful, which is facilitated by early discussion of money matters. The second is the therapist's ability to have a realistic perspective on money and be at ease with discussing the subject. This is the more insidious problem because many therapists remain in practice without having developed that ease. The need for psychotherapists to resolve their own "money neuroses" is basic and essential for their most effective work.

Chapter 9

FEE POLICIES

T he concern here is with the various possibilities for fee policies and their advantages and disadvantages. We will start with the two general approaches, sliding fee scales and fixed fees, then look at third-party arrangements, and conclude with other details of the therapist–patient contract, including cancellations, missed sessions, telephone time, and vacations.

FLEXIBLE FEES

Institutional Services

The central concept in flexible fee setting is that the fee is primarily based on the patient's ability to pay. The qualifier, "primarily," is a key word in the conception because there is a minimum overhead that the therapist (or an employer of the therapist) will want to satisfy, so it would be unusual for the patient to pay no fee even if the patient were at poverty level. Public institutions, training centers, and other situations where economic support is not dependent on patient fees tend to be the most likely source of low fees. The commitment is to the removal of the economic barrier so that those who need service can get it. Of course, these provider agencies have to get their funds from somewhere, so whatever they do get from patients is considered helpful. Thus, staff are expected to take the fee payment seriously. Furthermore, the belief remains prevalent in the field that it is therapeutic for patients to pay something, and this belief is usually accepted by patients. Patients are not as attracted to the need for payment as the providers are, and in situations where the therapists' incomes are not affected by patients' payments, fee policies may be quite loose as therapists merge with patients in fee avoidance. Identification with the patient's point of view comes easily when a therapist feels exploited, and that feeling is relatively common in public agencies or training programs.

The difficulties usually begin with the determining of the patient's ability to pay. Even relatively objective indices of income, such as pay stubs or withholding forms, may not reveal the patient's real income, and of course income is relative to expenses. So, determining what any patient can really afford is difficult and customarily results in an approximation that tends to be on the low side. This tendency is enabled by intake therapists who picture themselves as battling the institution on the patients' behalf. It is a poor way to start therapy because deceit is already being condoned, and a part of the therapeutic process is diminished needlessly. It is certainly a positive to have a society that provides low-cost therapy services, but those services are immediately limited in value if the patient is encouraged to be dishonest.

Even when therapists are not involved in some rebellion against authority, their tendency to minimize the financial aspects of psychotherapy may provide their patients with opportunities to be less than honest. A lack of thorough exploration of patients' financial resources is sufficiently common that too often therapy is partially undermined. The fee does not have to be high, or for that matter there does not actually have to be a fee in every instance, but whatever the fee policy it should be adhered to. This sets the tone for the structural aspects of any course of therapy. Patients and therapists are poorly served when either or both avoid these realities.

Private Practice

Of course in private practice where therapists are directly dependent on patients' fees for income, there is less leeway in the motility of payment scales and schedules. Lacking any external subsidies, therapists have a limit on how little they can charge. This limit is set by the reality of an individual therapist's expenses directly connected to the practice—rent, phone, utilities, etc.—and those costs in other areas of a therapist's life that are expected to be met by income from the practice. For purposes of our discussion, the assumption is made that therapists in private practice are expecting a significant portion of their income to be derived from the practice. Thus, the practice must be profitable, without specifying the amount, in order for it to continue for any extended time period. Therapists who do not fit this assumption, such as those who deliberately have a limited practice and receive most of their income from other sources, will naturally have less pressure on their limits, although they are also well advised to treat their fee policies as important structural components of the therapy.

Therapists' Image

Another factor in setting financial limits is the therapist's self-image. In addition to the desire to be seen as a relatively altruistic helper, there is the desire to be successful. In private practice this generally is translated into financial success. Some of this is required by life-style expenses such as support of the household and people for whom one is in some way responsible. Some of it is also part of being competitive, keeping up with if not surpassing the probable income of other practitioners, particularly peers, though with a style that avoids the appearance of smugness or greed. This latter motive is complex because it can clash with the selfless, helping image, which, as repeatedly noted, is particularly attractive to psychotherapists. Some therapists sidestep this conflict by using the number of hours they see patients as their world symbol of success. By doing this, they can have lower fees and make up for it in volume while letting other therapists think that all these hours are at the same fee, a high one. The inefficiency of this method is sacrificed to image preservation.

Negotiating Fees

Self-image is certainly a significant factor in determining fee policies. A sliding-scale approach has the appearance of fairness, which is appealing. Also, it is the majority method, keeping one in the mainstream. On the downside, it involves a thorough investigation early in the therapy of the patient's financial resources. This makes many therapists uncomfortable and in turn causes them to be hasty and superficial as well as defensive if they feel a challenge to their inquiries. As a result, either party may become disadvantaged, depending on the personalities involved. It is difficult at best to get more than approximations in determining income, and certainly there is a temptation for the patient to deceive. If deception does occur, it is usually in the direction of income understatement so that the therapist is the victim.

This deception can be a deliberate sociopathic maneuver on the part of patients, but that is less likely than a justified miscalculation. Given options, patients tend to choose fees they want to pay rather than those they can afford to pay. They consider the element of "fairness" but include in this conception their predetermined view of what psychotherapy is probably going to be worth to them, as opposed to what a therapist might indicate it ought to cost. Also included is the therapist's apparent willingness to negotiate, which from the therapist's viewpoint is designed to provide a service according to the patient's ability to pay but may appear to the patient as a bargaining situation in which some sort of a "deal" is commonplace. In essence, the patient's criteria of payment ability will be a mix of actual income, priorities of interest in spending available money, felt distress, expectations of relief, and perceptions of the therapist's attitude about the fee. Any patient can arrive at a fee that he believes is "okay" with the therapist and the patient when the therapist eagerly facilitates the "okayness." The result is that such a fee is often both less than the patient could pay and less than what the therapist wants.

Some type of negotiated fee will be all right if the therapist is comfortable with doing business this way. Some therapists are resigned to it, which may leave lingerng resentment. Others view it as reality, a way of getting what one can, following the supply–demand cycle and akin to selling a house or a car, where the American way is usually paying less than the asking price, depending on market conditions. Of course there is a temptation in that situation for the therapist to have an asking price that is sufficiently high enough to make the patient feel uncomfortable going too far below it as well as grateful in some fashion for the therapist taking a cut from his apparently usual fee. Of course this fee may not be usual but unusual in that the therapist has rarely received it and does not expect it but uses it as a possible preventive device as well as a fantasied part-object of a grandiose ego-ideal.

Another possibility is that an agreement is reached in which the therapist is unhappy and suspicious, but, caught in personally created contract boundaries, he suffers along. This is good material for paranoia as the therapist looks for evidence to increase the fee or considers ways to expedite this patient's departure from therapy other than, of course, raising the fee.

Effective Flexibility

The sliding-scale approach produces many opportunities for irrational contracts, a subject that has been discussed in some detail in earlier writings (Herron & Rouslin, 1984; Welt & Herron, 1990). However, these possibilities, as well as others that one might add that have not been depicted, do not have to be actualized. There are at least two ways to use a sliding scale effectively. One is to be an accurate investigator of patients' financial situations. Since this needs to be carried out rather early in the therapy relationship, there is a very definite need for tact and exploration. Furthermore, some patients will be put off by this, seeing it as an excessive monetary interest or a premature intrusiveness by therapists. Therapists using this approach will have to be willing to understand the possible range of patients' reactions and carefully explain the intent of their exploration as well as its advantages. Some patients will still be annoyed, even to the point of not continuing. However, these tend to be a minority and a group whose resistance to therapy would probably appear in some other form at some other stage. Nonetheless, they are lost at that point, and so is the possibility of handling the resistance if it had appeared later.

At the same time, for the majority of patients this relatively exacting approach will be effective in producing a fair arrangement with both parties ready to do more therapeutic work, since the fee issue is a substantial beginning. The catch is that many, if not most, therapists do not feel comfortable conducting such an inquiry, so they will not do it.

This leaves the second possibility, which has the best chance of being the most feasible solution. The basic element for success on the therapist's part when developing a fee arrangement is a feeling of satisfaction with what he is paid, which in turn reflects positive self-esteem. This is achieved when the individual transaction is satisfying, and that satisfaction is viewed in the context of one's overall economic situation. Thus, even if the therapist and patient engage in an open, detailed discourse about the fee, there is the probability of some inexactitude. However, the therapist can be comfortable with that because he has carried out his own method diligently and expects to live with the results. The therapist who wishes to be less exacting creates a different self-comfort zone. That therapist is willing to live with less evidence that the patient is being fair and honest and prefers to let the money dynamic evolve slowly. The possibility of getting lower fees is increased, but the therapist expects that, and of course all therapists can control the bottom of the range by selection. Any one therapist can afford only so many low-fee patients and needs to recognize the limit and not stretch it unduly, or the comfort zone will be invaded and negative countertransference is likely. As a result, even with a sliding scale, some patients will be turned away and have to be referred to still less expensive sources of therapy.

Hidden Dangers

Althoug sliding scales can be effective, they are really more insidious for therapists than is recognized. They have the surface appeal of fairness to the patient in that payment appears to be based on his financial situation. However, there is a limit to that for each practitioner. So, in order for the scales to be equitable, they also have to be based on therapists' needs. This means therapists have to present a range and have sufficient heterogeneity in the range to accommodate themselves and the available patient pool. If too many patients of one monetary extreme make up the sample, then the range is narrowed or disappears, as does the concept of a sliding scale. To be faithful to the concept requires a degree of social consciousness that may be hard to maintain if the therapist's practice becomes tilted. Too many patients at the low end may cause frustration and resentment, with the possible "curing" of too many too fast with the aim, albeit unconscious, of making room for the more affluent. In contrast, if the upper end of the scale is predominant, there may be less incentive to make room for lower-paying patients unless therapists' superegos have a persistent guilt-tilt. Lower payers may have more appeal to therapists when patients are in short supply or when one is beginning, but if one's practice develops to provide a certain living standard that becomes expected, it will be difficult to shift downward. In theory the scale slides down as well as up, but the impression is that therapists are less prepared for the possible reverses than for an upward progression in each patient.

Two other observations deserve mention here. One is that the current embrace of short-term therapy by many therapists may, in part, be a reaction to the problems of variable fees. An obvious part of a patient's concern with the fee is the proposed length of the therapy. When the fee is low, this is also a concern for the therapist. Short-term work takes a lot of the sting out of both sides because a higher fee will be more palatable for the patient when the possible total number of sessions will be lower. Even an arrangement where the patient finds himself returning every few years has a more manageable feel to it than anything that looks continuous. Since the therapist is operating on a high-volume philosophy, there will be a problem only if that supply is not maintained. Expectations are that it will, so short-term therapists can charge higher fees and stay within more patients' comfort zones for total psychotherapy expenditures. The relative affordability of briefer therapy has among its less obvious appeals the reduction of the need for therapists to bother so much with the cost issue. Of course, this may be a temporary vacation from the financial jungle because of two possibilities. The first is that recidivism could turn briefer into longer and even rather continuous therapy. The second is that managed health care could dominate the marketplace and try to pressure providers into lower fees per session, regardless of length. There already is a tendency in that direction that will undoubtedly increase if brief therapy is not as successful as it is currently purported to be. Nonetheless, at the moment brief psychotherapy is an easier sell for therapists.

This fact is actually exemplified even within the psychoanalytic community, which has a major commitment to long-term intensive work, yet also has a good proportion of analysts increasingly filling their practices with psychoanalytic psychotherapy. The latter is less cost-intensive, but was in fact originated for purposes other than that, namely, for people who were not, at the moment of entering psychotherapy, ready for psychoanalysis. However, as Gediman (1990) notes, an economic situation has developed in which many people who can afford psychoanalysis will not make the time commitment. What they are doing is all they are willing to do, and they are not convinced that more would be better. Gediman (1990) states:

> The private psychoanalytic practice of every analyst in America has decreased over the decade, whereas their relatively well-paying psychoanalytic psychotherapy practices have increased. More and more, analyses are offered at significantly reduced fees to the non-affluent . . . who are able to make the commitment in time but not in money. . . . Today's educated consumers . . . often reject our recommendations. . . . They have redefined, in terms of their own ethic, the value of the treatment modalities they seek. (p. 7)

She is describing psychoanalytic psychotherapy as two visits per week as contrasted with four for psychoanalysis. The current reality is that once a week is more common, so that for analysts as well as for those who believe in briefer therapy, there is an economic pull. The upper end of the sliding scale in essence can remove the analyst from practicing his preference. Sometimes this preference may result primarily from analysts' needs, but even when it does not, it is increasingly difficult to find patients who are both willing and affluent enough to spend the time in psychoanalysis. The message from patient to analyst is, "you can be as psychoanalytic as you want, but this is all the time I am willing to give you." That is an unfortunate limitation, and although it is true that some of these people would not give more time if the fee were less, the problem for analysts is that they might feel a need to work with a substantial number of such patients in order to be able to afford to do psychoanalysis with at least some patients in their practices. Sliding scales can make some patients worth more than others and thus influence decisions about patient selection and the type of therapy to be practiced.

The influence is an economic one, but it is probable that this may be discounted in favor of a theoretical point of view that highlights the previous undervaluing of briefer forms of treatment. Practical considerations may be the deciding factor in who gets what, so that psychoanalytic psychotherapy will be deemed appropriate more often because it pays better. The next step may be the alteration of the structure of that as well to fit consumer demands. Although the marketplace obviously has a strong voice in determining what analysts can do, what is done ought not to masquerade under solely theoretical motivations.

In the context, consider the following two statements: "Frequency and sequence of visits should depend exclusively on the patient's psychological condition, and financial considerations should not determine these decisions" (Lane & Hull, 1990, p. 263). "We should think, rather, of a broadening range of patients treatable by a broadened armamentarium of techniques, equally valued in their own right, derived from a unified psychoanalytic theory" (Gediman, 1990, p. 10).

The first sounds as if the authors are saying whatever the patient needs, the therapist should not let the fee stand in the way, thus affirming the value of a variable fee schedule. However, this follows an endorsement of the validity of referring patients who cannot pay either usual or reduced fees, which implies that financial considerations do play a part in decisions regarding what happens to an individual patient. It behooves therapists to face this and be open with patients about it. It is clear that Lane and Hull are sensitive to a patient's needs and would take the economic situation into account *as much as they could.* That last phrase is added because they manage to avoid saying that directly, and it needs to be said.

The Gediman statement, although written in an attempt to redress a perceived distortion in regard to the value of psychoanalytic psychotherapy, also leaves something unsaid. It provides a justification for psychoanalysts to indeed be psychoanalysts and still do psychoanalytic psychotherapy, for which it is easier to attract higher-paying patients. Now Gediman's motivation for her words need not have been economic, but her position is financially helpful to psychoanalysts because of its provision of a rationale that enables them to keep their identity, integrity, and income all at the same time. Again, what is not said directly is, this is a nice way to remain economically viable. Again, the possible money motive ought to be recognized.

Whitson (1989) notes:

> Regardless of what you choose to do, there probably is ample theoretical justification not to mention collegial support for your position. This can add to a sense of security but also can help us unattend to other reasons for what we do. The danger exists that theoretical explanations can be used to maintain a sense of correctness which limits therapist exploration of how their policies also reflect their personal attitudes toward money. (p. 6)

Thus far, mention has been made of one relatively obscured issue embedded in flexible-fee policies, namely, the need to maintain an economic equilibrium for the therapist and some methods taken to achieve this that present problems. The balancing act is also involved in the second concern as well, that is, reliance on insurance to bolster the lower end of one's scale. The patient is concerned about direct, out-of-pocket expenses, whereas the therapist is looking for a certain income. The degree of third-party payment available reduces the impact of the fee for the patient, because of course the fee charged is not the fee the patient pays directly. Again, this works particularly well with short-term patients where it is unlikely most insurance carriers will attempt to limit benefits. However, it is a risky long-term solution because therapist and patient tend to rely on that indirect subsidy, and the increasing tendency to find it limited comes as a shock. If payments are terminated, then the patient will probably want to pay only what he has been paying directly, resulting in a fee cut for therapists. Sometimes a compromise can be reached, although it will still mean less income for the therapist.

If the patient is using insurance, the therapist would do well to discuss in advance what is possible if those payments are stopped or limited. This guards against the shock effect for both parties and provides a way to continue the therapy, but it has to be a way that is understood clearly and is agreeable to both participants.

The potential value of insurance payments has also been known to induce cheating. Patients may offer possibilities (as may therapists) such as overbilling, billing for nonexistent sessions, and other forms of sociopathic collusion. In addition to being unethical and illegal, they are a therapeutic mistake. One may think insurance carriers deserve to be cheated and somehow come up with a justification to do it, but it is not going to help the therapeutic process. Staying within the boundaries of whatever the patient's insurance provides has to be incorporated in the sliding scale, along with the possibility that those boundaries may ultimately reduce the fee or require that the patient be asked to pay more or a compromise be developed. Such understanding and preparation are often missing, and therapy gets an unwelcome disruption that could be avoided or mitigated. One may note at this point that all these problems could be avoided by limiting one's practice to patients who do not use insurance, especially because of the possible dynamic implications in maintaining or disturbing the process. Although this is certainly an issue, economic realities make it impossible for most therapists. Also, a number of authors have indicated that the impact varies with patient populations (el-Guelbay et al., 1985) as well as the fact that the psychodynamic issues can be utilized profitably (Raney, 1982–83).

Policy Presentation

Assuming that the therapist understands all the advantages and disadvantages of a sliding scale and decides he will use it, there is surprisingly little said about just how one might present this policy to patients. The mammoth *Encyclopedic Handbook of Private Practice* (Margenau, 1990) gives fees limited coverage, with some generalities as: "For some, the use of a sliding scale that sets fees for service according to family size and income, ranging from zero to full fee, is a comfortable and practical way to temper idealism and function professionally" (Canter & Freudenberger, 1990, p. 220). These authors recommend getting a fee schedule from a community agency to provide a norm. They indicate that some people negotiate fees for each patient without having a usual fee, whereas others have a set fee but will reduce it depending on circumstances.

Specifically, we have suggested an explanation of fee policies, starting at least with stating the cost of the first session, prior to seeing the patient. Whether or not that has been done, the details of fee policies will have to be explained in the initial sessions. If it is a sliding scale, then the therapist should decide in advance what it will be, including the specific criteria. For example, the therapist could have determined the market in his area and, taking into account personal needs, arrived at a fee schedule that appears appropriate on both of these counts. Thus, for certain income levels, certain fees will be requested, providing a graduated payment system. In addition, the therapist needs to take into account the patient's available income for therapy, which is the amount after other necessary expenses that the patient is willing to spend for psychotherapy. It can be difficult to determine this amount accurately because what is a "necessary expense" from the patient's perspective may not be one from the therapist's. The therapist can question the priority of necessities, but it is important to avoid having the questioning turn into an argument. The therapist gets an impression of what the patient is willing to pay, assesses the reasonableness of this, forms some ideas about the patient's ego strength, discusses impressions of what is affordable for the patient to the extent congruent with the patient's ego functioning, and then decides whether or not to accept the fee being offered.

Although it may well be discomforting to turn a patient down on the basis of money, it is providing better service to the patient than working with the person when there is a strong possibility of negative therapist responses. Resentment about fees certainly can result in that, and the easiest way to avoid this possibility is to refer the patient to a lower-cost provider. If the therapist's fee schedule is set up in a realistic manner that takes into account patient supply and the therapist's appropriate needs, and if sufficient heterogeneity of payment is maintained to keep the needed balance between low and high fees, this is a workable method. If it becomes too concentrated in any area of its range, then the purpose is defeated because it has become a fixed-fee arrangement. It is a method that requires honesty by both parties and considerable vigilance by therapists if fairness and service are to be preserved. These attributes are not always forthcoming, so that in practice the method remains disproportionately elastic. The openness to discussing money matters is just not there yet for enough patients or therapists to take the inequities out of sliding-scale fee policies. The risks of deficiencies in service based on economic considerations are definitely present and are difficult to eliminate. However, they certainly can be mitigated, and therapists would help both themselves and their patients if they worked increasingly to do this in the ways that have been suggested thus far or using any better approaches to accuracy and fairness that may come to their minds.

At this point, or perhaps throughout the discussion, the reader may ask, well, what about giving it away? In essence, are therapists not here to serve, and how much money do they need anyway? The helping self is apt to bridle at the economic self, but the answer to these questions has to be within the context of this society and its market economy. The point has been made that psychotherapists are paid helpers who are comfortable with and desire a middle- to upper-middle-class life style. For those therapists who feel they do not need this, then to some extent it can be given away, particularly to those who need it and will not devalue it. However, since those therapists are a minority, and the situation is similar in all the helping professions, the majority remain enmeshed in the rules of capitalism. We caution against the belief that a flexible fee schedule will get one around these boundaries.

FIXED PAYMENT

Fixed payment is the method that charges all patients relatively the same amount. As with variable fees, a qualifier, "relatively," has to be used because patients enter practices at different points in time. This means that there is temporal variation in entry fees that usually results in some differential in a cross-sectional view of fees in a given practice. Usually fees are raised first for new patients, with most other patients brought up to that level before any new cycle of higher fees is initiated. The basic concept is that at any given time period the entry fees are the same for all patients. Exceptions to this policy can be and are made, but the policy is intended to limit these and keep fees fixed.

Advantages

The positive aspects of this policy begin with guaranteeing the therapist a fixed income and eliminating any need for negotiation. Patients' feelings about payment are still explored, but they do not affect the size of the fee. This approach also presents a clear structure that is fair in its approach to all who are in treatment with the therapist. Essentially all patients pay the same fee, so that there are no "favorites." This indicates the therapist is not open to reduction or manipulation and can be reassuring in regard to other aspects of the therapy. It also provides a clear economic screening device for patients and therapists in that selection is apparently based on ability to pay. The therapist's resentment is clearly taken out of the picture because he gets what is requested, so a major source of negative countertransference is eliminated, which certainly benefits the patient. The therapist also appears as a role model for believing in the self and asking for, as well as getting, what one feels is both needed and deserved.

Variations in this model include keeping the initial fee the same for the patient as long as he is in therapy but charging new patients (or former patients if they return) higher fees, having a time span probably relative to inflation during which the fee is not raised for current patients, and exercising flexibility in regard to existing patients if they encounter adverse circumstances such as payment deferral until their economic situation improves as well as at times taking a patient for a lesser fee because of circumstances that make this palatable to the therapist. Thus, a psychoanalyst might have an interest in demonstrating the effectiveness of his approach with patients who are often considered difficult to treat for reasons other than economic but who also are of limited means. Being in a training program where the reward is primarily completing requirements is another example. However, the fee flexibility is not a primary ingredient of the fee policy as it is in sliding scales. In contrast to the latter, the apparent image is of a market-determined fee that is tied to therapists' needs and competencies rather than appearing to be a function of what patients can or want to pay. As noted, flexible fee schedules in private practice are not nearly as patient-determined as they may look. Fixed-fee policies, in turn, are not as therapist-determined as they may look because in setting a realistic fee therapists have to take into account patient contingencies as well.

The fixed-fee approach makes the roles clear, namely, that the therapist is a paid service provider who expects a clearly defined monetary return for efforts expended. Although the option of meeting a particular patient need is there, if it requires a monetary sacrifice by the therapist, the therapist will not automatically give it. The preference is to get the desired fee, and generally patients who cannot provide this are sent to lower-cost providers. It is a policy that prevails among most health care providers, physicians for example, although less prevalent with psychotherapists, who have more ambivalence about their role. It is a comfortable policy with patients who share a similar philosophy in regard to their work efforts and therefore both expect and respect it. As a result it is a niche philosohy, but exactly in line with independent health service providers. The place it fills is a large one, and whereas consumers may want to pay less for health care, they are not eager to lower the income of the providers, assuming it is in a range they consider reasonable. Consumers just want somebody else, namely, third-party payers, to make up the difference. Thus, kept within reasonable limits, a fixed-fee policy will seem appropriate to most consumers of private psychotherapy services.

Disadvantages

The set-fee approach is not the one most frequently used by psychotherapists, so it puts the user out of the mainstream. Furthermore, it lacks an altruistic image, although the economic motivations of a sliding-scale therapist may be no less than those of the fixed-fee therapist.

Furthermore, it requires the ability to withstand more assaults on one's therapeutic intentions, the implication being that if a therapist will not vary his fee, then he is a cold, avaricious person. The helping image is placed under attack, but the attack is inappropriate, not the provider. Of course, the guilt is easy to stimulate, and so the fixed-fee approach is best suited for those therapists who are very clear about how they are going to enact their role. If clarity and resolve are missing, they will become sliding-scale providers without admitting it, and their supposed fee policy will be just another deception that undermines the effectiveness of therapy. A key issue, regardless of policy, is the honesty and integrity of the policy, because it sets the tone for the process. If mendacity underlies it and indeed surfaces, the therapeutic utility of fees is diminished if not lost.

Neither variable- nor fixed-fee policies provide that much of a way to service the poor. Flexible approaches appear to do this, but the individual practitioner needs a balance in patient fees to survive, so the poor can be served only to the extent that the rich pay more. Patient mix is a hidden issue that will surface in flexible fee schedules to limit the number of low-paying patients. Fixed-fee approaches do not even offer the appearance of serving lower-income patients, although any individual may choose to serve them, and many do. At the same time, their stated policy limits the number of lower-paying patients who will approach them, so it is less of an ongoing possibility.

The biggest problem in a fixed-fee approach is coming to terms with the ambivalence surrounding the role of the psychotherapist. Whereas it is easier to use with patients in the sense that there is no negotiating, it will never appear as fair as a flexible system to either patients or other therapists who use sliding scales. If therapists cannot come to terms with that impression, then they will periodically experience discomfort with fixed fees.

Overview: Variable- and Fixed-Fee Policies

Fee policies are determined by a number of factors, including tradition, practicality, and personal issues, with some overlap. Tradition involves what the field has suggested and sanctioned in the past. This is a sliding scale as the most common approach with the fee based on the patient's ability to pay. Some free or very low-cost provision of services have traditionally been sanctioned; most of the treatment of the poor in funded agencies, public or private; payment hierarchies based on status hierarchies, with psychiatrists at the top; and the use of third-party payments, a result of designating psychotherapy as a health service.

Tradition

Each of these characteristics has some hidden or less-noticed features that bear mention because they change the feature from its surface appearance to its actualized reality. Thus, the sliding scale is based on a balance between patients' paying abilities and therapists' needs, including status needs. Some therapists feel better with a majority of low-paying patients or just lots of patients, regardless of fees, but most therapists will limit the number of low-paying patients in their practices and also will dislike lowering fees that are already in place. In regard to free service, the adjective "some" can only be defined in individual terms. Any standard would be arbitrary, and considering the need to make a living, "some" will be limited. Thus, there is the necessity of funded treatment, as in different types of institutions. However, that treatment is usually considered inferior and often can be, which means rethinking how the poor and relatively poor are to receive better-quality treatment.

The payment hierarchies have undergone considerable restructuring in the private sector, although not that much in the public, which is part of the problem with treatment in the latter. Since psychiatrists are medical doctors, they kept pace with the rising fees of other medical doctors. Insurance carriers helped them do this, as did their ability to provide services directly that other providers could not, such as hospital admitting and prescription delivery. However, as other disciplines gained provider status with insurance companies, they in turn were able to increase fees so that disparity by discipline has decreased. As consumers gained greater freedom of choice with increased insurance coverage, they became aware that in regard to the customary verbal psychotherapies, psychiatrists were not per se more competent.

As other disciplines seek and gain a broader range of service capabilities, a leveling effect will probably move into place. Also, if managed health care drives down fees, psychiatrists would suffer the most because their fees, on average, remain the highest based on time spent per patient. The "biologizing" of psychiatry, with an emphasis on medication, many patients, and infrequent, brief visits has been one reaction to avoid income reduction. It is, of course, not promulgated on economic but on theoretical grounds, but it holds down costs per patient. As noted, other disciplines without the medication possibility have embraced the short-term philosophy, which has a similar cost-reduction effect. These approaches limit demands for accountability from third-party payers, provided they work and there is limited recidivism. Such effectiveness remains to be proven, and consumers are relatively unaware of this possible significant defect.

The embracing of psychotherapy as a health service also has an economic lure because it is tied to insurance coverage, whereas something like educational services are not. This view does not portray the health aspect as a facade but does make sure it is emphasized over anything else psychotherapy might do. Also, the insurance coverage has such an impact that it cannot be ignored, whether therapists are motivated to follow its whims and dictates or struggle with them, as is often needed to maintain one's integrity. Furthermore, managed health care is paradoxically eliminating much of the freedom of choice that insurance coverage provided as it expanded to disciplines beyond medicine, and unfortunately many consumers are unaware of these limitations.

Another aspect of tradition is the therapist's experience with therapy, including how the therapist was trained, and particularly what his therapist(s) and supervisors did. They were the primary models, and their fee policies have a significant effect on the therapists they analyzed and/or trained. If one was favorably impressed, then one is likely to follow suit, with differences appearing when one was dissatisfied with their approaches.

Practicality

This is a matter of doing what works and has even caused therapists to switch orientations and techniques to improve income, though again, these switches are usually attributed to seeing new theoretical truths rather than due to lucre. Basically, practicality means a realistic assessment of the potential for making a living as a psychotherapist in private practice. The extent of living is based on perceived needs, ranging from survival upward, and naturally affects what one is willing to do. Particular training is required, depending on specialization, and personal interests need to be met or the work will lose its attraction. Deciding on where to practice and establishing a continuing supply of patients are expedient concerns. The profession has become increasingly competitive, particularly in metropolitan areas where there are many psychoherapists, and managed health care is adding to the problem. Although the need for mental health services remains high, the economic returns are more difficult to come by. In turn, the need for marketing is stressed in most bulletins, newsletters, etc. emanating from the profession.

It is interesting that psychoanalysts are notable for their apparent avoidance of this concern, although they can't be unaffected by it. Consider the influential comments by Cummings (1987), in which he foresees the prevalent future therapy model as brief, sporadic life-cycle treatment. Forman (1990) adds that the desire for a practice of primarily long-term, intensive cases is unrealistic in the current market. Perhaps analysts are ostriches, or patient and philosophical, or flirting with poverty, or heavy on denial, or magical, or doing an increasing amount of relatively short-term psychotherapy.

At any rate, the psychotherapy profession is having to face practical issues. Forman (1990) describes the practice environment as being "market driven":

> Forces operating in the marketplace have superseded theoretical considerations. These include supply and demand, price sensitivity of psychotherapy consumers, rising health care costs, and managed care. . . . Brief therapy is likely to be the norm for most psychologists' practices. . . . It will be necessary to revise our thinking about the nature of our practice and how we go about our work. (p. 34)

The question really becomes, how can one maintain theoretical integrity and still be economically successful? If one's commitment is to brief therapy, which can actually be practiced within a variety of theoretical schools including psychodynamic (Bauer & Kobos, 1987), then the type of therapy frequently being asked for by the consumer is not a major problem. However, it does remain a minor problem even within that framework because therapists who use it acknowledge that it is not a solution for everybody, just as everybody is not a candidate for longer-term therapy. Of course, if one's commitment is to long-term, intensive therapy, then a major, larger difficulty is presented. Now the consumer has to be convinced of the value of such an investment. There is an economic temptation to switch allegiances and go with the consumer drive rather than to struggle with educating all concerned to the need for freedom of choice and the possible value of different types of psychotherapy.

This book has stressed the need for education to keep the consumer's options available as well as to enable all therapists to practice their specialties because the evidence on effectiveness is so far from conclusive that decisions about funding psychotherapy are being made from an economic viewpoint rather exclusively. There is a relatively easy rationalization for going short-term, for all therapists know that even one psychotherapy session can have some therapeutic value. At the same time, all therapists also know that dosage effectiveness is very dependent on patients' reactions, and in psychic matters these are extremely variable in duration and degree. Furthermore, they are not that predictable or controllable by therapists. No one really knows when psychic resistances diminish sufficiently for the therapeutic process to be effective.

To avoid a sellout, long-term therapists who work short-term because that is all the patients will agree to then have an obligation to indicate the limits, as they see them, of the procedures being carried out. Of course, they also have a right to stay away from treating patients who impose limits, but the way events are transpiring, this approach will increasingly restrict the size of their practices and their incomes. Thus, it is probable that psychoanalysts in particular will do more short-term therapy than in the past and that they had better get moving on the educating–lobbying front if they want to practice in a way they really consider most effective.

For many psychotherapists there is a difficult and painful provider tightrope to walk, at least in the immediate future. Helfmann (1990) puts it well with the following comments:

> To change the way we practice principally because we fear that's what third parties will reimburse for, or to compete with the evergrowing supply of specialty technicians, would be a major error. . . . It would be much better to educate further both insurance carriers and the public about the nature and efficacy of mental health services. . . .
>
> Nonetheless, as managed care takes over a larger percentage of our reimbursement pool, some of us certainly do need to consider making changes in how we practice. New and innovative types of delivery services will likely be required. . . . Yet for those who believe in psychodynamic principles, faith and experience might dictate that there will continue to be a need for longer-term, insight-oriented therapy.
>
> If we truly hold onto our belief in the worth of our profession, then jumping on a bandwagon which does not really meet the needs of our patients is unnecessary and a mistake. (pp. 4–5)

Thus, in practical terms psychotherapists will have to be more flexible in their requirements for each patient's structure or frame of the therapy. In particular, variations will probably be made in number and frequency of sessions as well as in length of the sessions and intervals between sessions. Accompanying this flexibility there should be education of all payers as to the probabilities of outcomes, as best one can determine, based on what is being done. Furthermore, the case for greater freedom and flexibility in reimbursement plans must be continually argued, and with financial sophistication.

A practical issue related to duration of treatment is cost per session. Managed health care aims at cost containment in two ways, limiting the amount of specialized service, that is, the length of a course of psychotherapy, and limiting the cost per session. The latter limit is easier to gain oppositional unanimity on because most psychotherapists do not believe their fees are excessive. *Psychotherapy Finances* (1991b) provides an annual survey for anyone who wishes to compare his fees with others. The 1990 national median fee for therapists other than psychiatrists was $80 (psychiatrists' median fee can be estimated at $90). Prevailing Medicare rates in New Jersey for 40- to 50-minute individual therapy sessions were $60 for psychiatrists, $48 for psychologists, and $36 for social workers (*Psychotherapy Finances*, 1990c, p. 4). Rates will vary from state to state, but these rates could be considered the low end of the scale and probably indicate what payers would like fees to be. The actual amount received by the therapist is somewhat higher than the amount paid by Medicare, which is 80% of the approved amount for the service, with the remaining 20% paid by the patient. There is a payment hierarchy by discipline, as depicted in the figures, and according to a formula suggested by *Psychotherapy Finances*, it appears that a psychologist could in total be paid about $62 per individual session. If this holds up, meaning exact payment figures were not available as this was written, then the payment is low but not a drastic reduction from the "usual fee."

However, private managed health care appears even lower. In an article titled, "How low will you go?" *Psychotherapy Finances* (1990b) reports one managed health care plan paying $30 for a 45-minute session. Although it is not clear what, if anything, the patient was to pay, most of these plans limit the copayment to a percentage of an approved fee, so even if it was 50%, which is often the top, the total possible would be $60, and it could be less. The lure is possible volume, but if that is not forthcoming, and in many cases it has not been, then providers drop out of the plan.

For therapists who have a sufficient supply of patients with less restrictive insurance coverage, or patients who do not rely heavily on such coverage, these plans are not practical. Managed health care plans put a ceiling on what the provider can charge anybody in the plan and then pay a percentage of that, with the rest coming from the patient. The ceiling is routinely under prevailing rates, plus the plans usually limit the number of sessions and require a lot of extra time in respect to paperwork and phone consultations with reviewers.

They seem to have little to recommend them to practitioners except the reality that their usage is on the increase by employers who in turn want, and often persuade, their employees to take them. Although consumers are often unaware of what they are really getting or, more accurately, not getting via these plans, people do not customarily pick a plan for its mental health benefits. In essence, most people are not anticipating the need for psychotherapeutic services relative to other medical services. As a result, although they do not anticipate this, more people who become therapy patients are in relatively restrictive plans. This makes therapists anxious, and they join as providers to insure a probable supply of patients, despite lower per-session fees and other restrictions.

Mental health services are a small portion of overall health costs and are mainly attributable to inpatient services, particularly those for substance abuse. *Psychotherapy Finances* (1990a) reports that mental health costs were actually slightly less in 1988 (10%) than 1980 (11%), and for the period from 1971 to 1988, they ranged from 8.6% to 11.2%. Furthermore, they describe still another study indicating psychotherapy reduces other medical costs. Thus, mental health services, particularly outpatient ones, are erroneously being targeted for cost reduction and other service restrictions. It is in the practical interest of psychotherapists to correct this error rather than to perpetuate it.

If one is dubious about the reasonableness of mental health costs, the following report on psychiatrics by Wiggins (1990) is useful. The most typical practice earnings in 1989 were $100,000 to $125,000 for a 55-hour work week. This group made up 21% of the sample. Only 9% earned more than $200,000, whereas 25% earned less than $80,000 yearly. Therapists in other disciplines earn even less, so it is hard to picture psychotherapists as having excessive incomes. In the survey cited by Wiggins (1990), psychiatry was actually the lowest-gross-billing medical specialty. Granted that surveys vary depending on sample size, location, etc. and that income may be understated relative to other professionals, psychotherapists' fees are quite reasonable. The only reason to lower them across the board for the profession would be a shift in the economy that resulted in a recession or depression limiting people's ability to pay. It is true that most practitioners are accustomed to an inflating economy where most costs and incomes rise; should the opposite prevail, then adjustments would have to be made.

Personal Issues

The need for a certain amount of income will cause therapists to adopt fee policies that indeed reflect this. Beyond that may come desires for a certain life style and economic status that will place a high premium on financial success. A sufficient amount has already been said about the practicality of approaches for therapists to make decisions accordingly based on personal needs and desires. However, these tend to be complex because of needs to be seen as selfless, helpful, altruistic, and, at the very least, a good person, all of which may feel or seem to be in conflict with making money. Most therapists perform some type of balancing act. There are undoubtedly some who charge as much as possible and are relatively careless as to how they get their fees, but they are a small number. There are also a minority who consistently undercharge and suffer accordingly. Most, however, run "benign businesses," meaning there will always be some flexibility around fees, and their aims are to have reasonable incomes and feel good about themselves and their work at the same time.

THIRD-PARTY PAYMENT

It is impractical and difficult to run a practice without having some patients use insurance. From the viewpoint of retaining an ideal therapeutic model, particularly a psychoanalytic one, that is a problematic development. In essence, it adds an outside influence to the therapy process, disturbing the frame. A dependency on the insurance copayment is created for both patients and therapists, and this can affect fees charged, responsibilities for payment, frequency of sessions, diagnosis, duration of treatment, and the general mood of transactions between patient and therapist. Certainly confidentiality is restricted, with somebody other than the therapeutic duo having rights to know and decide important issues relevant to the treatment. As a result, it is appealing when a patient has no need or interest in using insurance. However, insurance has made psychotherapy possible for many more people, and increased therapists' supply of patients as well as therapists' incomes. As a result, it is recognized as a presence that has to be worked with:

> In effect, third-party payment, in its variety of forms, has become the customary manner of reimbursing mental-health service. It has permitted such services to be within the reach of most people. The design of these programs and packages will continue to adapt to the needs of our society, and it is up to all concerned to ensure a good fit to quality standards of practice. (Cohen, 1990, p. 242)

The starting point for therapists is to find out what insurance coverage the patient has for mental health services, to discuss the details with each patient, and to be clear about accountability information that may be required. The insurance is factored into the manner of payment, meaning that a certain portion will be paid by the insurance carrier, the rest by the patient. From the therapist's viewpoint the best arrangement is to have the patient pay the entire amount per session or at whatever time interval one deems appropriate and have the patient collect the copayment directly from the insurance company. However, since some patients cannot afford to do this, an arrangement can be made to have the patient pay his portion directly to the therapist with the remainder due when the patient is reimbursed by the insurance carrier.

The key issue is always to have the payment coming to the therapist from the patient. Let the securing of the insurance payment, or any third-party payments such as those from spouse or parent, be as much the patient's responsibility as possible. Sometimes the therapist's direct intervention will be necessary, as when the patient is a minor or when some unusual payment arrangements are all that is possible, such as payment by an estranged spouse. It is certainly safer to avoid such arrangements, but they happen, and if one takes them on, it ought to be with an awareness that there is an increased possibility of personal frustration and economic loss.

Payment Plans

The customary form of insurance, namely, that a patient would have a lifetime limit for mental health along with a yearly limit and a copayment percentage that results in any licensed provider getting paid, is being at least paralleled, if not replaced, by more directly managed health care. There are a variety of plans, designated by an increasing barrage of acronyms, so that it is probable that by the time this is in print some additions and/or replacements will have been made. Nonetheless what follows should be relatively complete and illustrative of the concept.

The first type of plan is the Employee Assistance Program (EAP), which is primarily directed at emotional problems that limit working ability. Typical concerns would be undue stress and substance abuse. The programs are generally short-term, with little or no direct payment by the employee, and with in-house counselors of varying credentials who customarily refer to outside sources if the problem appears to require further assistance. It is also possible for an outside provider to contract with a company to do the in-house work. The EAP counselors tend to develop their own specialization, akin to alcohol and drug counselors, so a partially competitive discipline is also being created. Generally once the outside referral is made, the employee's regular insurance plan takes over, but the EAP screening person has influence as to the referral, or it may be tied to a particular plan with designated providers. Although the ostensible aim is to improve worker productivity, there is also a desire to hold down costs. This may result in the counselor/evaluator holding a few sessions and considering this sufficient or making referrals that appear to be the least costly rather than the most effective. Involvement with

EAP can be useful if referrals are made without restrictions that will hamper the therapist. In turn, the therapist needs to evaluate the mechanics of an EAP and make his decision accordingly.

Then there are a number of plans that provide prepaid services to members with a limited copayment. They usually involve providers that have agreed to operate within the rules of the plans. These rules are generally limits on the amount of the fee and the number of visits, and they usually have a primary care physician who operates as a "gatekeeper" for specialists. Psychotherapists are in the specialist category. Some plans have a few designated providers in each specialty, with patients restricted to these providers. Other plans allow the patients to choose their own specialists but require a larger copayment by the patient. All the plans aim to cut health costs, and this can be accomplished by limiting both the cost per unit of service and the amount of service. The plans operate from the principle that providers have been charging too much per service unit as well as performing unnecessary services. Psychotherapy is often categorized as too costly and lengthy, so these plans want to reduce its per-session cost as well as to keep treatment duration brief. The possible value to therapists is speculative and circumscribed, but unless a different viewpoint is established with employers and consumers, the psychotherapy field is increasingly going to have to face a contrasting approach from third-party payment.

The plans available include the Health Maintenance Organization (HMO), Preferred Provider Organization (PPO), Exclusive Provider Organization (EPO), and Independent Provider Association (IPA). A summary of possible plans is provided by Biegel and Earle (1990) and Nevin (1991). In addition, some organizations have become self-insured, which has allowed them to limit benefits, particularly mental health services.

The challenge here is to deal effectively with what the patient brings to therapy as payment sources. Since some of the source will so frequently be insurance payment, it is essential that therapists explore the details of the insurance coverage. Plans then can be made to integrate that money into the payment arrangements. It is important that this be explicit and that the role of the third-party payer be clearly understood, as well as the responsibilities of therapist and patient in regard to payment. Medicare, for example, appears to be structured in such a way that the therapist could deal directly with the patient only for the patient's copayment. The amount to be derived from Medicare must be gotten directly by the therapist, and some other managed health care plans also operate this way. Such procedures are time consuming and usually result in delays in payment. They remove a large part of the payment issue from the therapy as well, a factor that reduces its utility as a therapeutic concern.

Specific Arrangements

Other insurance arrangements are more palatable. For example, a patient may receive a total of $2000 per year, at the rate of 50% of a maximum $60 per session. If the therapist is charging $80 per session and sees the patient once a week and plans to do that for 40 sessions, then the patient will be paying a total of $3200 to the therapist. The patient will be receiving $30 per visit from the insurance company for a total of $1200 for the 40 sessions, so the patient's direct cost will be $2000. These details are to be discussed with the patient. Decisions have to be made as to the frequency and probable total number of sessions; the latter decision is difficult, so consideration has to be given to whether an estimate of duration can be given and, if so, in what terms. If the therapist does long-term work and sees that that is required, the patient will have to be made aware of the probable additional cost. Thus, in the example given, if the frequency were three sessions per week for 3 years, the patient would get a maximum of $2000 per year, or $6000 for the length of the therapy and would have to pay the difference directly. If the awareness of the cost is hidden or denied, then there is a risk of premature interruption that could have been avoided.

The reluctance to discuss money matters tends to result in limited advance discussion of the details of where payment is coming from, what is going to be involved in getting it, and how long it will be available. Understandably it is difficult to be precise in many instances, but that does not excuse treating payment as a relative "non-issue." The type of discussion suggested is in the service of the therapy because it grounds the work in the reality of what is possible. There is clarification of what each party is willing to do. For example, is the therapist willing to work within the limits of an insurance plan in regard to a set number of sessions? Is a patient willing and able to pay whatever insurance will not pay? What arrangements are acceptable to both parties if insurance payments are to be used? For example, in the $80 fee situation described, the patient may wish to pay $50 each week and the remaining $30 for each session when she receives this from the insurance carrier. The therapist has to decide whether this delay is an acceptable arrangement.

A structure is put into place that is designed to insure as much of a comfort and freedom zone for therapist and patient to do their work. The fee structure can be an impediment to this. The therapist has the opportunity to have the patient be as clear as possible about his feelings in this matter and to keep lines of communication about fees open throughout the therapy. The fee is part of the material that can, and most often will, need to be discussed more than once. However, the therapist, once he makes the payment contract, is relatively silenced. The therapist is supposed to know *at that time* whether or not the fee arrangements will work, and if he pays insufficient attention to this issue and enters into an essentially unworkable agreement, it will be difficult to modify it. The result will certainly be resentment, with the high probability that this will interfere with the actual therapeutic work.

Therapist Motives

Therapists are carrying out a variety of motive satisfactions in agreeing to particular fee arrangements. Usually when a third-party payer is involved, the therapist is furthering a personal security motive in that at least part of the payment is relatively guaranteed. Also, the patient is helped to make use of the service, often at a rate that is more in line with what the therapist wants than if that same patient had to pay a fee without using insurance. Even in managed health care plans, the participating therapist is motivated by at least short-term security, and there is the possibility of an increased or relatively continual flow of patients.

Some other possibilities include the opportunity to be the patient's advocate with insurance carriers and thus demonstrate an active stance on the patient's behalf that is necessitated by external forces. This can be avoided by having the patient bear the major responsibility in this regard, but some therapists may not want to avoid it because it provides a tangible, visible helping occasion that appeals to them. Also, it is rare that this can be avoided completely because insurance companies usually require certain information from providers, including completed forms and review information on the progress of the case. Transferential distortions are kept at minimum by keeping contact with third-party payers also at a minimum. Some therapists carry this to an extreme, and many would like to, in that they will have nothing to do with anybody other than the patient, but current reality makes that close to impossible. Others go to the other extreme and get caught up in dealing with the third-party payers in a variety of countertransferential modes. One is inappropriate advocacy. Merger and identification with the patient is another, where therapists start colluding with patients to defraud third parties who are perceived as common enemies. Still another possibility is to act out some hostility toward the patient by presenting a treatment situation in such a way that payment is denied.

The intrusive aspect, the presence of an "additional patient," does create problems for the treatment process. Nonetheless, insurance payments in particular have become necessary for many patients to be in therapy, particularly intensive, long-term work. As a result therapists have to stay aware of the potential impact and work with it as part of the transference–countertransference–resistance material that will emerge in the therapeutic process. Once it was a new and infrequent intruder, but now it is becoming a familiar variable.

THE CONTRACT

An arrangement is agreed on between therapist and patient that stipulates the responsibilities of each party as the therapist provides a service, broadly designated as psychotherapy, to the patient. This stipulation is a contract, with legal and ethical aspects. The development of the contract in therapy has been discussed in detail (Herron & Rouslin, 1984; Welt & Herron, 1990), with the conclusion that this is both an important and difficult task to carry out, since therapy contracts have both rational and irrational aspects, and the latter are frequently overlooked with resulting misunderstandings.

Two points should be noted. The first is that the irrational or unconscious elements involved in the therapeutic contract do not argue against making any contract but do argue for understanding the complexity and scope of contracts. As Handelsman (1990) points out, there is a growing consensus on the need to inform patients about all aspects of treatment, and this requires specific contracts.

The second is that these contracts include aspects that are interrelated, though many are not specifically financial. Thus, Chapman (1990) mentions both payment agreements and treatment contracts, though the latter are often broad enough to include the former. Welt and Herron (1990) describe rational therapy contracts as including what the patients want, what the therapist is willing and able to offer, and time and financial arrangements. The focus in this chapter is on the financial arrangements, but at times it is necessary to discuss the other ingredients of the contract because of the relationship between these aspects and fees. For example, the varying contributions of patient and therapist affect the monetary value of therapy and the assignment of responsibilities. Also time arrangements are directly connected to payment.

Written Contracts

Contracts have tended to be verbal agreements, with an increase in specificity as the psychotherapy profession has matured. Nonetheless, in many types of therapy, aspects of the contract can only be relatively precise, and therapists understandably do not want to be held liable for more than they can deliver. The need to be careful and the difficulty in explaining the therapeutic process promote an avoidance of specificity, but difficulties in one area do not have to be reflected in other areas of contracts. It is certainly possible, and useful, to be quite specific about financial arrangements.

Futhermore, there is a growing tendency to make written contracts (Handelsman, 1990). This is not what most therapists are accustomed to, and its impact on the therapeutic process remains to be seen, but it may be one of those new variables, similar to insurance payments, that therapists are going to have to consider as part of their endeavors. This is said not particularly to endorse written contracts but because there has been some political movement to mandate them. For example, a recent Colorado law requires the presentation to patients of some written material, such as therapists' credentials, patients' rights in psychotherapy, and the address of the State Grievance Office.

This is a complex issue because therapists do not want to appear to be resistant to accountability or to the protection of consumers, yet the manner in which protection is assured is of considerable importance. That issue seems to be relatively ignored in a rush to be politically correct and legally protected. For example, Callahan, an attorney advising therapists, has stated: "The most important area, and again, one more often overlooked than would seem possible, is that of entering into a written fee arrangement with your patients" (1989, p. 23).

Suggested ingredients are the length of sessions, policies about missed appointments and cancellations, payment procedures, emergency availability, confidentiality, and a general discussion of fees. In addition, a written acknowledgment from patients is expected. Whereas the areas covered are certainly appropriate, this work has usually been carried out verbally, allowing more room for timing and style variations in presentation. At the same time, it is probably easier to "forget" or postpone aspects of the verbal presentation, and it is also probably easier for patients to "misunderstand" or forget what was said to them. Thus, the written contract has the advantage of clarity and is a reference point for both parties if any confusion appears. Handelsman (1990) has shown positive effects from using written forms, but the studies were not concerned with real patients, so the matter requires further study.

Contract Details

The contract will involve an agreement as to what the fee will be, what the length of the session will be, how frequently the therapist and patient will meet, and when the fee will customarily be paid. For example, the fee will be $100 per 45-minute session for individual psychotherapy on a once-a-week basis, the total fee payable at the end of each month. If the therapy is closed-ended, then the total number of sessions will also be indicated, with whatever reservations are necessary. For example, the expected length of treatment may be 15 sessions, but the possibility of additional sessions may also be indicated at the outset. In contrast, if the therapy is open-ended, that needs to be stipulated. Fees for different types of therapy, such as couples, family, and group therapy, usually vary from individual fees, so their specifics would be mentioned if these modalities are to be used. Payment for group is sometimes set on a monthly basis regardless of the number of sessions (four or five) in the month, with an explanation of the fee if in a given month the group has met fewer than four times.

It is useful to suggest to patients that they pay at each session because this provides a positive cash flow and makes it less likely that any one patient will run up a large bill. However, many patients find this difficult to do, needing perhaps to follow the pattern of their earnings, such as biweekly pay checks, or insurance reimbursement, which is usually on a monthly basis. These patterns can certainly be accommodated, so that the common practice arrangements work out to be a mixture of payment times. The important issues are to agree as to the timing of payments and to follow up if the timing is not adhered to by the patient.

It is prudent to have an arrangement that fits well for both patient and therapist. Thus, the timing of payments, and all aspects of fee policies, would have that as a goal. At the same time it is probable that patients will use the fee as a resistance from time to time and also may not acknowledge or be aware of that. In addition, reality constraints may appear, so it is highly probable that the suggested fee payment pattern will not always be followed. Therapists should be flexible enough to work with this during the therapy, but it is particularly risky to begin this way. Chances of losing money are greater with people one does not know very well or people one is no longer seeing, particularly if the therapist has only seen them a few times.

Whatever fee payment pattern is agreed on, the idea is to make it one both parties feel comfortable with. It is possible these zones may change, so that contingency needs to be discussed as well. Requests for fee alterations may come from either therapist or patient, and that possibility needs to be acknowledged from the start, as does an exploration of the possible reactions. The latter will of course be more apparent if and when the occasion arises. Prior awareness of the possibility is helpful, so an indication of what may occur should be included in the initial discussion of fees.

From the therapist's side, lowering a fee is easy from an image perspective but painful from an economic perspective, whereas raising a fee is the reverse. From the patient's side, fee raises are generally experienced as unpleasant unless the initial fee was so low it embarrassed the patient and symbolized a consistently poor self-image. Lowered fees are usually accepted with relief and some appreciation, although if they are the result of a deteriorating economic situation for the patient, then there will be accompanying discomfort. The issue is the meaning of the increase/decrease, and fee changes provide opportunities to explore such meaning.

Fee Increases

In Chapter 5 the patient's need for a fee change, primarily a reduction, was discussed in detail, along with the therapist's possible reactions. Some notice was taken then that therapists will also have a need to change fees, primarily to increase them. Further attention is paid here to raising fees. If a sliding scale is being used, therapists can expect to raise fees only when their patients' financial conditions improve. This possibility is inherent in the fee policy, and therapists should exercise it as soon as it is prudent to do so. For example, a therapist should stay aware of the patient's finances, and, if these improve, indicate to the patient that a fee raise proportionate to the patient's increase in monetary position will be forthcoming within a stipulated time. Although such an indication may be met with resistance, and certainly there will be some feeling about it, the request is reasonable, and most therapists are comfortable doing this. This type of fee raise follows a reality principle reflecting the economic condition of the patient rather than arising from a monetary need of the therapist. Of course, it may coincide with the therapist's need, but it does not originate there. In accepting the original contract, the patient has agreed that if he gets more money, so will the therapist.

Possible resistances are that the patient has a dim realization of the intent of the contract so he is unlikely to broach it and/or the patient gives priority to other expenses despite now having more money. The patient has become accustomed to being gratified in a certain way by the therapist, and although the possibility of a fee raise is there, the reality of it will be experienced as a deprivation. The patient will feel disillusioned, and the therapist wounded, by the patient's reluctance either to agree to or to feel comfortable with the new fee.

Some therapists may be put off by this unenthusiastic response or the anticipation of it, but most therapists will not because ego and superego forces are well attuned here in the direction of the raise. It is the responsible, mature approach for the fee to rise, so the change is primarily viewed as being in service of the patient with the therapist's needs being secondary.

The fixed-fee situation tends to be more difficult for the therapist because the need originates from the person requesting it, who is not the patient. It is true that the original contract did not require an economic tilt in the patient's direction. All patients pay the same, with the fee being set by the therapist's need from the start. As a result, there is less likelihood of initial patient gratification based on the fee. Also, it is true that the therapist can explain in advance that fee increases may occur if the therapist's expenses rise to the point where greater income is needed. Nonetheless, when this happens the burden of proof will be on the therapist, which can lead to defensive and inappropriate detailing of the problem or postponement to avoid anticipated patient displeasure.

Resistance may be encountered in expressions that the fee is already substantial enough, that the patient does not accept the therapist's need, or in patient protestations of an inability to pay any more. Disillusionment may appear, with the therapist perceived as a greedy person taking advantage of the patient's dependency. Since the raise is based on reality, namely, an increase in the therapist's living costs, and equity, that the therapeutic contract makes the patient the therapist's source of income as needed, it is crucial that these ego and superego factors be carefully considered before the institution of a raise. Assuming the raise is appropriate in respect to the factors mentioned, then the therapist should introduce it and be willing to work with the patient's reactions.

When a sliding scale is used, the patient's finances are basically the stimulus for a raise. The therapist needs to monitor these because the aim is to have the patient paying a fee in accord with income level, but it is understandable that the patient may not be eager to let the therapist know of his improved financial status. Once the therapist does know, then the patient should have the opportunity to discuss both the size and timing of the fee increase. A similar opportunity should be made available to the patient in a fixed-fee situation, although the stimulus is the therapist's need. Experience suggests that in the inflationary economy that has existed, a fee increase of $10 every 2 years would be sufficient and not experienced as excessive in fixed-fee situations; the fee increases can be initiated with new patients first and then passed on to existing patients with at least a few months' notice.

In making requests for fee increases, it is always necessary to keep in mind what this will mean to the patient in terms of both dollar cost and emotional reaction. The number of times per week the patient comes and how long each patient is likely to be in therapy certainly have to be considered. The aim of increasing the fee is not to cause anyone to have to leave therapy, and if that could be the result, then in specific instances the therapist needs to leave the financial arrangements as they are. Within the totality of any practice, the number of patients who cannot continue if the fee is increased tends to be small. An increase of $10 per week, for example, with a once-a-week patient for 45 weeks is $450 per year, which most people would view as reasonable. Also, people who remain in therapy generally improve their financial situations, so therapists are more likely to experience postponements than total inability to have a fee increase with any long-term patient. This is true whether the fee policy is sliding-scale or fixed.

The preceding remarks are made in the context of an economy that has expanded and been inflationary. Rising medical costs, of which psychotherapy is a part, are resulting in a desire to reduce expenditures. If coupled with a recession, this could result in decreasing revenue for therapists either because a sufficient number of therapists compete by lowering fees or because a sufficient number of potential patients stay away from mental health care even though they need it. It is important to remember that psychotherapy functions in a market economy and can be subject to price fluctuation. Over the past 20 years these have gone primarily in one direction, up, but that does not have to be the case. Thus, realistic pricing of services needs to be kept in mind.

However, the equating of fees with personal power and status can obscure the economics of the profession, so that therapists view fee increases as primarily affirmations of self-esteem and societal respect. The result tends to be that therapists either act as though they were not subject to monetary concerns and use inefficient and inconsistent fee policies, or they are insecure and become preoccupied with marketing in order to stock up on patients a potpourri of fees and without much regard for quality service. Such a lack of a realistic appraisal of the marketplace coupled with an unwillingness to educate consumers could indeed be problematic.

Service Packages

Therapists provide a package of services to patients with a common thread, namely, availability. Therapists make themselves available to patients, generally at set times, but the services have to go beyond that, and there have to be ways to compensate therapists when patients request availability but fail to use it.

The size of the package and how costs for components are to be assessed is up to the therapist and should be indicated in the original contract. One possibility is to charge a fee for time spent with the patient in a scheduled session, with additional fees for additional services such as phone calls and filling out insurance forms. However, most therapists tend to include these as part of the basic package unless they take an excessive amount of time, with the judgment of what is excessive left to the therapist. The specifics of all such contingencies are rarely known in advance, but a general statement could be made that if any such events arose, they would be discussed at that time to determine their cost to the patient.

Most therapists attempt to schedule patient sessions within a given time period for specific therapeutic work. Sessions a patient misses without advance cancellation are routinely charged to the patient, but canceled sessions, meaning that a reason for not attending is given, tend to be handled differently. Some therapists charge for all scheduled sessions regardless of the patient's reasons for missing any of them. Thus, a classical psychoanalytic position would be that if an analysis is contracted for, then the patient is expected to pay for whatever number of sessions the analyst made available. Other therapists charge for all scheduled sessions but will offer make-up sessions at no charge to take care of any reasonable cancellations. A reasonable cancellation is the patient having to work unexpectedly at the time of the usual session or some event over which the patient has little or no control. Unreasonable cancellations are those over which the patient does have control, such as "I forgot," or "I just didn't feel like coming."

From an analytic point of view, all missed sessions are resistances, since they limit or interfere with the progress of therapy. Thus, the charge is not based on determining the existence or degree of resistance but on the concept that the therapist and patient have contracted to use a certain amount of time, and the therapist is to be paid for that time even if the patient chooses to use it by avoiding the therapist. Make-up sessions provide flexibility for reality factors that can result in an interference, but they are to be used with discretion to avoid collaborating with possible acting out by patients. Therapists try to create a consistent schedule for themselves and their patients as both a practical and therapeutic tool because structure is useful and a guarantee of the therapist's reliability and durability. If therapists have to miss sessions or change times, then they would be expected to provide alternatives.

Some therapists allow cancellations without charge if they are given sufficient notice, which is often construed as 24 hours. However, this is both impractical, for psychotherapists fill hours in advance and do not have easy substitutes, and misses the point of the importance of the session. Also, some therapists differentiate between cancellations and vacations, as do many patients. Patients are encouraged to have their vacations coincide with their therapists', but that is not always possible. Vacations can also be used as resistances by patients so that considerable time is taken away from the therapy. Make-up sessions can be used to alleviate this, though discretion has to be used because if they get excessive, continuity is limited, and a therapist may end up putting in time at personally inconvenient hours that does not make for the best of sessions.

The Availability Model

From a psychotherapeutic and an economic point of view, the therapist wants to make the best use of the time he has available. This is a reasonable position that should be made explicit to patients and certainly can be understood. The arrangements regarding payment are in accord with this position, but they are not universal and will be constructed in different ways, but always with an underlying rationale that they are to be helpful to both therapists and patients.

Granting the availability of more than one model, a model suggested here is the availability package. Thus, with a given year of 52 weeks, the therapist could guarantee availability for 46 of them, eliminating therapist's vacations or conference time and holidays when by mutual agreement both therapist and patient would not meet. During the available time, the therapist would provide therapy sessions on, for example, a once-a-week basis as well as additional services, such as phone calls, itemized bills, completed insurance forms, unless they become excessive, for a set fee per session. The length and the time of each session would be the same each week unless changed by mutual agreement. Any likely fee increase would be discussed in advance, as would arrangements for when payments are to be made. All scheduled sessions would be charged to the patient. If the therapist had to cancel any scheduled sessions, he would offer the patient an alternative. If the patient canceled, then both therapist and patient would work out make-up times. If the patient was uncooperative in this, meaning that he just couldn't seem to agree to a time, then the patient would have to pay the fee without the session being made up. Phone sessions would also be used from time to time to ameliorate this problem. Missed, as opposed to canceled, sessions would be paid for by the patient. Of course, whatever alternatives occurred in the usual schedule would be discussed as to their meaning for the therapy process.

It is useful to discuss these arrangements in advance, but the details may seem overwhelming to both patient and therapist, so some of the procedures could get conveyed over time, although if possible prior to the event that will require the information. If written contracts indeed become more popular, then it will be easier to spell out all the possibilities as well as to have an acknowledged reference point. For example, Callahan (1989) includes such items as the patient paying for services although these may be mandated by a third party, such as subpoenaed testimony in a contested custody case, late fees for overdue accounts, and expenses paid to collect overdue balances.

Some of these are features that most therapists would not bother about, such as late fees, and there are still other things that occur, as fees charged by a bank to the therapist if a patient's check is returned. All contingencies probably will not be anticipated, even by the most obsessive therapist, and even in attempting to anticipate and cover every eventuality, the manner of presentation is very important. Indicating what will occur if a person does not do what he said he would do implies that at least one of the therapist's patients has indeed failed to keep the agreement, and any patient may resent the implication. Therapy is, after all, a very personal matter. Thus, a general statement about contingencies, whether written or verbal, appears to be the most appropriate option, with details clarified if the event does occur.

For example, most patients do not give therapists bad checks, whereas most patients will change a session over time, and many patients will alter their payment schedules even though they will pay with relative consistency. Thus, creating a contract that covers basic issues and still permits flexibility is important because it utilizes the fee arrangements as therapeutic tools. Getting too businesslike can destroy that possibility. A bank, for example, does not usually care why a customer pays her mortgage before or after a certain date but just assesses an extra fee if the payment is late. Therapists do care about the why of the timing of payments and can be flexible without running at a loss. Fee policies are put in place to develop structure, to indicate the professional nature of the relationship, and to provide therapists with reasonable ways to make a living. They do not exist to maximize profits or punish patients for their resistances or even particularly to motivate, although sometimes they have that effect. They do meet personal needs, and that will be reflected in how much the therapist charges as well as in his preferences for payment patterns and in the degree theoretical conceptions are played out in fee arrangements, as well as the flexibility–rigidity balance that is comfortable for the therapist.

ETHICAL CONCERNS

In addition to, or along with, getting into trouble in the therapeutic process because of fee policies, there are possible legal and ethical complications. Pope (1988) has provided a useful summary of potential trouble spots, namely, patients' informed consent, insurance billing, carrying patients, legal redress, therapy quality, record keeping, bartering, and contingency fees.

Informed Consent

Therapists should be as clear as possible in advance about their fee policies and try to insure that these are understood and agreed to by their patients. Along this line of reasoning Pope (1988) indicates the amount of the fee, length of the session, time of payment, charges for other services, policies about cancellations and missed sessions, and procedures if the patient cannot or does not pay what is owed. Failure to be clear about these issues can indeed result in legitimate complaints by patients that make after-the-fact enforcement impossible as well as resulting in complaints being filed with ethics committees. So, even if one does not like to have much of a discourse about fees, some money talk is essential.

Insurance

Kovacs (1987) has provided a helpful summary of the pitfalls in regard to insurance billing, which if construed as fraud can also lead to criminal penalties. Some of these ought to be obvious, such as billing for services not rendered by the person signing the bill, creating false data and/or diagnoses, in essence cheating the insurance carrier. One that is more problematic is billing for missed or canceled sessions. The therapist needs to find out in advance if the insurance carrier will pay for these, and Kovacs (1987) indicates they usually will not. Once this is established, the therapist then needs to indicate to the patient that if the policy is that canceled and missed sessions are to be paid for, they will be billed to and paid directly by the patient. Make-up sessions can eliminate much of this issue because those can be billed to the insurance company, but if and when these are not used, then the patient has the full payment responsibility.

Essentially if the therapist understands the insurance carrier's rules and bills accordingly, then there should be no risk. It is by intentionally violating these, such as by billing the insurance company for one amount and allowing the patient to pay only the percentage reimbursed, that gets therapists into trouble. If, for example, a therapist were to say, "But I 'forgive' the amount not reimbursed," the admission will not hold up in court, in addition to all the other therapeutic problems it could create.

Unpaid Bills

Many therapists have carried patients when the patients' circumstances made it difficult or impossible for them to pay regularly. Most reports indicate this works out, meaning that the therapist eventually gets paid in full (Hofling & Rosenbaum, 1986; Welt & Herron, 1990). However, it is possible that a malpractice suit could be brought based on the idea that the therapist was taking advantage of the patient and that termination, transfer, or free service are more appropriate alternatives (Pope, 1988). Thus, financially carrying patients needs even more scrutiny than usual, although the therapist in such a situation already knows there is the possibility of just not getting paid.

It appears that reasonable bills can get paid even by using external agencies, but a large unpaid bill allowed by the therapist will not fare so well in the legal or ethical system. Furthermore, any type of external enforcement attempts may be met by malpractice accusations about the services. Pope (1988) states "consider carefully the ways in which attempts to collect fees via third parties affect not only aspects of therapy such as privacy, confidentiality, and privilege but also the psychological welfare of the client" (p. 28).

If therapy is provided for little or no money, then the quality needs to meet the standard of full-fee-paying patients. Contingency fees and bartering services are not considered acceptable. The basic principle is, take care of fee issues promptly and carefully, and keep detailed records for 3 years, a summary for 15, just in case.

As Pope (1988) notes, "fraudulent billing" has risen in popularity to trail only "sexual intimacies with client" as a cause of license revocation. Whereas it is probable that many of the billing practices involved were attempts by therapists to aid their patients in some way, they were misguided attempts and were deemed inexcusable. The ultimate benefit for therapists is fair, clear, legal, and ethical fee practices. Every therapist has the responsibility to know and carry out such policies.

PART IV

INTEGRATION

I n the final section we tie together patients' concerns about using psychotherapy, most of which are related in some way to cost. These include sufficient willingness to adopt the patient role, to resolve fee ambivalence to the point of agreeing on monetary arrangements, to work with fee resistance, to understand the purpose of fees, and to be well aware of the possibilities and limitations of psychotherapy.

Then we summarize the monetary issues for psychotherapists. A major problem has been developing an integrated image and role as a paid helper. The concept of a helping relationship has a long history of conflict with a monetary one: the holding environment versus the business environment. This is a simplistic and false dichotomy, but the complexity and unusual aspects of the therapeutic situation make the conflict understandable, as does the overdetermination of money. With the current economic climate, the cost of psychotherapy has become a public issue and has markedly increased the visibility of the economic aspect. Managed mental health care has gained prominence as a response to the cost issue and in turn raised questions about the degree of emphasis on cost as opposed to quality. Since guilt about fees of any size has always existed, managed care feeds on that as well as on having the support of professionals opposed to long-term psychotherapy and attracts therapists who need patents as well as those who want to move into the managing part of mental health services. Actually, outpatient mental health services are not the culprits in cost increases, yet they have been rather indiscriminately targeted so that the manner of funding service is of increasing concern to all practitioners. Although struggles within the field about who should get what and how are not pleasant, they have made therapists' roles as paid providers more obvious.

Shifting to the future, it is vital that psychotherapists be involved at the policy level of funding, both to insure quality of care and to provide for the needs of those who are economically disadvantaged. The role of the fee is shifting, with managed care turning some therapists into employees and taking the fee out of visibility, whereas in contrast, other therapists will insist on independence and make the transactional nature of psychotherapy ever more visible. Furthermore, in order to insure treatment quality, therapists will have to be both convinced and convincing about the dollar value of their services.

Chapter 10

THERAPEUTIC
FEE ARRANGEMENTS

W e have traced the evolution of the fee in psychoanalysis and psychotherapy from known inception to the present day. We started with the importance and yet paradoxical nature of money matters in the process of therapy, traced that to the many meanings of money in our society, and then elaborated the philosophy of service for a fee that underlies the current practice of all psychotherapies. With that as a context, we considered both patients' and therapists' attitudes about fees. As a result, we concluded that although money issues are less of a taboo topic now than they had been for many, many years, they are still a major source of discomfort for both therapists and patients. This discomfort can too often become a major contributor to ineffective therapy. In turn, there is a pressing need for developing fee arrangements that are indeed therapeutic. To do this we will first summarize the problems from the patients' points of view, then the therapists', and conclude with suggestions for the future designed to improve the practice of the psychotherapies for all concerned.

PATIENTS' CONCERNS

When psychotherapy is the medium, many people with problems that would be helped by it nonetheless avoid it. Psychotherapy for many people will always be for others, ranging from "crazies" to the more moderate, "those who need that sort of thing." Nonetheless, the possible consumers of therapy still outnumber the potential suppliers, so there was, is, and probably always will be a need for psychotherapeutic services.

However, many of the service users come with reluctance and underutilize the services in respect to what is needed for effective dosage. Some of this results from ambivalence about being a patient or client, some from poor service, and some from the necessity to pay the fee. In addition, all of the reasons have an economic interconnection, regardless of the type of society, because services are funded, directly or indirectly, in all forms of government.

So, for example, if people are educated to make more extensive use of psychotherapeutic services, and there is good reason to consider this a valuable effort for all societies, this usage has an economic cost. Even if one disguises the services with more palatable names such as counseling, pastoral guidance, etc., and does the same for the providers, the tab still has to be paid. Furthermore, the increase in usage increases the need for providers, who in turn are now "in business," and businesses are everywhere, including professions that are not so keen on the label, such as organized religion and, of course, psychotherapy.

For example, Kovacs (1989) presents an impassioned plea for the survival of professional psychology depending on the movement of providers out of the mental health profession and into being "consultants on life-span developmental challenges." His ostensible motivation for this change appears to be both economic and ideological, with more attention on his part to the latter. Although the same type of patient problems will still be worked with if patients so desire, the names will be changed to such more palatable alternatives as "unhappiness." Whereas Kovacs is not looking to bill himself as a mental health provider, nor to get third-party payment, he does note that insurance reimbursement is getting scarce and that the psychotherapy profession is feeling an economic pinch that probably will get worse. At the same time, he does want to get paid for his services as "an expert on life-span human development and on the family life cycle." He is, in effect, attempting to provide himself, and those who use his services, with an alternative that will be more likely to attract paying consumers than by using terms such as "patient" and "psychotherapist." We are not suggesting his motives are primarily economic, especially since he is giving up the possibility of at least some insurance reimbursement. However, he is trying to tap into a consumer group that does not like the patient designation and so would not be available if the usual categories of service were used. The approach is a marketing tool that contains economic motivation.

For a person to be a productive consumer of psychotherapeutic services, it is necessary that she feel a sufficient degree of comfort using such services. People need a way to look at their role in the therapy situation that will enable them to get past whatever apparent philosophical, religious, or psychodynamic reasons they have for disliking the role to the point that they cannot allow it for themselves. Psychotherapists need to be aware of this probable ambivalence on the part of many potential and actual patients. This awareness contains the potential for discussion and for sufficient amelioration of what can be a very basic and devastating resistance. It is not necessary to eliminate such feelings completely, and in fact this may not be either necessary or desirable. It is necessary for the patient to be comfortable enough, however, to do the work that is indeed required.

How any therapist will assure this comfort zone is certainly a matter of customizing the fit between patient and therapist. The therapist is the diagnostic expert, and that means describing to the patient what would be the probable best course. The patient is entitled to questions, skepticism, other opinions, etc., but within limits because if there is too much ambivalence, the treatment cannot proceed. Therapists will try to deal with perceived distortions by patients, but there is a degree of commitment that must be made, that degree varying in each patient–therapist dyad but generally understandable to the therapist if the patient's ambivalence is indeed appreciated.

As Canter (1991) points out, that degree does not have to be the same as what the therapist has in mind, because patients can still realize something from therapy that is less than ideal. However, regardless of length or intensity of the therapy, the starting point is that the patient is enough of a patient for therapy to take place. It is part of the work of all therapists to try to implement that much motivation. Patients expect help with overcoming resistance both to being in therapy and to working while there. If therapists give up too quickly or easily, then potential patients are lost.

Part of the motivational block is economic. This operates in two ways. One is that it is inherent to the patient role, especially for those who are feeling negative about that role to start with, that the prospect of paying enhances patient negativity. However, most patients who spend sufficient time in therapy to benefit from it have satisfactorily fit to the role yet still have a variety of ambivalent feelings about the fee. Patients generally expect to pay a fee, but they do have their own views about both what they would like to pay and what they are willing to pay. These views are not automatically in accord with therapist expectations, but therapists have many options to come to terms with patient–therapist needs and expectations.

As Sitkowski and Herron (1991) reported, it is not necessary for patients and therapists to have the same attitudes about money in order for patients to begin therapy, to remain in it, or to make progress. It is necessary that they agree on the monetary arrangements, however, and this can be a powerful stumbling block. People can take the view that relatively cheap psychotherapy is inferior, yet "better therapy" is too expensive, so either way, they do not enter therapy, or they do not remain in it long enough for the process to be effective.

Even when this barrier is removed, at any time during therapy patients can and will use the fee as a source of resistance. Therapists should expect this, try not to be rattled by it, develop an understanding of it, and try to work out a solution. Distinctions have to be made between a real inability to pay and fee resistance, with therapists prepared to cope with both possibilities. It is probable that most patients remain ambivalent about fees throughout psychotherapy but resolve the issues sufficiently so that payment is not an ongoing problem. Therapists can facilitate this resolution by continually being open to any discussions of money matters.

The positive resolution is tied to perceived effectiveness. Patients use therapy as long as they feel it is worth it. Although criticism has been directed against possible overutilization, underutilization is the norm and thus a serious mental health concern. This certainly suggests skepticism by consumers regarding the value of psychotherapy, and the lack of agreement about the specifics of effective treatment that prevails in the field does not help. It is to be expected that patients will be confused and uncertain about the best means for alleviating their distress as well as how much they should pay. Therapists have to be patient with this uncertainty and be willing to explain and reexplain the workings of psychotherapy, including its possible limitations. The best sales pitch is accurate representation of what will take place, and if that is acceptable to patients, then demonstrated competence ought to produce satisfied customers who will serve as the best advertisement for subsequent consumers.

Thus, when patients' attitudes about fees are summarized, ambivalence will be the major pattern. This may pertain to the role of a patient, particularly the demonstration of vulnerability, to uncertainty about the effectiveness of the psychotherapies, and of course to the payment of fees for services that engender such mixed emotional reactions. Patients can make effective use of "free" service, and they are more comfortable with it than therapists. As a result, since therapists want to get paid, the selling of psychotherapy services is their concern. This is most effectively carried out by recognizing and working with the patients' ambivalence. Certainly a significant part of the value of the fee is structural and motivational for the patient, but its primary purpose is to enable psychotherapists to make a living. This reasonable expectation needs to be shared with, not hidden from, all patients.

THERAPISTS' CONCERNS

Therapists struggle with the development of an integrated image, namely, the paid helper. They like the look and sound and feel of the helping part but worry that due notice of the paid part will somehow destroy their perceived helpfulness. This has led to considerable guilt, soul searching, disavowal of monetary interest, and motivational disguise. Therapists have been reluctant to discuss money matters with patients, particularly fees, and therapists and patients have suffered because of the resulting secrecy.

It is a very understandable conflict. Most psychotherapists did not go into the profession primarily for monetary reasons, have not gotten rich (nor will they), and in fact are living in more difficult economic times. Ten years ago the assurance of earning a reasonable middle- to upper-middle-class living via private practice was quite reliable. Now it is more of a struggle with troubled times still ahead. The number of psychotherapists has increased, but this has been primarily in disciplines that expect lower fees, such as social work, as contrasted with psychiatry. Also, the number of women entering the profession is moving it in the direction of a female majority, and as *Psychotherapy Finances* (1991b) reports, women charge lower fees. So, although fees have continued to increase, being higher now than 2 years ago, the pressure of managed health care is beginning to be felt.

Sitkowski and Herron (1991) found that relative to both their patients and the general population, psychotherapists were more concerned about financial security. In the current economic climate, it is increasingly difficult for therapists to hide or disguise their economic interest. Money matters are coming more into the open, and that aspect of the current environment is really quite a positive factor for the psychotherapy profession.

At the same time, psychotherapists are still uncomfortable about having an explicit economic motivation and requiring reasonable return for their work. The overdetermined meanings of money certainly stimulate discomfort, and it is going to take more time and effort before the conflict is appropriately mitigated. Furthermore, as in all helping professions, there will be a need to provide services for people of all income levels. The helping motive has to be primary, with creativity required to provide services to as many as possible who need it yet still derive a comfortable return for the expended effort. Social, political, and economic activism are going to be required with still another shift in the image of psycho-therapists away from a decorous anonymity. This type of shift indeed has appeared from time to time, as, for example, when insurance coverage was extended to psychologists as a result of their lobbying efforts, so it is a role that can be well played.

Marketing already has become a much-discussed and written-about area of concern, but it has focused primarily on how to attract clients. Now the move will have to be toward the direct selling of the service once the client has shown interest. This is hardly a detached role, and it calls for personal investment, honesty, and integrity so the possibilities and limitations of service are as definitely articulated as possible. Inherent in that is the frank and open discussion of fees.

Psychotherapists have in the past experienced private practice as relatively secure despite the probability of cash flow problems. Many therapists had other, mainstay jobs to fall back on if necessary. With time, private practice became more attractive as a full-time occupation. It became clear that one could make a relatively good living at it, and although there was a fee hierarchy depending on discipline, that same structure existed in institutions as well. Private practice was more lucrative, gave practitioners considerable independence and freedom to operate in ways that expressed personal beliefs and preferences, and, particularly with the increased insurance coverage that became available, was relatively secure. More and more mental health professionals entered the field, and because of the need, there seemed to be plenty of room.

Now the field is struggling with unwanted and unexpected changes for the practitioners. Two major issues are beliefs that psychotherapy is too costly and demands for specifics of accountability that are often difficult to produce. The cost issue comes from employers via insurers and is part of the view of the rapidly increasing national health cost. Psychotherapeutic services are wrapped up in this in a disproportionate manner and have become a major target for cost containment. Since they have often been a "capped" service, this should not be a surprising development. But before the caps gave sufficient room for quality work. Now the emphasis is on "quick and cheap," and of course this is disillusioning to psychotherapists. Coupled with this are demands for specific accountability that are difficult to conceptualize, no less satisfy, considering the nature of psychotherapy. The result has been the increased use of managed health care that threatens most of the features of private practice that had attracted professionals in the past, namely, independence, freedom, and enhanced income.

The threat of reduced practices appears to be playing on the insecurity of practitioners so that a certain number are joining managed health care networks. How many have done so is still unknown, though *Psychotherapy Finances* (1991b) reports in its survey of approximately 1,700 practitioners that about 50% had signed reduced-fee contracts. There were no psychiatrists in the survey, and about half the sample were psychologists. These data were not broken down by profession; however, it can be speculated that professionals with lower fees or lower patient loads would be most likely to join such networks. They have the least to lose and the greatest chance of being selected for referrals because they are the least costly. This is a very disturbing possibility when referrals are not based on competence or tied to quality of service. Furthermore, it is a striking development in light of the comments elicited by *Psychotherapy Finances* in regard to the effects of managed care. These included reductions in number of patients and income, more claims disallowed, and different and briefer courses of therapy. From the point of view of care managers, the approach is successful, but it is hard to see how it benefits the caretakers.

Despite this, the apparent threat has been sufficient to cause many practitioners to become involved and essentially to hand over significant control to less knowledgeable others. Carville (1991) provides a detailed account of the problems encountered when practitioners do this, but the inevitability of some form of managed care is also noted. Although the majority of people in private practice do not like it, the trend in the field is to induce professionals to embrace managed care as a positive event for their practices.

Thus, Broskowski (1991) describes the opportunities for psychologists in managed care, indicating that such care has potential benefits for current practitioners. He concludes with "be prepared, however, to participate in these, or better, managed care solutions, and not simply argue for more of the same private, uncontrolled, and often guild-oriented fee-for-service systems of the part" (p. 13).

Richardson and Austad (1991) present a rather balanced description of life in the HMO, yet they too are firm about the inevitability of managed mental health care. A similar theme is echoed by Haas and Cummings (1991). Reservations about specifics are noted, and the point is made that this type of practice may not suit all psychotherapists, but very little is suggested as to what one can do if unsuitability indeed prevails. Whether said gently or with intensity, the message is, cut a deal or suffer. In addition, it is clear that the most frequent suggestion is to practice short-term therapy. Although proponents of managed care will argue for a variety of quality controls, they have no interest in long-term therapy, particularly if it is continuous.

Of course, this represents a major disservice to a very large theoretical orientation, psychoanalysis, as well as to all long-term providers and patients who would want or need such services. Apparently many providers are willing enough to go along with ignoring the complexity of mental health problems. Unfortunately, those who know better have been relatively content to ignore the short-term insistence of managed care and the narrowing of options or dismiss it with anger as though it could never have personal relevance. Now it is becoming clear that such an approach can affect the livelihood of all practitioners, including those believed to be untouchable. It is a rare practitioner in the current market who does not have some of her patients on insurance, and many practitioners have most of their patients using insurance reimbursement. Up to now, sufficient options remained open so that a large group of patients could still choose plans with considerable provider choice. However, these options tend to cost the consumers more directly, and employers tend to discourage them. The options are being decreased, and providers have felt it in terms of the decrease in new patients. Thus, the pressure is on providers to accept managed health care or have fewer patients and, in turn, less income. Of course, managed care could give them less income anyway, but it suggests that the patient supply will be sufficient to offset any loss—and even possibly provide a gain. At the very least, the hope is for a stable case load. However, also at the very least, per-hour earnings could decrease, hardly an incentive. One could have to work more either to make less or to break even.

With the industrialization of mental health services, some new possibilities appear that provide mental health professionals with ways out of the actual practice of psychotherapy. A major criticism of managed care is that it sacrifices quality for cost containment. Major players in creating the sacrifice are the decision makers, who determine how much treatment is needed, as well as what type for what disorder. These decision makers have often been criticized for their lack of experience, training, and/or knowledge. Thus, job opportunities are open in the system for better-trained people who would not be open to such criticism.

Broskowski (1991) has a number of alternatives to clinical practice, such as organizing and managing case-management services, serving as consultants or managers within the industry, and conducting research into clinical and financial accountability. These are roles related to clinical practice and certainly could be more effective if performed by experienced practitioners with additional capabilities. As such, they have an appeal to many who are either tired of the routine and/or the struggle of maintaining an independent practice. Managed care has created job opportunities for therapists to function as part of the management, and the appeal of "getting a piece of the action" in that way seems to be increasing.

As far as job opportunities go, it has also created opportunities for practice. The practice, however, must be short-term, and the most-favored orientation is behavioral (Broskowski, 1991). DeLeon, VandenBos, and Bulatao (1991) describe the origins of managed health care. In its evolution, a major development was the passage of the Health Maintenance Organization Act of 1973, which provided funding and developed standards for HMOs. Unfortunately, as Richardson and Austad (1991) point out, what is mandated as minimal coverage becomes the maximum benefit in many plans. An example is the frequent limit of 20 outpatient visits per member each year, which is below the effective dosage rate (Howard et al., 1986) yet above the average rate of therapy attendance. Phillips (1988) argues that the average rate of attendance is what therapists ought to accommodate to, and such a view is in accord with an increasing emphasis that others—the on-line consumer, corporate America, the national government—ought to write the prescription and therapists ought to learn how to fill it. We disagree with this approach, but many practitioners and policy makers in our field are using it. At the same time, it is true that many people in the field are just beginning to become aware of the implications of managed care. Also, a number of people who now have, or always had, reservations are realizing that different ways of financing mental health services need to be developed and that providers from all disciplines need to be noticeably involved in policy formation (Herron, in press).

THE FUTURE

The first thing that psychotherapists will have to face is that psychotherapy is indeed a business. Freud recognized this immediately, but he had a rather humane way of looking at the situation. The fee was considered beneficial to the patient, a sacrifice for motivational purposes, yet the sacrifice needed to provide a living for the therapist. Over the years it has become apparent that the primary reason for the fee involves the needs of psychotherapists. This is understandable and not an issue to be defensive or devious about, nor does it take away from the fee as a valuable force for the therapy. It is indeed a defining boundary, a motivational force, and multidetermined. A major difference, however, between the future and both past and present will be the awareness of all parties concerned that monetary transactions and economic forces are an integral part of the psychotherapeutic relationship.

This is put rather bluntly in the following statement by Terris, in which one could substitute the word "psychotherapist" for "physician."

> Physicians paid by fee-for-service are small businessmen, like lawyers, investment counselors, dry cleaners, and auto mechanics, who also sell services, and like small manufacturers, farmers, and retail merchants, who sell products. In common with other businessmen, physicians are in the business of making profits, and their profits depend on the prices they receive for their services and how many services they sell. (1990, p. 3)

Therapists will be able to accept the fact that they are in business by integrating their helping skills and motivations with their economic needs. Psychotherapists can actually be more proficient at what they do because they get paid than if they provided free or low-cost services. They retain the option for the latter if and when it is needed, and it is understood both that the helping professions have special ethical and moral obligations to those they serve and that the economic status of those to be helped has a significant part in determining the fee to be charged. The key point, however, is the willingness of psychotherapists, given the concept of the psychotherapeutic relationship, to resolve their own conflicts about giving and getting. The resolution means therapists will be open with their patients about indicating what therapists will do for patients and what they expect patients to do for them—in particular, pay them for services rendered. After all, from its formal inception with Freud, psychotherapy was a job. Making that point visible and explicit between therapist and patient will only help matters by reducing an unnecessary and potentially harmful role distortion.

A second issue that will have to be faced is that the role of the fee will change if the trend toward managed mental health care continues, as is so frequently predicted. In this regard, a number of issues have to be considered. The first is that mental health benefits historically have had limits based on the belief of potentially runaway costs because of an associated belief that mental disorders are both hard to define and hard or impossible to cure. These limits have been on the increase, based on the assumption that treatment is both too costly and too lengthy with the associated idea that mental disorders are curable quickly and cheaply except in the case of the chronically mentally ill, who are left to fend for themselves along with the poor. The expectation is that these groups are the burden of government, which, in limited ways, accepts the burden. Underlying all the limitations, past and current, is probably the assumption that with the exception of organic mental disorders the rest of the problems could by avoided if the people with them just had more moral fiber.

In essence, it is a case of blaming the victim, with the idea being to provide some assistance but not too much, because this mental illness stuff is something people do not have to get. Obviously more knowledgeable people have held out different views, and to some degree, these prevail. That is, mental disorders are within the realm of illness and are thus considered a health problem. However, there is an increased emphasis on finding biological causes, and even without discovering them, treating them primarily by medication. In addition, treatment of substance abuse disorders, which account for much of the increase in mental health costs, generally aims at control. The idea is that the patient has a disease—alcoholism, drug addiction, or food addiction—that cannot be cured in the sense that such a person could ever be free to use the substance as she saw fit but must always be controlled in a specific way. Thus, alcoholics cannot drink, drug addicts cannot take drugs, and overeaters must limit their food intake. Once this discipline is established, then periodic support can be used for maintenance. Hence, the person is cured in a limited sense. Not much credence, or money, is given to personality exploration as a causative or useful preventative factor.

A similar thrust is seen in regard to serious mental disorders, such as the psychoses, which are increasingly being depicted as genetic disorders without much convincing evidence and are treated by medication and frequent hospitalizations accompanied by attempts to mainstream such patients. These approaches have not been very successful, yet they remain popular. They have an appealing surface logic, and they appear less costly than more lengthy alternatives.

The problem is not so much that the current approach is terrible or even totally ineffective but that it is a narrow focus on a broad, complex problem. For example, much of the cost of mental health services results from inpatient treatment, particularly for substance abuse. Lowman (1991) indicates that the typical mental health benefits design is to pay more for inpatient care, which tends to make it more attractive to the insured and therefore increases its usage. The design appears to be based on the ideas that inpatient care is superior to outpatient and that longer hospitalization is better than brief hospitalization. Furthermore, cost containment tends to be directed across the board, rather than at high-cost cases, which in fact are few but are the main users of the benefits.

Lowman notes that the literature does not support the typical design, and he concludes: "Were form to follow function in benefit design, if the goal is clinically effective, cost-contained treatment, then inpatient care would be limited and outpatient care would be made much more accessible. . ." (1991, p. 43).

Thus, benefit redesign is needed and likely to occur. National mental health coverage is an increasing possibility. The fact that a few people count for a relatively disproportionate amount of cost supports the contention that opening up mental health benefits to everybody will not be a relatively costly enterprise provided the emphasis is on outpatient care.

Furthermore, outpatient benefits can be liberalized. Lowman (1991) offers one way to do this in which the first 10 visits are paid 100% by the third party, the next 10 at 75%, the next 10 at 50%, and the next 10 at 25%, with visits after 40 getting no reimbursement. This plan emphasizes short-term care as though it had been proven superior, and it does not seem that concerned with specific effective dosages, but it is in a direction we see as appropriate. Instead of focusing on length of treatment, we would leave that as open as possible but tie the amount of patient copayment to her income, with the wealthier patient paying more and the poorer patient having a greater percentage paid by the insurance company. Since people tend to have an average length of stay in treatment of 4 to 6 visits (Richardson & Austad, 1991), there seems little cost risk in uncapping treatment length. Also, even if therapists wanted to keep patients in therapy for lengthy periods of time, patients do not stay. Thus, the assertion that psychotherapy as it has been practiced takes too long appears false.

Also, in terms of relative incomes, psychotherapists are not particularly wealthy. In turn this indicates, as do fee surveys, that psychotherapy per-session costs are not excessive. The culprit in rising mental health costs is inpatient care, which in turn can be traced to the design of mental health reimbursement plans that typically encourage such care and for longer, rather than shorter, time periods.

Wiggins (1991) indicates that substance abuse costs have been con-suming about 40% to 45% of mental health benefits, and in conjunction with this, the greatest increases in costs have been 28-day admissions to alcoholism and substance abuse hospital units as well as adolescent hos-pitalization in private facilities. These are expensive, questionable solutions that are of limited long-term therapeutic value.

Lowman (1991) concludes that a number of cost-containment measures exist, without sufficient research to be definitive about their effects. How-ever, he makes the point that inpatient services are the problem and that outpatient services are an inappropriate target for cost reduction.

Although the average patient uses a very limited number of psycho-therapeutic sessions, this fact has been translated into the idea that therefore it must be all that is generally needed. Even many critics of managed health care tend to support the concept of brief therapy, thus threatening psychoanalytic methods in particular. Psychoanalysts will have to address this, and there are signs that at least some recognition of the problem is taking place.

For example, Maltin (1991) states:

> As psychoanalysts, many of us are already experiencing our practices shrink in the face of our patients' reduced incomes and insurance com-panies diminished reimbursements. This raises some serious questions about the long-term effect of the recession on private practice, particularly psychoanalytic work. . . . The challenges are there. Perhaps psychoan-alysts will have to reach out more to the community to demonstrate that our skills are readily adaptable to meeting any pressing emotional needs. (pp. 1–2)

That is a gentle understatement, considering the current economic climate and its interface with employers' views of the need for wholesale cost containment. There is not a great deal of sympathy for psychoanalytic work, primarily because of its length and consequent potential cost. Psy-chiatrists are increasingly turning to medication as the treatment of choice, and practitioners from other mental health disciplines, such as psychologists, are making a strong pitch for prescription privileges. In addition, there is a movement toward subspecialization, as in substance abuse, with the idea that such an approach can be a profitable niche. There has also been a rather widespread embrace of short-term therapies. Psychoanalysts will have to struggle to sell their wares to the public, and they are just beginning to take that work seriously.

In truth, there is not much about managed care we like. At the same time, we are sympathetic to the idea that employers have limited responsibilities to their employees. In that respect there are going to be limits on mental health coverage, and therapists and patients will have to work with these limits. For some, this will mean briefer therapy, probably at lower fees. For others, this will mean patients themselves will be paying for therapies that extend beyond an arbitrary limit, such as more than 20 sessions. Certainly the idea that therapists or patients can depend on lengthy insurance coverage is dubious. At the same time, more attention will probably be paid to the excessive cost of inpatient services, and this should benefit outpatient coverage, particularly if attention is paid to medical cost offsets that are attributable to the use of psychotherapy.

The treatment of the poor and the chronically mentally ill is going to require some form of national mental health insurance. In advocating that we are aware that it will be limited and managed and that national health plans of other countries, such as Canada, have their difficulties. Nonetheless, this is a pressing social problem that requires the attention of all mental health professionals.

Also, what bothers us the most about the current trend in funding of mental health services in this country is that it limits freedom of choice, both by patients and by therapists. The literature on the effectiveness of psychotherapy consistently indicates the need for a "good fit" between patient and therapist. Managed health care shows limited interest in this fit, yet the chances of success without attunement to the "fit" seem diminished. In particular, long-term therapy is essentially discouraged without considering individual differences in patient needs or without demonstrating superiority, or even equality, of short-term work.

The restriction of choice affects both consumers and therapists. The more obvious cost-containment measures are increasing the percentage paid by patients, which, depending on the patient's income, limits the amount she can expend. This in turn limits either the length of treatment or the therapist's fee and promotes a yearly cap for services or number of sessions. Then, treatment can be restricted to certain diagnoses or treatments; such practice creates incentives to distort, disagree, or practice only a particular way regardless of what the patient may wish or what the therapist may consider most appropriate. Then, there are limitations through gatekeepers as well as preselected providers who agree to the cost-containment procedures.

In addition to restricting choice, the limitations are not designed to improve service quality. A possible exception to this is limits on inpatient services, but if applied indiscriminately they too would cause problems for certain patients who may need more lengthy hospitalization. There are insidious aspects to managed mental health care that merit attention. The gatekeeping method in which one person, frequently one not trained in mental health care, approves specialty care such as psychotherapy as well as the use of financial incentives to limit such care, would appear subject to legal liability. Newman and Bricklin (1991) point out that although no case involving mental health has yet been filed, challenges to other forms of medical care are pending, and providers will probably take heed and do something about such practices. Furthermore, if liability is established, and the treating provider has not protested the limitations, then she will be sharing the liability along with the third-party payers.

A further difficulty is that if a patient exhausts her benefits and further payment is denied, yet the therapist and patient believe further treatment is needed, the possibilities are limited. The therapist cannot accept payment of the fee from the patient, even if the patient is willing, and regardless of the size of the fee, because the health plan prohibits this. The therapist can see the patient for no fee, obviously a hardship on the therapist, or refer the patient to another therapist if the patient is willing to pay a fee and not use insurance, again a financial disincentive for the therapist as well as a severe disruption of the therapeutic relationship. The obvious motivation is to avoid such a situation by "curing" the patient in whatever paid time is allotted, and the patient may well have a similar motivation to be "cured," regardless of the degree of "curing" that really takes place.

DeLeon et al. (1991) have noted three major problem areas for managed mental health care: access, quality, and consumer–provider awareness. If such care is indeed going to be a significant force in the future, then it is going to have to make access easier and more reasonable, improve quality, and have informed consumers, because in the last category it is clear that many people are relatively unaware of what they are buying.

In regard to access, it is clear that high-risk populations—which refers to both heavy users of mental health services, a relatively small group, and those currently unprotected by mental health insurance, a relatively large number—require service provisions. This, we suspect, will have to be carried out on a national level, via some form of federally mandated preventive programs as well as national health insurance. Despite difficulties with this approach in other countries and difficulties with various federal assistance programs already in place for those needing them, the scope of the problem is such that other approaches do not appear likely. As a result, more concrete efforts toward disease prevention and health insurance for all are likely to be made and are necessary.

The mechanics of access are of course a related problem. The lack of sophisticated knowledge on the part of gatekeepers and the presence of incentives to restrict usage that have been found in managed care will have to be remedied along with paradoxical incentives to use more costly inpatient services that have not been demonstrated to be more effective.

Medical cost-offset data support the need for easy access to mental health care. Furthermore, the effectiveness of outpatient treatment supports uncapping the use of that approach, as do data on effective dosage. We see this as a cost-effective approach in that it is more likely to insure quality and reduce recidivism as well as prevent the more costly inpatient treatments. For example, although Haas and Cummings (1991) appear to favor time-sensitive treatment, which appears as courses of treatment relatively circumscribed but probably to be repeated, at least for severe problems, they do not favor specific limits on the number of sessions as either clinically or ethically appropriate.

In fact, they do include as an option what we favor as the best approach.

> A program may impose no limitations on outpatient treatment . . . it has proven viable when carefully implemented. . . . This policy option is clinically safe (patients who need more extensive treatment will get it); it is economically risky (the plan has no way of limiting the amount of expenses it is exposed to); and it is ethically sound (the competent and ethical provider decides in conjunction with the patient what treatment is indicated). (Haas & Cummings, 1981, p. 47)

Thus, the basic objection comes back to the fact that such an approach *may* cost too much, yet this possibility can be reduced, and outpatient mental health services are inappropriate for cost-cutting efforts. The probability that there will be some limits as well as accountability are issues psychotherapists already expect, but more limits are counterproductive. If therapists want to keep freedom of choice for themselves and their patients, then complaints will be insufficient, and proof of effectiveness, particularly economic effectiveness, will have to be demonstrated.

The people who are the decision makers need appropriate information, which is available. For example, the quality of providers needs to be emphasized so that plans will not be designed based primarily on who offers to perform services for the least amount of money. Then, in particular, consumers need to be better informed. An example of this is the useful brochure published by the Psychological Association of Northeastern New York (1991), which recommends the minimum benefits that ought to be in a mental health insurance plan. Not surprisingly, this suggests that an appropriate plan allows a choice of licensed mental health professionals as well as 60 outpatient sessions per year, 30 inpatient days, 3 crisis visits, and coverage for any diagnosable mental health condition. The point is made that what may at first appear cheap can turn out to be costly if it provides insufficient coverage and that although most people do not expect to need mental health benefits, one in five will indeed require them.

An additional point needs to be made with regard to informing consumers. One of our most persistent objections to managed mental health care is the limitation on duration of outpatient treatment. This objection is motivated by a number of factors, including the fact that we believe change takes a long time and that much of that time is better spent in therapy than out of it, as well as the fact that we are accustomed to doing longer-term therapy, prefer it, have experienced it ourselves, and generally consider it more effective than short-term work. At the same time we are aware of research attesting to the effectiveness of brief therapy (Koss & Butcher, 1986) as well as the lack of empirical support for the superiority of unlimited therapy. Both approaches work, neither is appropriate for all, but what has to be kept in mind is that they are *different*, especially in regard to their goals. For example, in listing common characteristics of brief treatments, limitation of therapeutic goals is invariably included. Also, Koss and Butcher (1986) respect the fact that change takes a long time, but they do not believe all that time has to be spent in therapy. That may be, but again the type of change desired tends to be different, and our concern is with the restriction imposed by a mandated prevalence of short-term work.

Third-party coverage has always limited coverage for mental health services. Currently disturbing are further limitations and the relative embracing of such limitations by mental health professionals on the grounds of inevitability rather than the appropriateness of the dyads, namely, therapist–patient, patient–treatment method, and therapist–treatment method. This is clearly a field where there are numerous possibilities, and it is hoped that future clinicians will work to make and keep options available.

The Role of Fees

It appears that a layered system of payment is in the process of developing with its rudiments in the past division of poor people being seen in institutional settings where therapists were salaried and had limited interest in fee structures or fee payments and the rest of the population being served by private practitioners on a fee-for-service basis, generally using a sliding-scale method tied to patient income and therapist need. Theoretical orientation was also an influential variable, with psychoanalytic therapists considering the fee a significant part of the therapeutic process, at least in theory, regardless of the setting. As insurance coverage increased, a portion of the fee entered into the process in still a different way. Most therapists tried to keep the fee in the same position it had been by assigning total payment responsibility to the patient, but that was not always possible.

With more extensive reliance on insurance coverage, a new, powerful, and at times rather arbitrary Oedipal component was introduced to the patient–therapist interaction. Both members of the dyad could use the additional member to act out with, or against, so that the dyad became a triad, and some of the fee responsibility was shifted to the therapist.

For example, accountability moved from being solely an issue of the patient's satisfaction to becoming a question of the insurance carrier's approval, generally regardless of patient satisfaction, with the burden placed on the therapist to convince the third party that payments should continue. For many therapists the advantages of insurance payments, namely, that the patient pool was increased by making therapy more affordable and the fact that fees could be charged that were appropriate to an inflationary economy, outweighed the disadvantages. Also, for some time insurance carriers were not either that intrusive or that restrictive. If therapists and patients were prudent enough to take into account the insurance payment portion of the fee and work with its implications and ramifications, then it was workable. From a clinical viewpoint now the fee offered additional opportunities for the exploration of transference, countertransference, and resistance because in totality it had additional derivatives. This did not eliminate the problems of intrusiveness and determination of what was in or out of the patient's control in regard to payment, but the problems were not exceptional.

The future seems less promising, because many managed health care plans make the therapist into their employee who gets a significant portion of her payment from them, essentially based on plan approval. At the same time, based on whatever copayment is in place, the therapist also has to work with the patient about that portion of the fee. The task has become more complex, yet it is moving therapists in the direction of being salaried employees who can end up simplifying financial matters by agreeing on direct payment from their employers, the people for whom the patients work. This way patients and therapists will not have monetary exchanges, and the fee will have practically vanished from the therapeutic process.

Some therapists may welcome this since they disliked the monetary transaction aspect anyway, but the therapist–patient dyadic control of the therapy will also have vanished. This is a freedom that is clinically, ethically, and economically worth keeping instead of expending effort to fit into whatever system is currently being imposed under the guise of necessary efficiency.

A starting point is the recognition that the degree to which people are entitled to health coverage is by no means settled, nor is it likely to be any time soon. The trend is to decrease the amount of mental health coverage for those who already have it and to consider ways of funding limited coverage for those who do not. The first part of the trend is based on the idea that what existed cost too much, whereas the second has a more humanitarian motivation.

In order to facilitate the availability of mental services for all who need them, psychotherapists will have to be involved at the policy level. Furthermore, they will have to demonstrate that their services are effective, including cost-effective, and in turn be prepared to offer ways to fund such things as national mental health coverage. They will also have to be more united in their efforts, keeping in mind that many possibilities are effective in the mental health field and that is is foolish to restrict options.

At the same time, it is unwise to believe that a broad conception of mental health will gain either ascendance or funding. What can be hoped for is the extension of at least some mental health insurance to those who lack it and greater freedom in regard to the duration of outpatient therapy benefits. In support of this, more attention needs to be devoted to research on effective dosages of psychotherapy as well as to the delineation of benefits that accrue from different types and durations of therapy. There is a lack of both information and understanding in these areas, and this lack can be remedied. With such remediation, it is then possible to illustrate better to consumers, policymakers, and employers what is available and its value and cost.

On the firing line what could therapists do? Well, by understanding themselves that third-party coverage is but one way for patients to pay for their services and, at best, always can limit confidentiality, therapists can offer patients realistic appraisals of what psychotherapy is going to mean to them. If there is open discussion of possible financial arrangements, then patient and therapist can decide together what each is willing to do to work together. Treating insurance as though it is the determiner of the price, type, and duration of psychotherapy is a distortion. Insurance appears to have developed into a funding source that, during its reliable days, fed the dependency of therapists and patients but now threatens to deliver withdrawal effects. Put back into perspective, insurance is a limited funding source for psychotherapy and may be useful depending on the conditions determining its use.

Patients are interested in quality care, and whereas there are many opinions in the mental health field about the specifics of such care, that does not rule out presenting one's case. In fact, it basically mandates it, or somebody else will do exactly that for whatever they consider valuable. There is a great deal of competition in the psychotherapy arena, as well as a large potential pool of people who could use the services. It is unrealistic for therapists to believe that, if managed care sweeps the nation, and if many employers were to eliminate mental health coverage, people would stop using the services. Certainly it is facilitative to have ways to defray costs, and it is to therapists' and patients' benefits to influence policy and law in the direction of extensive coverage or at least some coverage. Yet the standards of the psychotherapy profession and its existence are not that dependent on corporate policy or the insurance industry. Ultimately the use of psychotherapy is the consumer's option as she asserts dollar priority for spending.

Good-Fit Fees

Psychotherapists are in the business of offering services whose mechanics and results are not well understood by a large number of people. Thus, psychotherapy will have to be "sold" to consumers, and part of the sales pitch is pricing. Although corporations, insurance carriers, and government are not in control of how people spend their personal funds, they certainly influence the money supply and the atmosphere for spending. Their message has been that health costs including mental health are too high. So, the purchasing environment is attuned to the goals of quicker and cheaper treatment based on the belief that quality service can be purchased this way and that lengthier and/or more costly approaches are unnecessary. Although this belief is valid only in some instances, it is insidiously translated into something approaching a universal, putting many people at risk. This belief will undoubtedly remain until evidence accumulates to refute it, but in the meantime, how will the psychotherapy profession market itself?

Certainly there will be pressure for funding therapy for those who cannot afford it, which probably means mandated mental health coverage in existing private plans and some form of national mental health insurance. All of this will also probably be minimal and is not designed to facilitate the economic status of psychotherapists but is a necessary ethical concern for all therapists. This will mean that a greater percentage of psychotherapy practice time will be devoted to lower-income people paying relatively low, subsidized fees and who will have relatively short courses of therapy.

Then there will be a variety of managed mental health care plans. In some of these therapists will be salaried employees following prescribed therapeutic procedures with patients who follow the payment rules of the plan. These plans will offer relatively guaranteed results within set time periods, generally brief. They will stress cost-effectiveness, usually lock in consumers for a fixed price range, and endure as long as they are able to satisfy consumers as well as employers who hire them to put plans in place. Their attraction to therapists will be the apparent security of employment. In addition, they offer other employment possibilities, particularly in administration, and some therapists may become the management and have others do the treatment. Also, these plans will vary in the freedom allowed their providers, so therapists who are already doing short-term work, or those who feel comfortable being eclectic, will find opportunities still within a fee-for-service context linked to a health care plan. The goodness of fit will depend on whether the therapists and patients involved feel comfortable within the time and cost boundaries that are the hallmarks of these plans.

Managed health care alters the significance of fees. It places an initial responsibility with the potential consumer to pick a plan, and what appears cost-effective may be deceptive, or choices may be excessively limited. The consumer will also have some burden in meeting paperwork requirements and then in appraising the effectiveness of service as well as selecting a strategy if she is dissatisfied. Whatever the plan, its monetary value is part of the employee's wages, although, depending on the degree of copayment, direct cost to the consumer may be hidden, thus minimizing the issue of the fee as part of the therapy process.

The therapist now will have more responsibility to get paid, but much if not most of the payment may come from an employer other than the patient. The therapist could be more accountable to the criteria of a particular plan than the patient desires. Control of the therapy could move away from the therapist–patient dyad and into the hands of third-party enforcers who are supposed to be both quality and cost conscious but could easily be swayed in the direction of the latter.

Therapists and patients who dislike these restrictions will tend to stay out of managed health care plans or be involved only with those that allow sufficient latitude for discretionary practice. In these situations the fee will retain its traditional magnificent significance, though it will probably be harder to come by because of the competition with promises of quality care for less time and cost. The income incentive to become a psychoanalyst, for example, will diminish because the profession will be a "harder sell," and this is currently reflected in declining applications to analytic institutions. The incentive to medicate is increasing among psychiatrists, and other disciplines want that possibility as well, and some of this clearly comes from economic interest. Along with this is the tendency toward subspecialization, connected to apparent need, but also to dollar flow.

So good-fit fee arrangements are undergoing quite a revolution in their definition, and this shakeout is only in its inception. This can be disturbing, particularly when it threatens arrangements that are personally important and truly believed in as effective and/or when it threatens the quality of care. Professional responsibilities have not changed, however, in that psychotherapists should be committed to providing the best mental health care they can. This means involvements in all aspects of provision, including research, planning, policy, cost, delivery, and accountability. In particular, it will be a time for education, of the self and others, as to the most appropriate and effective ways to provide psychotherapy.

REFERENCES

Abraham, K. (1923). Contributions to the theory of the anal character. *International Journal of Psychoanalysis, 1,* 400–418.

Bacon, K. (1990, July 23). Private drug abuse treatment centers try to adjust to life in the slow lane. *The Wall Street Journal,* pp. B1, B2.

Balsam, R. M., & Balsam, A. (1984). *Becoming a psychotherapist: A clinical primer* (2nd ed.). Chicago: University of Chicago Press.

Bar-Levav, R. (1979). Money: One yardstick of the self. *Voices, 14,* 24–30.

Bauer, G. B., & Kobos, J. C. (1987). *Brief therapy: Short-term psychodynamics intervention.* Northvale, NJ: Jason Aronson.

Beigel, J. K., & Earle, R. H. (1990). *Successful private practice in the 1990s: A new guide for the mental health professional.* New York: Brunner/Mazel.

Béland, P., & Cronin, I. (1986). *Money myths and realities.* New York: Carroll & Graf.

Benjamin, J. (1988). *The bonds of love: Psychoanalysis, feminism, and the problem of domination.* New York: Pantheon.

Bergler, E. (1959). *Money and emotional conflicts.* New York: International Universities Press.

Berle, A. A. (1969). *Power.* New York: Harcourt, Brace, & World.

Bleuler, E. (1911). *Dementia praecox or the group of schizophrenias.* New York: International Universities Press.

Bloom, B. L. (1984). *Community mental health* (2nd ed.). Monterey, CA: Brooks/Cole.

Blum, H. (Ed.). (1985). *Defense and resistance: Historical perspectives and current concepts.* New York: International Universities Press.

Bolter, K., Levenson, H., & Alvarez, W. (1990). Differences in values between short-term and long-term therapists. *Professional Psychology: Research and Practice, 21,* 285–290.

Bornemann, E. (Ed.). (1976). *The psychoanalysis of money.* New York: Urizen Books.

Bowlby, J. (1969). *Attachment and loss. Vol. I. Attachment.* New York: Basic Books.

Bowlby, J. (1973). *Attachment and loss. Vol. II. Separation. Anxiety and anger.* New York: Basic Books.

Broskowski, A. (1991). Current mental health care environments: Why managed care is necessary. *Professional Psychology: Research and Practice, 22,* 6–14.

Budman, S. H., & Gurman, A. S. (1983). The practice of brief therapy. *Professional Psychology: Research and Practice, 14,* 277–292.

Budman, S. H., & Gurman, A. S. (1988). *Theory and practice of brief therapy.* New York: Guilford Press.

Burnside, M. A. (1986). Fee practices of male and female therapists. In D. W. Krueger (Ed.), *The last taboo: Money as symbol and reality in psychotherapy and psychoanalysis* (pp. 48–54). New York: Brunner/Mazel.

Burrell, M. (1987). Psychotherapy and the medical model: The hypocrisy of health insurance. *Journal of Contemporary Psychotherapy, 17,* 60–67.

Callahan, T. R. (1989). Get it in writing. *The Independent Practitioner, 9,* 21–23.

Canter, A. (1991). A cost effective psychotherapy. *Psychology in Private Practice, 8,* 13–17.

Canter, M. B., & Freudenberger, H. J. (1990). Fee scheduling and monitoring. In E. A. Margenau (Ed.), *The encyclopedic handbook of private practice* (pp. 217–232). New York: Gardner Press.

Cantor, D. (1990). I am not a dinosaur. *Psychotherapy in Private Practice, 8,* 11–19.

Caroff, P. (1990). The application of theory to practice. In E. A. Margenau (Ed.), *The encyclopedic handbook of private practice* (pp. 844–855). New York: Gardner Press.

Carville, D. J. (1991). Managed care: Challenges and opportunities for psychologists. *The Independent Practitioner, 11,* 4–43.

Chapman, R. (1990). Sole proprietorship. In E. A. Margenau (Ed.), *The encyclopedic handbook of private practice* (pp. 5–17). New York: Gardner Press.

Chodoff, P. (1964). Psychoanalysis and fees. *Comprehensive Psychiatry, 5,* 137–145.

Chodorow, N. (1989). *Feminism and psychoanalytic theory.* New York: Columbia University Press.

Citron-Bagget, S., & Kempler, B. (1991). Fee setting: Dynamic issues for therapists in independent practice. *Psychotherapy in Private Practice, 9*(1), 45–60.

Cohen, H. M. (1990). Third-party payments. In E. A. Margenau (Ed.), *The encyclopedic handbook of private practice* (pp. 233–242). New York: Gardner Press.

Cummings, N. A. (1987). The future of psychotherapy: One psychologist's perspective. *American Journal of Psychotherapy, 41,* 349–360.

DeLeon, P. H., VandenBos, G. R., & Bulatao, E. R. (1991). Managed mental health care: A history of the federal policy initiative. *Professional Psychology, 22,* 15–25.

Ehrenreich, B. (1989). *Fear of falling. The inner life of the middle class.* New York: Pantheon Books.

Ehrenwald, J. (Ed.). (1976). *History of psychotherapy. From healing magic to encounter.* New York: Jason Aronson.

el-Guelbay, N., Prosen, H., & Bebchuk, W. (1985a). On direct patient participation in the cost of their psychiatric care. Part I. A review of the empirical and experimental evidence. *Canadian Journal of Psychiatry, 30,* 178–183.

el-Guelbay, N., Prosen, H., & Bebchuk, W. (1985b). On direct patient participation in the cost of their psychiatric care. Part II. Access to services, impact on practice and training implications. *Canadian Journal of Psychiatry, 30,* 184–189.

Epstein, L., & Feiner, A. H. (Eds.). (1979). *Countertransference.* New York: Jason Aronson.

Epstein, R. S., & Simon, I. (1990). The exploitation index: An early warning indicator of boundary violations in psychotherapy. *Bulletin of the Menninger Clinic, 54,* 450–465.

Fairbairn, W. R. D. (1952). *An object relations theory of the personality.* New York: Basic Books.

Fenchel, G. (1981). The psychoanalysis of the money complex. *Issues in Ego Psychology, 4,* 11–18.

Fenichel, O. (1954). The drive to amass wealth. In *The collected papers of Otto Fenichel* (pp. 89–108). New York: Norton. (Original work published 1938).

Ferenczi, S. (1952). *First contributions to psychoanalysis.* New York: Brunner/Mazel.

Forman, B. D. (1990). Media, marketing and psychology. *The Psychotherapy Bulletin, 25,* 34.

Forrest, D. V. (1990). Further developmental stages of the interest in money. *American Journal of Psychoanalysis, 50,* 319–335.

Freud, S. (1900a). Infantile material as a source of dreams. In J. Strachey (Ed.), *The standard edition of the complete psychological works of Sigmund Freud* (Vol. 4, pp. 189–219). London: Hogarth Press.

Freud, S. (1990b). Some examples—Calculations and speeches in dreams. In J. Strachey (Ed.), *The standard edition of the complete psychological works of Sigmund Freud* (Vol. 5, pp. 405–425). London: Hogarth Press.

Freud, S. (1901). The forgetting of impressions and intentions. In J. Strachey (Ed.), *The standard edition of the complete psychological works of Sigmund Freud* (Vol. 6, pp. 134–161). London: Hogarth Press.

Freud, S. (1905). Three essays on the theory of sexuality. In J. Strachey (Ed.), *The standard edition of the complete psychological works of Sigmund Freud* (Vol. 7, pp. 125–245). London: Hogarth Press.

Freud, S. (1908). Character and anal erotism. In J. Strachey (Ed.), *The standard edition of the complete psychological works of Sigmund Freud* (Vol. 9, pp. 167–175). London: Hogarth Press.

Freud, S. (1909). Notes upon a case of obsessional neurosis. In J. Strachey (Ed.), *The standard edition of the complete psychological works of Sigmund Freud* (Vol. 10, pp. 153–318). London: Hogarth Press.

Freud, S. (1913a). On beginning the treatment. In J. Strachey (Ed.), *The standard edition of the complete psychological works of Sigmund Freud* (Vol. 12, pp. 123–144). London: Hogarth Press.

Freud, S. (1913b). Two lies told by children. In J. Strachey (Ed.), *The standard edition of the complete psychological works of Sigmund Freud* (Vol. 12, pp. 305–309). London: Hogarth Press.

Freud, S. (1913c). Totem and taboo. In J. Strachey (Ed.), *The standard edition of the complete psychological works of Sigmund Freud* (Vol. 13, pp. 1–161). London: Hogarth Press.

Freud, S. (1918). Anal erotism and the castration complex. In J. Strachey (Ed.), *The standard edition of the complete psychological works of Sigmund Freud* (Vol. 17, pp. 72–88). London: Hogarth Press.

Freud, S. (1964). Analysis terminable and interminable. In J. Strachey (Ed.), *The standard edition of the complete psychological works of Sigmund Freud* (Vol. 23, pp. 209–254). London: Hogarth Press. (Original work published 1937).

Friedman, R. C. (1991). Psychotherapy without fee. In S. Klebanow & E. L. Lowenkopf (Eds.), *Money and mind* (pp. 207–221). New York: Plenum Press.

Fromm, E. (1941). *Escape from freedom.* New York: Avon.

Frosch, J. (1990a). *Psychodynamic psychiatry. Theory and practice* (Vol. 1). New York: International Universities Press.

Frosch, J. (1990b). *Psychodynamic psychiatry. Theory and practice* (Vol. 2). New York: International Universities Press.

Fuqua, P. B. (1986). Classical psychoanalytic views of money. In D. W. Krueger (Ed.), *The last taboo. Money as symbol and reality in psychotherapy and psychoanalysis* (pp. 17–23). New York: Brunner/Mazel.

Gabbard, G. O. (1990). *Psychodynamic psychiatry in clinical practice.* Washington, DC: American Psychiatric Press.

Gediman, H. K. (1990). The pure gold in psychoanalytic psychotherapy. *The Round Robin, 6,* 6–10.

Gedo, J. (1981). *Advances in clinical psychoanalysis.* New York: International Universities Press.

Glazer, N. (1988). *The limits of social policy.* Cambridge, MA: Harvard University Press.

Glennon, T. M., & Karlovac, M. (1988). The effect of fee level on therapists' perception of competence and nonpossessive warmth. *Journal of Contemporary Psychotherapy, 18,* 249–257.

Goldberg, C. (1986). *On being a psychotherapist—The journey of the healer.* New York: Gardner Press.

Goldstein, A. P. (1971). *Psychotherapeutic attraction.* New York: Pergamon Press.

Gorkin, M. (1987). *The uses of countertransference.* Northvale, NJ: Jason Aronson.

Gutheil, T. G. (1986). Fees in beginning private practice. In D. W. Krueger (Ed.), *The last taboo: Money as symbol and reality in psychotherapy and psychoanalysis* (pp. 175–188). New York: Brunner/Mazel.

Haas, L. J., & Cummings, N. A. (1991). Managed outpatient mental health plans: Clinical, ethical, and practical guidelines for participation. *Professional Psychology: Research and Practice, 22,* 45–51.

Handelsman, M. M. (1990). Do written consent forms influence clients' first impression of therapists? *Professional Psychology: Research and Practice, 21,* 451–454.

Harari, C. (1990). Collections. In E. A. Margennau (Ed.), *The encyclopedic handbook of private practice* (pp. 243–249). New York: Gardner Press.

Hartmann, H. (1964). *Essays on ego psychology. Selected problems in psychoanalytic theory.* New York: International Universities Press.

Helfmann, B. (1990). Psychological service plus recession minus third party reimbursement = anxiety. *New Jersey Psychologist, 40,* 4–5.

Herron, W. G. (in press). Managed mental health care redux. *Professional Psy-*

chology: Research and Practice.

Herron, W. G., & Rouslin, S. (1984). Issues in psychotherapy (Vol. 1). Washington, DC: Oryn.

Herron, W. G., & Sitkowski, S. (1986). Effect of fees on psychotherapy: What is the evidence? Professional Psychology: Research and Practice, 17, 347–351.

Hofling, C. K., & Rosenbaum, M. (1986). The extension of credit to patients in psychoanalysis and psychotherapy. In D. W. Krueger (Ed.), The last taboo: Money as symbol and reality in psychotherapy and psychoanalysis (pp. 202–217). New York: Brunner/Mazel.

Howard, K. I., Kopta, S. M., Krause, M. S., & Orlinsky, D. E. (1986). The dose–effect relationship in psychotherapy. American Psychologist, 41, 159–164.

Hurvitz, N. (1979). The radical psychotherapist and the American dream. Voices, 14, 66–76.

Jacobs, D. H. (1986). On negotiating fees with psychotherapy and psychoanalytic patients. In D. W. Krueger (Ed.), The last taboo: Money as symbol and reality in psychotherapy and psychoanalysis (pp. 121–131). New York: Brunner/Mazel.

Jasnow, A., Raskin, N., Klein, A., & Stren, E. M. (1979). The selling and/or sellings of the psychotherapist—Trade-offs included. Voices, 14, 2–8.

Jones, E. (1918). Anal–erotic character traits. In Collected papers (pp. 438–451). Boston: Beacon.

Jordan, J. V., Kaplan, A. G., Miller, J. B., Stiver, I. P., & Surrey, J. L. (Eds.). (1991). Women's growth in connection: Writings from the Stone Center. New York: Guilford Press.

Kaufmann, W. (1976). Some emotional uses of money. In E. Bornemann (Ed.), The psychoanalysis of money (pp. 227–257). New York: Urizen Books.

Kiesler, C. A. (1983). Psychology and mental health policy. In M. Hersen, A. E. Kazdin, & A. S. Bellack (Eds.), The clinical psychology handbook (pp. 63–82). New York: Pergamon Press.

Klebanow, S., & Lowenkopf, E. L. (Eds.). (1991). Money and mind. New York: Plenum Press.

Klein, M. (1975). Some theoretical conclusions regarding the life of the infant. In M. Klein (Ed.), Envy & gratitude & other works, 1946–1963 (pp. 176–235). New York: Free Press. (Original work published 1952)

Klein, M. (1975). Envy and gratitude. In M. Klein (Ed.), Envy & gratitude & other works, 1946–1963 (pp. 176–235). New York: Free Press. (Original work published 1957)

Klein, M. (1975). On mental health. In M. Klein (Ed.), Envy & gratitude & other works, 1946–1963 (pp. 176–235). New York: Free Press. (Original work published 1960)

Koss, M. P., & Butcher, J. N. (1986). Research on brief psychotherapy. In S. L. Garfield & A. E. Bergin (Eds.), Handbook of psychotherapy and behavior change (3rd ed., pp. 627–670). New York: John Wiley & Sons.

Kovacs, A. L. (1982). Survival in the 1980s: On the theory and practice of brief psychotherapy. Psychotherapy: Theory, Research and Practice, 19, 142–159.

Kovacs, A. L. (1987). Insurance billing: The growing risk of lawsuits against psychologists. *Independent Practitioner*, 7, 21–24.

Kovacs, A. (1989). The uncertain future of professional psychology. *The Independent Practitioner*, 9, 11–18.

Krueger, D. W. (1986a). Money, success, and success phobia. In D. W. Krueger (Ed.), *The last taboo: Money as symbol and reality in psychotherapy and psychoanalysis* (pp. 3–16). New York: Brunner/Mazel.

Krueger, D. W. (1986b). A self-psychological view of money. In D. W. Krueger (Ed.), *The last taboo: Money as symbol and reality in psychotherapy and psychoanalysis* (pp. 24–32). New York: Brunner/Mazel.

Krueger, D. W. (Ed.). (1986c). *The last taboo: Money as symbol and reality in psychotherapy and psychoanalysis*. New York: Brunner/ Mazel.

Krueger, D. W. (1991). Money meanings and madness: A psychoanalytic perspective. *Psychoanalytic Review*, 78, 209–224.

Kudirka, N. (1977). Trading therapy for art. *Voices*, 14, 51–54.

Lambert, M. J., Shapiro, D. A., & Bergin, A. E. (1986). The effectiveness of psychotherapy. In S. L. Garfield & A. E. Bergin (Eds.), *Handbook of psychotherapy and behavior change* (3rd ed., pp. 157–212). New York: John Wiley & Sons.

Lane, R. C., & Hull, J. W. (1990). The role of fees in psychotherapy and psychoanalysis. In E. A. Margenau (Ed.), *The encyclopedic handbook of private practice* (pp. 260–272). New York: Gardner Press.

Lane-Palés, N. (1989). Explicit clinical assessment and planning for appropriate longer-term therapy. *Psychotherapy in Private Practice*, 7, 3–12.

Langs, R. (1982). *Psychotherapy: A basic text*. New York: Jason Aronson.

Lapham, L. H. (1988). *Money and class in America: Notes and observations on our civil religion*. New York: Weidenfeld & Nicolson.

Lasky, E. (1984). Psychoanalysts' and psychotherapists' conflicts about setting fees. *Psychoanalytic Psychology*, 1, 289–300.

Lathrop, D. (1979). Money, money, money. *Voices*, 14, 31–33.

Lesse, S. (1989). Current attempts to control health care costs—Blueprint for disaster. *American Journal of Psychotherapy*, XLIII, 1–3.

Levenson, E. (1983). *The ambiguity of change*. New York: Basic Books.

Liss-Levenson, N. (1990). Money matters and the women analyst: In a different voice. *Psychoanalytic Psychology*, 7, 119–130.

Lowman, R. L. (1991). Mental health claims experience: Analysis and benefit redesign. *Professional Psychology: Research and Practice*, 22, 36–44.

Luborsky, L. (1984). *Principles of psychoanalytic psychotherapy: A manual for supportive–expressive treatment*. New York: Basic Books.

Maltin, M. S. (1991). President's message. *ASPP Newsletter*, 5, 1–16.

Manos, N. (1982). Free psychotherapy: The therapist's and the patient's view. *Psychotherapy and Psychosomatics*, 37, 137–143.

Margenau, E. (Ed.). (1990). *The encyclopedic handbook of private practice*. New York: Gardner Press.

Mayer, T., Duesenberry, J. S., & Aliber, R. Z. (1984). *Money, banking, and the economy* (2nd ed.). New York: W. W. Norton.

Mayer, S., & Norton, P. (1981). Involving clinicians in fee collections: Implications for improving clinical practice and increasing fee income in a community mental health center. *Community Mental Health Journal*, 17, 214–225.

McGrath, J. J. (1986). Long-term psychotherapy and psychoanalysis in a changing health economy. In D. W. Krueger (Ed.), *The last taboo: Money as symbol and reality in psychotherapy and psychoanalysis* (pp. 253–256). New York: Brunner/Mazel.

Menninger, K. A. (1958). *Theory of psychoanalytic technique.* New York: Basic Books.

Meyers, H. (Ed.). (1986). *Between analyst and patient: New dimensions in countertransference and transference.* Hillsdale, NJ: Analytic Press.

Mollica, R. F., & Redlich, F. (1980). Equity and changing patient characteristics—1950 to 1975. *Archives of General Psychiatry, 37,* 1257–1263.

Morgan, R. F. (Ed.). (1983). *The iatrogenic handbook: A critical look at research and practice in the helping professions.* Toronto: IPI Publishing.

Morrison, J. K. (1990). Techniques for expansion. In E. A. Margenau (Ed.), *The encyclopedic handbook of private practice* (pp. 274–283). New York: Gardner Press.

Moses, R., & Moses-Hrushovski, R. (1990). Reflections on the sense of entitlement. *Psychoanalytic Study of the Child, 45,* 61–78.

Nelson, M. C. (1979). Comment. *Voices, 14,* 33.

Nevin, D. A. (1991). "The new scrabble"—Letter games with insurance plans. *New York State Psychologist, 42,* 48–49.

Newman, R., & Bricklin, P. M. (1991). Parameters of managed mental health care: Legal, ethical, and professional guidelines. *Professional Psychology: Research and Practice, 22,* 26–35.

Newman, F. L., & Howard, K. I. (1986). Therapeutic effort, treatment outcome, and national health policy. *American Psychologist, 41,* 181–187.

Nickerson, E. T. (1991). The therapist as paid friend. *Psychotherapy in Private Practice, 9*(1), 131–134.

Olsson, P. A. (1986). Complexities in the psychology and psychotherapy of the phenomenally wealthy. In D. W. Krueger (Ed.), *The last taboo: Money as symbol and reality in psychotherapy and psychoanalysis* (pp. 55–69). New York: Brunner/Mazel.

Paris, J. (1982–83). Frame disturbances in no-fee psychotherapy. *International Journal of Psychoanalytic Psychotherapy, 9,* 135–146.

Peplau, H. E. (1964). Professional and social behavior: Some differences worth the attention of professional nurses. *The Quarterly Magazine, 50*(4), 22–33.

Peplau, H. E. (1969). Professional closeness. *Nursing Forum, 8,* 342–359.

Perloff, R. (1990). Examining the psychological correlates of poverty: Toward advancing psychology in the public interest. *Advancing the Public Interest, 2,* 7.

Phillips, E. L. (1985). *A guide for therapists and patients to short-term psychotherapy.* Springfield, IL: Charles C. Thomas.

Phillips, E. L. (1988). Length of psychotherapy and outcome: Observations stimulated by Howard, Kopta, Krause, and Orlinsky. *American Psychologist, 43,* 669–670.

Phillips, L. (1986). *Human adaptation and its failures.* New York: Academic Press.

Pine, F. (1988). The four psychologies of psychoanalysis and their place in clinical work. *Journal of the American Psychoanalytic Association, 36,* 571–596.

Pine, F. (1989). Motivation, personality organization, and the four psychologies of psychoanalysis. *Journal of the American Psychoanalytic Association, 37,* 31–64.

Pine, F. (1990). *Drive, ego, object, and self.* New York: Basic Books.

Pope, K. S. (1988). Fee policies and procedures: Causes of malpractice suits and ethics complaints. *Independent Practitioner, 8*(4), 24–29.

Pope, K. S., Tabachnick, B. G., & Keith-Spiegel, P. (1988). Good and poor practices in psychotherapy: National survey of beliefs of psychologists. *Professional Psychology: Research and Practice, 19,* 547–552.

Prochaska, J. O., Nash, J. M., & Norcross, J. C. (1986). Independent psychological practice: A national survey of full-time practitioners. *Psychotherapy in Private Practice, 4,* 57–66.

Psychological Association of Northeastern New York. (1991). *Mental Health Benefits.* Latham, NY: PANNY.

Psychotherapy Finances. (1990a). Are mental health treatment costs growing faster than other health care costs? *Psychotherapy Finances, 16*(10), 8.

Psychotherapy Finances. (1990b). How low will you go? *Psychotherapy Finances, 16*(9), 5–6.

Psychotherapy Finances. (1990c). How much will medicare pay for covered services? *Psychotherapy Finances, 16*(10), 4.

Psychotherapy Finances. (1990d). *Managed health care strategies.* Hawthorne, NJ: Ridgewood Financial Institute.

Psychotherapy Finances. (1991a). Practice survey: How do your professional expenses stack up? *Psychotherapy Finances, 17*(2), 1–2.

Psychotherapy Finances. (1991b). Survey report. *Psychotherapy Finances, 16*(14), 1–8.

Raney, J. O. (1982–83). The payment of fees in psychotherapy. *International Journal of Psychoanalytic Psychotherapy, 9,* 147–181.

Raney, J. (1986). The effect of fees on the course and outcome of psychotherapy and psychoanalysis. In D. W. Krueger (Ed.), *The last taboo: Money as symbol and reality in psychotherapy and psychoanalysis* (pp. 88–101). New York: Brunner/Mazel.

Reich, W. (1949). *Character analysis.* New York: Orgone Institute Press.

Richardson, L. M., & Austad, C. S. (1991). Realities of mental health practice in managed-care settings. *Professional Psychology: Research and Practice, 22,* 52–59.

Rowland, M. (1990, May 9). When women manage money. *New York Times,* p. 17.

Schoenewolf, G. (1990). Spirituality vs. power: The art of therapy and the business of private practice. In E. A. Margenau (Ed.), *The encyclopedic handbook of private practice* (pp. 863–869). New York: Gardner Press.

Searles, H. F. (1979). The patient as therapist to his analyst. In H. F. Searles (Ed.), *Countertransference and related subjects* (pp. 380–459). New York: International Universities Press. (Original work published 1975)

Shueman, S. A. (1989). Perspectives on the financing of longer-term outpatient care. *Psychotherapy in Private Practice, 7,* 21–27.

Shulman, J. M. (1988). Psychologists must "position" themselves in the market place. *Psychotherapy in Private Practice, 6,* 115–127.

Sincoff, J. B. (1990). The psychological characteristics of ambivalent people. *Clinical*

Psychology Review, 10, 43–68.

Sitkowski, S., & Herron, W. G. (1991). Attitudes of therapists and their patients toward money. *Psychotherapy in Private Practice, 8*, 27–37.

Spitz, R. A. (1980). Countertransference: Comments on its varying role in the analytic situation. In H. P. Blum (Ed.), *Psychoanalytic exploration of technique: Discourse on the theory of therapy* (pp. 441–451). New York: International Universities Press.

Steiner-Adair, C. (1991). New maps of development, new models of therapy: The psychology of women and the treatment of eating disorders. In C. Johnson (Ed.), *Psychodynamic treatment of anorexia nervosa and bulimia* (pp. 225–244). New York: Guilford Press.

Stricker, G. (1989). Reflections on longer-term care. *Psychotherapy in Private Practice, 7*, 29–33.

Strupp, H. H. (1986). Psychotherapy: Research, practice, and public policy (How to avoid dead ends). *American Psychologist, 41*, 120–130.

Strupp, H. H., & Binder, J. L. (1984). *Psychotherapy in a new key. A guide to time-limited dynamic psychotherapy.* New York: Basic Books.

Taube, C. A., Burns, B. J., & Kessler, L. (1984). Patients of psychiatrists and psychologists in office-based practice: 1980. *American Psychologist, 39*, 1435–1447.

Terris, M. (1990). Failing health: A wasteful system that doesn't work. *Gray Panther Network, 19*, 1–4.

Tomes, H. (1990). Consumerism in mental health. *Advancing the public interest, II*, 4–5.

Tulipan, A. B. (1983). Fees in psychotherapy: A perspective. *Journal of the American Academy of Psychoanalysis, 11*, 445–463.

Waelder, R. (1976). The principle of multiple function: Observations on over-determination. In S. A. Guttman (Ed.), *Psychoanalysis: Observation, theory, application* (pp. 68–83). New York: International Universities Press.

Warner, S. L. (1991). Psychoanalytic understanding and treatment of the very rich. In S. Klebanow & E. L. Lowenkopf (Eds.), *Money and mind* (pp. 183–195). New York: Plenum Press.

Weiner, M. F. (1986). *Practical psychotherapy.* New York: Brunner/Mazel.

Welling, K. M. (1990, June 11). The sickening spiral. *Barron's*, pp. 8, 9, 18, 20.

Welt, S. R., & Herron, W. G. (1990). *Narcissism and the psychotherapist.* New York: Guilford Press.

Whitson, G. (1989). *Money matters in psychoanalysis: The analyst's coparticipation in the matter of money.* Unpublished manuscript.

Wiggins, J. (1990). Office expenses as percent of income. *Independent Practitioner, 10*, 29–30.

Wiggins, J. (1991). Managing health care by deregulation. *Psychotherapy Bulletin, 26*, 12–13.

Willis, D. J. (1990, Summer). APA's task force on American Indian mental health. *AAP Advance Plan*, p. 6.

Winokur, D. (1973). Does anybody really need psychotherapy? Consequences for retaining a mental illness model. *Psychotherapy: Theory, Research and Practice, 10*, 41–43.

INDEX